The Other War

Lael Brainard, Carol Graham
Nigel Purvis, Steven Radelet, Gayle E. Smith

The Other War

Global Poverty and the Millennium Challenge Account

Center for Global Development

Brookings Institution Press
Washington, D.C.

THE BROOKINGS INSTITUTION
1775 Massachusetts Avenue, N.W., Washington, D.C. 20036
www.brookings.edu

and

CENTER FOR GLOBAL DEVELOPMENT
1776 Massachusetts Avenue, NW, Suite 301, Washington, D.C. 20036
www.cgd.org

Library of Congress Cataloging-in-Publication data
The other war : global poverty and the Millennium Challenge Account / Lael Brainard . . . [et al.].
p. cm.
Includes bibliographical references and index.
ISBN 0-8157-1114-X (cloth : alk. paper)
ISBN 0-8157-1115-8 (pbk. : alk. paper)
1. Economic assistance, American. 2. United States—Foreign relations—2001– I. Title: Global poverty and the Millennium Challenge Account. II. Title: Millennium Challenge Account. III. Brainard, Lael.
HC60.O84 2003
338.91'73—dc21 2003008638

9 8 7 6 5 4 3 2 1

The paper used in this publication meets minimum requirements of the American National Standard for Information Sciences—Permanence of Paper for Printed Library Materials: ANSI Z39.48-1992.

Typeset in Minion

Composition by Circle Graphics
Columbia, Maryland

Printed by R. R. Donnelley
Harrisonburg, Virginia

Contents

Foreword

The plight of the poorest around the world has been pushed to the forefront of America's international agenda for the first time in many years. The debate triggered by the war on terrorism and its extension to Iraq has focused attention on third-world poverty—even though the links between poverty and terrorism are far from clear—and the HIV/AIDS pandemic is making the challenge of development even more formidable.

In March 2002, in the context of the UN Conference on Financing for Development, President Bush announced his intention to request an increase of $5 billion a year over current foreign assistance levels (ramped up over three years) through the creation of a new bilateral development program, the Millennium Challenge Account (MCA). To implement the program, the administration subsequently recommended the creation of an independent agency, the Millennium Challenge Corporation (MCC), to allocate the new funding on the basis of objective selection criteria, measuring a nation's commitment to sound economic policy, social investment, and good governance. Not surprisingly, this proposal has sparked a broader debate about U.S. foreign assistance policy.

The proposed MCA represents the largest single-year increase in U.S. bilateral development aid in decades. The increase in resources for foreign assistance is an important departure from a flagging U.S. commitment to foreign aid, which has been welcomed by the development community, other donors, and officials from poor countries around the world. It presents a rare opportunity to not only create from scratch a new blueprint for distributing and delivering aid effectively but also to strengthen U.S. development policy more generally. The MCA offers a critical opportunity to deliberately shape the face that the United States presents to people in poor nations around the world. Recognizing this as a rare and important opportunity, Brookings and the Center for Global Development jointly assembled a multidisciplinary team of scholars to study how best to fashion the MCA to make it an effective tool in its own right and also for transforming U.S. development policy and reinforcing international aid cooperation.

Not surprisingly, a number of unanswered questions remain as the MCA moves from idea to blueprint to reality. First and foremost is the tension between development and foreign policy objectives. The intent to create a new blueprint for delivering foreign assistance and to depart from an aid track record that is checkered with multiple, often conflicting objectives and myriad actors and directives coincides with renewed interest in foreign assistance as a foreign policy tool in the war on terrorism. Tensions between those two objectives are already evident. The MCA resources are meant to go to the poorest countries—a development objective. But the administration is also proposing that in its third year the MCA provide assistance to somewhat richer countries, such as Colombia and Egypt, where America has particularly important foreign policy objectives. The MCC, which has been given a "pure" development mandate, is to be established independently of the U.S. Agency for International Development (USAID), the federal agency that has international development as its core mandate. The administration proposes that the MCC board be chaired by the secretary of the State Department, which has foreign policy as its primary objective, and not include the head of USAID.

Tension between development and foreign policy objectives is not the only outstanding question. How will the MCA coordinate its efforts with those of other donors, and in particular with new mechanisms for donor coordination established in recent years by the Bretton Woods institutions? What countries will qualify for the MCA, and what criteria will be used to evaluate them? What kinds of programs and policies will be supported? How will the MCC, with its proposed small staff of 100 people, select countries and proposals and manage, monitor, and evaluate annual aid flows of $5 billion? How will the MCC coordinate with the myriad of existing programs for developing countries, and particularly with USAID? Will funds and attention going to the MCA be at the expense of bilateral assistance to weaker-performing poor countries? What role will Congress play? More broadly, will the MCC continue operating according to strict development criteria if both budgetary constraints and foreign policy objectives become more pressing in the coming years?

This book—a joint project of the Brookings Institution and the Center for Global Development (CGD)—addresses these questions from a vantage point that bridges the oft-observed divide between policy and operational considerations, between foreign policy and development economics, and between Congress and executive branch. The project was directed by Lael Brainard and authored by Brainard, Carol Graham, Nigel Purvis, and Gayle E. Smith of Brookings, and Steven Radelet of CGD. This book is a companion to *Challenging Foreign Aid: A Policymaker's Guide to the Millennium Challenge Account,* published by CGD and authored by Steven Radelet, which provides an economic analysis of the MCA in the light of lessons regarding the effectiveness of foreign aid in supporting economic growth in poor countries.

The authors of this joint study propose a number of operating principles for the MCC. These include strategies for guiding its coordination with other donors, methods for improving the qualifying criteria for applicant countries, and suggestions for the structure of its board and for the oversight role played by Congress. They also explore the broader questions that the existence of a major new player poses for U.S. assistance policy. The study is intended to inform the public and congressional debates, to provide concrete recommendations for the architects of the MCC, and to engage students and scholars of foreign assistance and global poverty. The authors bring to bear on the topic a range of experience and expertise—from government, academia, the international financial institutions, and the developing world.

The book could not come at a better time, as the public, Congress, the administration, and the wide community of development and foreign policy experts are beginning to engage in an important debate on the future of foreign assistance. For this major new effort in U.S. foreign aid to go forward successfully, the debate must address the tensions and identify the complementarities between development and foreign policy objectives. The authors hope that the book will further the debate in a constructive manner and result in the development of concrete policies for more effective aid.

The authors benefited from the collaboration and expertise of many colleagues throughout the course of the project. At Brookings, Ann Florini made an important contribution to the manuscript on the appropriate balance between government and civil society, and James Lindsay, Thomas Mann, Susan Rice, Ivo Daalder, and Jim Steinberg were generous with their time and expertise and provided helpful feedback on early drafts. Robert Cavey of the Carnegie Endowment for International Peace was a member of the core group of project advisors and contributed importantly to consideration of the appropriate role for the private sector. The authors are also grateful to Janet Ballantyne, Marc Schneider, George Ingram, Jennifer Windsor, Phyllis Forbes, Paul Oostburg, Mary Locke, Jim Greene, Tony Blinken, Heather Flynn, Dani Kaufmann, Michael Clemens, Carol Lancaster, Tom Carothers, and many others who provided thoughtful suggestions and reflections on what works and what does not in foreign aid. We are grateful to Lant Pritchett, Anne C. Richard, Colin Bradford, and George Ingram for providing thoughtful and constructive comments on the manuscript, which we hope are done justice by the book. Andrew Eggers, Maggie Kozak, Margaret MacLeod, and Shannon Leahy from Brookings and Sabeen Hassanali and Prarthna Dayal from CGD provided excellent research and administrative assistance. We also thank Sheila Herrling from CGD for helpful input and guidance. The project could not have succeeded without Allison Driscoll, who was the invaluable project coordinator and facilitator throughout the entire process. The authors also wish to thank Holly Hammond for excellent (and rapid) editing, Gary Harding for help with the web version, and Janet Walker and Larry Converse of the Brookings Institution Press. The authors collectively remain responsible for the manuscript and its content and any errors or omissions. Not all the authors necessarily agree with all the recommendations.

This book was made possible by a generous grant from Richard C. Blum, which enabled Brookings to establish the Global Poverty Reduction Initiative. This book is the first major product resulting from this initiative. The work of the Center for Global Development on the MCA has been made possible by the ongoing support of Edward C. Scott Jr., chairman of the board of the Center, and by a special contribution from George Soros. We are delighted to have had the opportunity for our institutions to work together to contribute to a common objective of the Brookings initiative and the Center: the reduction of poverty in the developing world.

STROBE TALBOTT
President, The Brookings Institution

NANCY BIRDSALL
President, Center for Global Development

Washington, D.C.
April 2003

The Other War

1

Introduction

We meet at a moment of new hope and age-old struggle, the battle against world poverty. . . . We fight against poverty because hope is an answer to terror. We fight against poverty because opportunity is a fundamental right to human dignity. We fight against poverty because faith requires it and conscience demands it. And we fight against poverty with a growing conviction that major progress is within our reach.

—President George Bush, *United Nations Conference on Financing for Development, Monterrey, Mexico, March 22, 2002*

In March 2002 President Bush announced his intention to request an increase of $5 billion per year over current assistance levels through the creation of a bilateral development fund, the Millennium Challenge Account. To implement the program, the administration subsequently recommended the creation of an independent agency, the Millennium Challenge Corporation (MCC), to allocate the new funding on the basis of objective selection criteria based on a nation's commitment to "governing justly, investing in people, and encouraging economic freedom."[1]

The proposed Millennium Challenge Account (MCA) is nearly double the size of existing U.S. bilateral assistance programs that are devoted specifically to development (as opposed to humanitarian assistance, politically directed aid, and other programs)—the largest increase in decades. It presents a rare opportunity to create from scratch a new blueprint for distributing and delivering aid effectively. For these reasons the MCA offers a critical opportunity to deliberately shape the face that the United States presents to people in poor nations around the world. This book examines how best to fashion the MCA to make it an effective tool, not only in its own right but also in transforming U.S. development policy and reinforcing positive trends in international aid cooperation.

Although the MCA presents an enticing opportunity, the risk is at least as great that the new fund will simply add to the confusion of overlapping policies, agencies, aid programs, and eligibility criteria targeted at developing nations. This initiative will fall short of expectations unless it squarely addresses the tension between foreign policy and development goals that chronically afflicts U.S. foreign assistance. It will fall short unless there is a clear-eyed vision of how the MCA can complement the operations and country coverage of existing U.S. programs for developing nations, particularly those implemented by the U.S. Agency for International Development (USAID). The president's decision to establish an independent agency was interpreted as a vote of no confidence in the 10,000-strong USAID, which will retain responsibility for providing foreign assistance to the vast majority of the world's poorest. And finally the MCA will fall short if it is interpreted as one more instance of the United States going it alone instead of buttressing international cooperation in the fight against global poverty. These are serious risks.

The Context: Global Poverty and the War against Terrorism

The risks are particularly acute because of the heightened sense of urgency about both global poverty and global terrorism, demands that may pull in different directions. The MCA is being crafted at a time when security has returned to the forefront of the nation's consciousness to a degree not seen since the height of the cold war. Indeed President Bush cited terrorism as a central rationale for the creation of the MCA: "We also work for prosperity and opportunity because they help defeat terror. Yet persistent poverty and oppression can lead to hopelessness and despair. And when governments fail to meet the most basic needs of their people, these failed states can become havens for terror."[2] But the central tenet of the MCA is that it would be committed to supporting the "best performers" in the developing world, regardless of whether these countries are political allies or strategic partners in the U.S. war against terrorism. With allocations based solely on economic performance and governance, the MCA would be protected from political interests and be the closest to a development purist's blueprint for aid that the United States has ever attempted. Indeed, security experts were puzzled by the proposal to sharply increase pure development assistance at a moment of greatly increased need for political funding to reward allies in the antiterrorism coalition, to shore up "frontline" states, and to stabilize failed states. In fact few such countries could meet the MCA's economic performance and governance tests.[3]

The broader international community is equally focused on the scourge of global poverty. In recent years donors and recipients have increasingly agreed on the policy environment and objectives conducive to poverty reduction and growth and on making aid more effective, including by ensuring greater coordination among donors in support of plans designed and implemented from the bottom up. It is significant that President Bush announced the MCA in anticipation of the UN Conference on Financing for Development, a summit designed to secure substantial new funding aimed at growth and poverty reduction, with a special focus on achieving the UN millennium development goals (MDGs). The MDGs are internationally agreed-upon quantifiable targets for halving poverty and improving health, education, and environmental outcomes by 2015.[4]

President Bush's announcement of a $5 billion per year increase in bilateral aid was warmly welcomed by development advocates and poor nations. Together with other donor nations, the development community has lobbied for years for an increase in U.S. foreign aid and increased U.S. engagement in the fight against global poverty. Indeed President Bush made an indirect reference to this in his remarks: "All of us here must focus on real benefits to the poor, instead of debating arbitrary levels of inputs from the rich."[5] It is notable that, since the Monterrey summit, coordination with the efforts of other donors and with international financial institutions has been absent from the discussion, and the administration's draft legislation makes no reference to MDGs and scant mention of multilateral aid cooperation.[6] It would be a terrible irony if the MCA were seen as one more instance of American unilateralism. But this risk is real, since both the MCA and the president's Emergency Plan for AIDS Relief (proposed in the 2003 State of the Union address) bypass international efforts and existing aid agencies in favor of bilateral U.S. programs with idiosyncratic eligibility criteria and newly invented institutional arrangements.

The Promise and the Pitfalls

At best the MCA could transform U.S. policy toward the poorest countries over time—driving greater coherence among U.S. trade, aid, and investment policies and helping to rationalize existing programs. With clear criteria and substantial sums of money with enticing terms, the MCA could create incentives for governments to improve economic policies and governance, while helping strong performers sustain growth and improve investment climates. By establishing a record of success, the MCA could earn both a measure of independence from political meddling by the executive branch and the trust of Congress, freeing it from the burdensome restrictions and procurement requirements faced by other agencies. At best a successful MCA would also have salutary ripple effects on other U.S. aid programs, by strengthening public support, clarifying missions, and leading to greater overall coherence. Such a best-case scenario could strengthen USAID, helping it to more clearly focus on challenges that the MCA does not address: humanitarian crises, transition in postconflict countries, and social investments in weaker-performing states.

Unfortunately darker scenarios are at least as plausible, wherein the MCA becomes one more pot of money among a morass of overlapping U.S. programs and conditions.[7] At one extreme the MCA could become the preferred fund, not only for the best performers but also for politically salient countries. This outcome could very well emerge if the increased calls on aid for geopolitical reasons and the rapidly deteriorating budgetary environment conspire to undermine the MCA's purity. In this case the lines between the MCA and other forms of assistance would blur, and Congress would feel compelled to constrain the MCA as it currently constrains existing assistance programs.

In fact the administration's November 2002 decision to expand the MCA pool of eligible countries to include not just the poorest but also countries with per capita incomes up to $2,975 moved in precisely this direction, taking development advocates by surprise. With this change the eligibility pool encompasses nations that are already among the largest beneficiaries of politically directed U.S. assistance but that no longer qualify for concessional lending from the World Bank, such as Russia, Jordan, Egypt, Colombia, and Peru.[8] In fiscal 2002 these five nations received $1.32 billion in U.S. economic assistance—one-fifth the total of nonemergency aid.

At the other extreme, by maintaining too high a degree of purity, the MCA might remain beyond the reach of most poor nations. It would thus become a marginal player in development assistance rather than the key player, relevant only for the few stellar performers with substantial local capacity to formulate and implement proposals, while USAID would remain the main source of U.S. funding for the far more numerous, less capable countries. Analysis presented in chapter 3 suggests that countries most likely to be initially eligible for the MCA include only 12 percent of the population of sub-Saharan Africa, the poorest region of the world. Prompted by this concern, critics have proposed greatly expanding the MCA's country coverage.[9]

The combination of growing challenges and tighter resources raises the stakes. Vast new foreign assistance needs are anticipated related to the war on terrorism and in Iraq, including for coalition building and reconstruction, as well as the skyrocketing costs of combating the HIV/AIDS pandemic, which estimates put as high as $10 billion per year. Meanwhile the budget outlook is grim and growing worse. The danger is not to the survival of the MCA (although it is far from certain that it will ever receive the full $5 billion a year the president pledged). The greater danger is that less prominent and less popular development programs will be squeezed over time from a combination of budget pressures and deterioration in the beneficiary pool, as the best performers migrate to the MCA.

Achieving the Full Promise of the MCA

This book presents analysis and recommendations to help the MCA achieve its full promise. It is informed throughout by analogies and lessons from U.S. independent agencies, private foundations, and innovative international efforts, such as the poverty-reduction strategy papers (PRSP) process and the Global Fund to Fight AIDS, Tuberculosis, and Malaria (Global Fund). It strongly endorses many of the guiding principles of the administration's proposal and suggests concrete ways for implementing them. The MCA design should emphasize selecting countries in a transparent, objective manner on the basis of their policy environments. It should allocate funds on the basis of a competition for the best proposals, supporting country ownership of development projects from design through implementation and evaluation, and holding recipients accountable for concrete results.

The discussion below provides concrete recommendations on how best to elaborate these core elements of the MCA policy framework. The analysis shows how modest adjustments to the selection criteria and their application can result in important changes to the pool of countries competing for MCA funds and how this process can continue to be improved over time. It suggests how to strike a better balance on eligibility—not too narrow and not too broad—as well as between political discretion and objective indicators. It recommends that the MCA should have a narrow mission to support growth, poverty reduction, and sustainable development in poor nations with sound policy and good governance, by underwriting meritorious strategies designed and implemented by recipients. It advocates that MCA grants focus on a few areas of core competence, selected because of their demonstrated contribution to poverty reduction and growth and consistency with MDGs, evidence that the market alone will not ensure the socially optimal outcome, and a good track record for foreign aid. These include some but not all of the areas highlighted by the administration, such as primary education and basic health, and would add areas where the administration is out of step with the international community and many in Congress, such as the environment.

It explains in concrete terms how to implement a fundamental shift in U.S. development aid—away from the top-down, donor-driven approach to one that supports countries in designing, implementing, and evaluating plans. It suggests how to structure the grant competition so as to strengthen accountable, reformist governments while also ensuring space for civil society. In examining the operations and structure of the MCA, the book weighs the pros and cons of establishing a new agency from scratch, as opposed to creating an independent corporation within USAID, and sketches out how the latter alternative could be constructed. It also compares the proposed governance structure of the MCA with other independent agencies and recommends an alternative approach that provides for greater congressional and outside input and greater assurances of independence from political interference. And it details the instruments of operational flexibility that are most important to the MCA's central mission.

The MCA will not be accorded such operational flexibility nor succeed in breaking new ground on development aid unless Congress is a committed partner, no matter how compelling the blueprint. The MCA will be able to win trust and flexibility only if its program design contains adequate self-executing safeguards and mechanisms to ensure congressional input and oversight. Our analysis suggests a workable balance of concrete obligations and authorities.

Even if the MCA succeeds on its own terms, it may fail in making the United States a better development partner, in the absence of greater effort to ensure coherence among the many U.S. programs and agencies oriented toward development and to work with and learn from international efforts more broadly. The MCA cannot and should not go it alone in crafting development aid. One of the best-known pitfalls of foreign aid is lack of coordination among donors, which places substantial burdens on host countries and often undermines the effectiveness of assistance efforts. Recent years have witnessed an emerging, unprecedented, and important consensus at the international level about what works in poverty reduction and growth. This consensus has been made operational in a variety of new processes, agreements, and institutions. American taxpayer dollars could be greatly leveraged if they piggybacked on and learned from the efforts of the PRSP process and the Global Fund to pioneer the country ownership model that animates the MCA—underwriting development plans developed by recipient governments, with input from civil society as a central element. Similarly the MCA could rely on the MDGs as broad organizing principles, reflecting their central role in a host of mutually reinforcing international and bilateral efforts.

Likewise even a lot of money and a great idea are not enough to make a difference to U.S. foreign assistance, unless the MCA is designed to reflect the lessons from past aid failures and to enhance and complement other U.S. programs for developing countries. This is not the first time an administration has created a new agency to address U.S. foreign assistance goals. Since the inception of the Marshall Plan in 1948, successive administrations have attempted to overhaul U.S. foreign assistance programs, with responsibility—and direction—volleying back and forth between the Department of State and various independent agencies. What is different about the MCA is that it would create a new development agency without either replacing or triggering the reorganization of already existing foreign assistance programs. This has the potential to lead to bureaucratic duplication and misalignment of staff responsibilities and performance evaluation on the ground in countries that become eligible for the MCA, almost all of which already have USAID missions.

The analysis calls for articulating a clear division of labor between USAID and the MCC (whether as a new agency or as an affiliated entity) and giving greater clarity to USAID's remaining missions: to provide humanitarian assistance, support growth, sustainable development, and good governance in geopolitically important countries and in weaker-performing poor nations, and helping establish stability in failing states and postconflict situations. For those countries that nearly miss qualifying for the MCA, it is recommended that MCA funds be used under USAID's supervision to address those areas that are weak.

The MCA holds the promise of greatly increasing U.S. development assistance and pioneering a fundamentally new approach. But success is by no means guaranteed. A failed Millennium Challenge Corporation would quickly become yet another example—and the most expensive one—of wasted aid, and it could undermine political support for foreign assistance for decades to come. The United States must get it right the first time.

2

Global Aid Trends and Donor Coordination

President Bush announced the Millennium Challenge Account as the U.S. contribution to the United Nations Conference on Financing for Development in Monterrey, Mexico, in March 2002. The central purpose of the conference was to coordinate and increase donor efforts to combat global poverty. Yet since that summit—and including the November announcement of the Millennium Challenge Corporation (MCC) as the institutional home for the increased aid funds—coordination with other donors and with international financial institutions and other multilateral development banks has been surprisingly absent from the discussion. This chapter focuses on the question of how the operations of the MCC—as well as our foreign assistance approach more broadly—could and should coordinate with and learn from related international efforts in order to maximize the likelihood of successful development outcomes.

One reason for the administration's lack of emphasis on coordination may be its clearly stated objective of distinguishing the assistance programs supported by MCA funds from past aid "failures"—failures that are in part associated with multilateral development banks and international financial institutions (IFIs).

These institutions have lost a surprising degree of confidence among the U.S. polity in recent years. The 2000 Meltzer Commission's report to Congress, for example, recommended abolishing the International Monetary Fund and the World Bank in their current forms. And, from its inception, the incoming Bush administration publicly expressed its skepticism of IMF bailouts, both reflecting and reinforcing the lack of confidence in international financial institutions more generally (although in practice the administration subsequently supported several large IMF packages).[1]

While these may seem compelling reasons to go it alone, there are equally if not more compelling reasons for the MCC, and U.S. foreign assistance efforts more generally, to coordinate more and better with other donors, while still pushing for international reforms. One of the best-known pitfalls of foreign aid is lack of coordination among donors, both at the policymaking level and at the operations level in recipient countries, which places substantial burdens on host countries and often undermines the effectiveness of assistance efforts.[2] World Bank president James Wolfensohn has called attention to the plethora of 63,000 aid projects in the developing world, which often take different procurement, evaluation, environmental, and social approaches. A United Nations study found 1,500 projects in Burkina Faso alone and as many as 850 in Bolivia. According to the World Bank, developing countries are contending with an average of thirty aid agencies sending at least five missions a year to oversee projects across a wide range of social sectors.[3] As a result, reporting requirements are no small task for developing nations. Multiple conditions by multiple donors can generate competing and even contradictory policy objectives and can overwhelm the administrative and economic absorptive capacity of small, poor countries.[4]

In addition high levels of aid from multiple donors concentrated in a few poor countries with good policies can raise resource flows to the point that their relative size causes "Dutch disease" types of macroeconomic distortions. For instance, aid inflows contributed to persistent inflation despite tight credit policy in Ghana in the 1980s, while in recent years in Uganda they have raised concerns about the increasing difficulty of macroeconomic management.[5] Better coordination does not completely eliminate these problems—particularly when star performers such as these attract large amounts of funds from a few donors—but it certainly can ameliorate them.

Four important facets of donor coordination relate specifically to the operations of the MCC and are the focus of this chapter. First, recent years have witnessed an emerging, unprecedented, and important consensus at the international level about what works in poverty reduction and growth.

This consensus has been made operational in a variety of new processes, agreements, and institutions. To achieve success the MCC must at minimum learn from these innovations and ideally in some cases incorporate explicit linkages to them. Below we point to important lessons from the international poverty-reduction strategy papers (PRSP) process, the highly indebted poor country (HIPC) debt initiative, and the Global Fund to Fight AIDS, Tuberculosis, and Malaria (Global Fund) as particularly informative for key elements of the MCA design.

Second, the international community has agreed that priority should be placed on a limited set of goals deemed to be the mutually reinforcing foundations of poverty reduction and economic growth as well as on quantitative targets for assessment. The IFIs have adapted policies to incorporate this learning and to coordinate assistance efforts around the principles established by MDGs. The MCC should consider consistency with the MDGs in its grant making and include MDG targets in its assessments where appropriate.

Third, a critical determinant of aid effectiveness is that resources from multiple donors be directed in a consistent way to support priorities and plans that are determined locally. The nascent PRSP process, now part of all major World Bank and IMF loans to low-income countries, provides an established mechanism for donor coordination and for input from recipient countries into the lending process, including from representatives of civil society as well as from governments. The PRSP experience and process (discussed in detail below) is important to the MCC, both because it provides a vehicle for donor coordination and because it provides key lessons on involvement of civil society and from its experience with the country ownership model that the MCC is adopting. Many MCA-eligible countries already have PRSPs in place. The MCC should therefore take the PRSP as a starting point for a country's development strategy and encourage MCC proposals to be consistent with the country's PRSP. Like the PRSP process itself, this will require working to establish the appropriate balance between civil society participation and government direction.

Finally, an additional component of policy learning comes from donor coordination efforts during disaster relief and reconstruction efforts.[6] These circumstances are distinct from most aid operations, in that urgency fosters collaboration and allows the cumbersome regulations that usually constrain donor agencies to be waived. Precisely because the MCC is set up as an independent corporation with a mandate to disburse funds rapidly and effectively, disaster relief may provide important lessons for the MCC and in particular demonstrate the potential benefits of donor coordination.

The issue of coordinating the operations of the MCC with those of other donors and multilateral efforts raises the broader issues of the international community's management of a host of issues related to economic integration and global public goods and what sort of leadership role the United States should play. Emerging international consensus has pushed in the direction of greater coherence at the international level, while in parallel pushing ownership down to government and civil society in recipient nations. The highly indebted poor country (HIPC) debt initiative, for example, depended for its success on complete coherence among donors, because the value of donors' outstanding claims was interdependent and because donors had to share the accounting cost of financing the debt forgiven by multilateral institutions. The PRSP framework likewise was negotiated among donors, reflecting its purpose of directing the proceeds from HIPC debt relief as well as new multilateral financing. Shortly after the PRSP was launched, the international community took the unprecedented step of agreeing to MDGs. The rising premium placed on coordination at the international level is also evident in the launch of the Global Fund, which pools contributions from official donors as well as the private sector to fund projects defined locally.

Although the proposed MCC design reflects the emerging international consensus in its emphasis on country ownership, its bilateral approach and idiosyncratic eligibility criteria do not promote cooperation with international efforts. An important and relevant parallel here is the $15 billion global HIV/AIDS initiative announced by President Bush in January 2003. The administration's initiative would contribute $200 million annually to the Global Fund over five years—which is actually a reduction from the $350 million Congress appropriated in fiscal 2003.[7] For purposes of comparison, UN Secretary General Kofi Annan has requested contributions of $8 billion to $10 billion per year to the Global Fund. This would imply a U.S. contribution ranging between $1.5 billion (based on the U.S. share of IMF and World Bank capital) and $3.7 billion per year (based on the U.S. share of Organization for Economic Cooperation and Development donor GDP).[8] Both the MCA and the global AIDS initiative—the two flagship initiatives announced by President Bush for poor nations—are determinedly bilateral in orientation. The tension between multilateral and bilateral approaches raises a number of more general questions for our foreign assistance strategy going forward. While a full discussion of these questions is beyond the scope of this chapter, the challenges that they pose to effective foreign assistance policy are directly relevant to the operations of the MCC.

Framing Objectives: Millennium Development Goals

In September 2000, at the United Nations Millennium Summit, world leaders agreed to a set of time-bound and measurable goals and targets for combating poverty, hunger, disease, illiteracy, environmental degradation, and discrimination against women. A final goal calls for a global partnership to better marshal the efforts of the international trade and intellectual property rights regimes so that they work better for the poorest countries. The Millennium Summit also outlined a wide range of commitments to human rights, good governance, and democracy. Millennium development goals, whose primary objective is to reduce poverty by half by the year 2015, were an outgrowth of that summit. These goals have become a framing and coordinating principle for foreign assistance efforts worldwide. While the goals are ambitious and some are loosely defined, they capture the essence of what is required to reduce global poverty and promote development.[9]

The specific goals and their definitions are as follows:

—Eradicate extreme poverty and hunger: Reduce by half, between 1990 and 2015, the proportion of people living on less than a dollar a day.

—Achieve universal primary education: Ensure that, by 2015, all boys and girls complete a full course of primary schooling.

—Promote gender equality and empower women: Eliminate gender disparity in primary and secondary education, preferably by 2005 and at all levels by 2015.

—Reduce child mortality: Reduce by two-thirds, between 1990 and 2015, the mortality rate among children under five years of age.

—Improve maternal health: Reduce by three-quarters, between 1990 and 2015, the maternal mortality ratio.

—Combat HIV/AIDS, malaria, and other diseases: Halt by 2015 and begin to reverse the spread of HIV/AIDS and the incidence of malaria and other diseases.

—Ensure environmental sustainability: Integrate the principles of sustainable development into country policies and programs, reverse loss of environmental resources, by 2015 reduce by half the proportion of people without access to safe drinking water, achieve significant improvement by 2020 in the lives of at least 100 million slum dwellers.

—Develop a global partnership for development:[10] Develop further an open trading and financial system that is rule-based, predictable, and nondiscriminatory; address the special debt and trade needs of the least developed countries and landlocked and small island developing countries;

in cooperation with developing countries, develop decent and productive work for youth; in cooperation with pharmaceutical companies, develop access to affordable drugs; in cooperation with the private sector, develop the benefits of new technologies.[11]

In addition MDGs provide a benchmark against which development progress can be measured. A number of efforts to measure progress—by countries, by international institutions, and by nongovernmental actors—are already under way. These efforts involve actors ranging from the United Nations Development Program to the World Economic Forum to a host of nongovernmental organizations worldwide.[12] While critics dismiss MDGs as too ambitious to be useful, they are instrumental in quantifying the vast development and poverty challenges that still need to be addressed, achieving near universal consensus around a set of goals and concepts, and providing benchmarks against which progress—or lack thereof—can be measured.

The MDGs have become the organizing principle for a host of mutually reinforcing international poverty reduction efforts. The Latin American and Caribbean region of the World Bank is currently operationalizing its country programs around the MDGs. The Inter-American Development Bank has made the MDGs one of its two top-priority policy goals. The incoming World Health Organization director-general Jong-Wook Lee has targeted achievement of the health MDGs as his top priority, and many bilateral donors, such as Canada, the United Kingdom, and some other European countries, have made the MDGs the central focus of their programs.[13]

As elaborated in chapter 4, the mission of the MCA should be defined more specifically and concretely than meeting the MDGs and should include some additional areas vital to sustainable development and growth. Nonetheless the MCA's stated objectives should contribute to the recipient countries' meeting the MDGs. Thus it makes sense for the architects of the MCC to embrace MDGs in principle, as well as to take advantage of the efforts of the wide range of actors and institutions involved in promoting and evaluating progress toward meeting those goals. Indeed close collaboration with these efforts could help the limited staff at the MCC with its momentous challenge of developing ways to monitor and measure the results of its own assistance efforts.[14] A simple way of ensuring that MDGs are incorporated into those operations would be to encourage MCC proposals to include their possible contribution to one or more of the goals, where appropriate, as well as some concrete assessment of the contribution.

Coordination Mechanisms: The PRSP Process

While the millennium goals have begun to serve as broad organizing principles for development assistance efforts, the poverty-reduction strategy papers (PRSP) process is their operational embodiment in the international financial institutions. PRSPs are strategy documents that are prepared by recipient countries, based on a dialogue between the government and representatives of civil society. The introduction of this process as a channel for donor coordination and the lessons that have been learned in its two years of existence have major implications for the MCC.

Starting in late 1999, the IMF and World Bank announced a new, two-pronged strategy for their assistance to low-income countries in late 1999. The first prong is to base concessional lending and debt relief efforts to low-income countries on PRSPs. The second and related prong is use of the completed PRSPs to provide IMF concessional lending through a revised program, the Poverty Reduction and Growth Facility (PRGF), which has a stronger poverty reduction focus than predecessor programs.

The PRSP process is a sea change in the manner in which IFIs operate, at least in principle. The rationale and approach underlying the PRSPs dovetails with the emphasis of MDGs on nationally owned poverty reduction strategies. The PRSP process is based on five key principles. It is country-driven, with broad-based participation of civil society; it is results-oriented; it has a long-term perspective; it addresses the many dimensions of poverty and the policies needed to reduce it; and it entails partnership among all stakeholders and donors, particularly between the IMF and the World Bank.

The change in approach by the Bretton Woods institutions was in part a response to the grass-roots movement in support of debt relief. The movement spanned both ends of the spectrum, bringing together the Catholic Church Jubilee 2000 campaign, with a host of nongovernmental organizations and famous entertainers such as U2's Bono. The campaign had unprecedented success in forcing debt relief and poverty reduction onto the international public policy agenda.[15] The relationship of the two was made explicit by linking eligibility for debt relief under the HIPC initiative to countries' completion of a PRSP.

Since their inception PRSPs have been completed by twenty-nine countries and twenty more are pending. (See table 2-1.) The efforts of both the World Bank and the IMF in the arenas of poverty reduction and capacity building hinge to a large extent on the PRSP process, and expectations of success have been heightened among both the donor community and the

Table 2-1. *PRSP Status of Likely MCA Countries*[a]

	Poverty-reduction strategy papers (PRSP) status		
MC eligibility	*Full*	*Pending*	*None*
Incomes less than $1,435	Bolivia Ghana Guyana Honduras Nicaragua Senegal Sri Lanka Vietnam	Armenia Lesotho Mongolia	Bhutan China[b] Nepal Philippines Swaziland Syria[b]
Incomes between $1,435 and $2,975	. . .	. . .	Belize Bulgaria Jordan Namibia South Africa St. Vincent and the Grenadines
Ineligible	Albania Azerbaijan Republic Benin Burkina Faso Cambodia Cape Verde Ethiopia Gambia Guinea Kyrgyz Republic Malawi Mali Mauritania Mozambique Niger Rwanda Tajikistan Tanzania Uganda Yemen Zambia	Cameroon Central African Republic Chad Congo Côte d'Ivoire Djibouti Georgia Guinea-Bissau Kenya Lao, PDR Macedonia Madagascar Moldova Pakistan São Tomé and Principe Serbia-Montenegro Sierra Leone	All other countries

Source: PRSP status is from International Monetary Fund (www.imf.org).

a. The status of countries is constantly changing.

b. Eliminated from receiving U.S. aid for statutory reasons.

countries involved. The introduction of this process represents major progress in providing a framework for coordinated donor support for country-owned programs. Yet there is still room for improving the process, as well as for better understanding the outcomes, as more countries complete PRSPs.

A 2002 review of the PRSP process by the IMF and the World Bank, aided by outside experts, details the major achievements and challenges. These achievements are: a stronger sense of ownership among most governments, a more open dialogue, a prominent place for poverty reduction in policy debates, and an acceptance by the donor community of the principles of the PRSP approach.[16] Not surprisingly the review also reported that substantial challenges remain, both in the policy design phase and in the less-tested implementation phase. Linkages between the PRSP process and poverty outcomes are unclear, for example.

Some of the most important challenges hinge on the participatory nature of the process. While most observers agree that country ownership is a desirable objective, it is not clear how much extensive debate about policy alternatives contributes to better outcomes. In some cases PRSPs have become mired in polemical debates that have significantly slowed the debt relief and lending processes. These debates often suffer from lack of adequate data on poverty and on the records of alternative policies. In other cases dialogue seems to have been curtailed or circumvented by the urgency of debt relief needs, resulting in justified criticisms that the process can be less than democratic. A few countries even contracted outside consulting firms such as PricewaterhouseCoopers to draft their interim PRSPs.[17] The requirement that PRSPs be formulated with the input of civil society was intended to remedy weaknesses in governance and accountability in many countries. Yet, ironically, delays and prolonged political debates are more likely to occur in better-governed countries than in less democratic ones. Bolivia, for example, a country that ranks fairly high in civil liberties and other governance indicators relative to other PRSP countries, had fallen off track in the process.

The PRSP process depends largely on governments and their ability to gain the participation of nongovernmental actors. The capacity of governments varies, particularly in the poorest countries, as does their degree of transparency and political openness. The structure of civil society and the sophistication of nongovernmental organizations also vary among countries. Parliaments have often been excluded from the process, either by government design or because the mechanisms for coordination are too weak. And while including representative institutions in the dialogue is the democratic ideal, in countries with weak institutional capacity or where such institutions are marginal to the policy process, making the effort to include them can be costly to timely and effective policy outcomes. Thus the outcomes of the PRSP process are diverse, both in the extent to which the design process is genuinely participatory and in the capacity of nongovernmental actors to play effective and productive oversight roles during implementation, which is particularly important in contexts where there is limited representation in official government institutions.

Expectations of the process, meanwhile, both within recipient countries and in the donor community, are often far beyond the institutional capacity in the countries. Monitoring and evaluation systems are still nascent. And while the process provides a new venue for donor coordination, the modalities for incorporating the involvement of donors from outside the Bretton Woods institutions are still limited. In sum, while the introduction of the PRSP process is a marked change in the approach taken by the IFIs, it is a matter of learning by doing.

Evaluations from both within and without the international financial institutions note this high degree of variance, both in terms of process and outcomes, stemming from limited institutional capacity, a lack of adequate poverty data, and weak democratic institutions, among other factors. Criticisms of the PRSP process range from those that emphasize its complexity and the difficulties that poor countries have in marshaling the institutional capacity required to complete the process, to those that question the extent to which the process is participatory at all.[18]

As the nascent PRSP process goes forward, two important questions remain unanswered, questions that are important not only to the PRSP process but to the proposed structure and operations of the MCC. The PRSP experience is germane to the MCC as a mechanism for coordinating with other donors and also as an experience with incorporating input by local civil society into the assistance process and combining the priorities and efforts of government and nongovernmental actors.

The first question is how much the outcomes of the process hinge on the transparency and capacity of recipient governments. The second is how much value is added by the participation of nongovernmental actors in both design and oversight. The answers to these questions determine how much the PRSP process can contribute to resolving critical issues of ownership, institutional capacity, and the relationship between foreign assistance and technical know-how and homegrown policies and efforts. They can also better align expectations of the process—both inside and outside the countries—with institutional capacities. Study after study of aid effectiveness highlights the need for ownership and institutional capacity in order to achieve positive development outcomes.[19] The learning that is occurring in these areas as the PRSPs go forward is invaluable.

An additional point, which relates to the need to better coordinate the efforts of donors, is the need for more and new kinds of technical assistance as the PRSP process moves into the implementation phase. At present the World Bank and the IMF, as well as other donors, attempt to identify areas where assistance is necessary in the PRSP process. As the operation enters the more difficult implementation phases, and new actors and institutions are needed (such as nongovernmental bodies capable of providing neutral oversight on budgets and expenditures), additional technical assistance will be required. New providers—for example, institutions that already play those roles effectively in other developing (or developed) countries, can fill this role.[20] Without such assistance many countries lack the institutional capacity necessary to manage a process whose success hinges on the ability of governments to solicit broad and transparent participation and on nongovernmental organizations to play a sustained, neutral role in oversight and evaluation.

Virtually all the challenges faced by the PRSP process—in both design and implementation phases—are relevant to the MCC, in both coordinating with other donors and incorporating inputs and proposals from actors in the recipient countries. The MCC's emphasis on proposals designed by the countries, incorporating input from nongovernmental and subnational organizations as well as national governments, is likely to face the same kinds of challenges as the PRSP process in incorporating genuine popular participation and addressing the limited capacity of many recipients for program design, implementation, and monitoring.

Even a cursory look at the list of countries that qualify for MCA funds in the first year suggests that the inclusion of civil society or representative institutions in the formulation of aid proposals might be arbitrary and less than democratic in some of them. This is likely to result in the same kinds of questions and criticisms that have been raised about PRSPs. (See table 2-1.)

Another problem is the ability of the countries to develop and produce the kinds of detailed proposals that the MCC is seeking. Certainly the challenge of producing PRSPs has proved daunting for many countries because of weak institutional capacity. How will the MCC overcome such constraints, given its limited staff? These challenges are equally if not more important in the project implementation phase, something that has not yet been fully evaluated in the case of PRSPs. The PRSP process is also challenged by the lack of adequate neutral oversight organizations in the poorest countries, organizations that play an important role in monitoring and evaluation. This is a key issue for the MCC as well, given that its small size leaves it with very little in-house capacity for monitoring and oversight.

An equally important challenge is that of donor coordination. While the PRSP process has proven an effective way to coordinate efforts of the World Bank and the IMF, it has been less successful at providing a channel for other donors, even though this is an explicit objective of the process. Will the MCC operate completely independently of this process, or will it attempt to give it impetus by using it as a starting point? The latter would surely be a more effective approach from the point of view of donor coordination and of contributing to country-owned poverty reduction strategies.

In sum, the PRSP process provides some important opportunities for the MCC to coordinate its efforts with those of other donors through a process that includes the recipient countries in a meaningful manner. The nascent process has significant challenges to overcome, but it has already broken new ground and provided important lessons. Given everything that we know about the respective roles of ownership, institutional capacity, and donor coordination in ensuring aid effectiveness, the MCC—the new player on the block—cannot afford to bypass this process. Rather, those involved in the management of the MCC should do their utmost to both coordinate with and build from the PRSP process. This is particularly important in MCC-qualifying countries that have initiated or completed the PRSP process.

As in the case of MDGs, coordination mechanisms need not be cumbersome. Proposals should reflect knowledge of and coordination with the overall poverty reduction objectives laid out in the country's PRSP, for example, as well as provide a more concrete description of how the proposal would contribute to meeting one or more of those objectives. Some simple method for assessing those potential contributions would give the coordination process more structure and credibility.

An additional reason for coordinating MCC efforts with those of other donors is economies of scale. The MCC will reach only a small number of countries, leaving other donors to play the leading role in roughly fifty countries whose poverty is sufficiently severe to warrant inclusion in the World Bank's International Development Association (IDA). If a genuine objective of the MCC is to strengthen the way the aid business works more generally, then it will need to leverage its influence in the countries in which it operates with the efforts of other donors in countries where it does not. Cooperating via the PRSP process is an obvious channel for doing that. To date there has not been any effort to design in coordination between MCA activities and those of the international financial institutions, perhaps because the initial focus has been on structuring the MCC and determining its relationship with other U.S. agencies. But now, as the MCC begins to establish operating principles and procedures, is the time to build effective coordination mechanisms into its operations.

Lessons for MCA Design from the Global Fund and HIPC

The architects of the MCA should also look carefully at the Global Fund and HIPC for valuable lessons on particular design issues. The Global Fund grew from a proposal at the G8 Okinawa Summit in July 2000; a year later it was officially launched by the G8 and UN Secretary General Kofi Annan.[21] The fund has, since its inception, received the endorsement of many international actors. In April 2001 the World Health Organization's Commission on Macroeconomics and Health endorsed funding a global fund for HIV/AIDS, tuberculosis, and malaria.[22] The same month the Organization of African Unity supported the creation of a global fund for AIDS.[23]

The Global Fund is pioneering precisely the sort of demand-driven, results-oriented grant-making approach that the MCA will adopt, based on competition among locally designed proposals. As such the Global Fund provides useful comparisons on many operational issues, such as proposal review, participation by NGOs, staffing, and monitoring and evaluation, as well as on governance, which will be examined in greater detail in chapters 4 and 5. It also provides informative contrasts. The Global Fund has a single-issue focus, unlike the MCA. And, lacking the strict selection criteria envisaged for the MCA, the Global Fund covers a vastly broader group of countries, which is valuable for assessing whether the MCA's demand-driven approach could be compatible with broader coverage of poor countries over time.

The Global Fund seeks to take advantage of expertise and resources across countries and sectors by reaching out to the various players in the global fight against these diseases. Developing and developed countries, nongovernmental organizations, the private sector, and the United Nations are responsible for selecting their own delegates to a governing board, with seats apportioned as follows: developed nations, seven; developing nations, seven; NGOs, two; and private sector, two. In nonvoting capacities, representatives from UNAIDS, WHO, the World Bank, and a person living with one of the three diseases also serve on the board. The inclusion of outside experts on the MCA board should likewise be considered.

The Global Fund awards grants on a demand-driven competitive basis, as the MCA seeks to do. And it goes beyond PRSP-style consultations in incorporating nongovernmental actors in the proposals. It requires recipient countries to establish a country coordinating mechanism (CCM), which integrates proposals from local actors into a single national proposal. The CCM must include a wide range of local stakeholders: government (national and subnational), members of parliament, NGOs, the private sector, religious groups, academics, representatives of local communities, and people afflicted with AIDS, tuberculosis, or malaria. The CCM approach gives the national government the central role as chair of the committee, but this is offset by allowing CCMs to submit more than one proposal (although these must be on different diseases) to the Global Fund and by encouraging organizations to submit proposals through the CCM.[24] Even so, controversy erupted when the South African Ministry of Health objected strenuously to the Global Fund directly funding KwaZulu Natal province (controlled by a different political party) and threatened to block delivery of funds unless they went through the federal Ministry of Health.

Finally, in line with the strong emphasis on results-oriented proposals designed by the recipients is a strong emphasis on multiple levels of monitoring and evaluation, with important components contracted out to private auditing firms.

The Global Fund's start-up was complicated by differences among key members regarding its structure and operations as well as the time-consuming nature of soliciting high-quality proposals from recipients and selecting outside monitors.[25] This too is instructive as Congress considers the budget for the MCA in its early years.

On the issue of selection criteria, the highly indebted poor country (HIPC) debt initiative may provide the most interesting parallel. HIPC differs from the MCA in key respects. It has a narrow mandate, it is a multilateral initiative, and it provides relief on the basis of strict formulas. Moreover, the HIPC quantitative eligibility criteria select for unsustainable debt burdens, while judgments on policy performance are largely qualitative. Nonetheless HIPC is among the first and best-known development programs that determine eligibility strictly on the basis of a set of quantitative indicators that are freely available, making possible a transparent and open selection process. Debt relief advocates and the official community take sharply different views on the particulars of the HIPC eligibility indicators. But even the fiercest critics would agree that the quantitative indicators are a great improvement over bureaucratic discretion, both in making possible an informed public debate and in creating valuable predictability for developing countries. As Congress considers how much detail on the MCA selection process to write into law, it is helpful to recall that, three years into the life of HIPC, public criticism of the slow pace and short eligibility list led to a significant modification of the eligibility criteria (and enhanced relief).

Lessons from Disaster Relief and Reconstruction Efforts

Much of U.S. foreign assistance is plagued by burdensome and time-consuming restrictions. Many funds are earmarked, setting aside specific amounts for particular purposes, such as child survival and health programs, as well as for specific countries and regions. In addition U.S. Agency for International Development (USAID) funds are also hostage to over 250 policy directives—implicitly binding recommendations that, among other things, often direct AID activities to favored U.S. universities.[26] Not surprisingly those procedures limit the flexibility of our aid programs and make it more difficult to coordinate with other donors.

Disaster relief funds, in contrast, which are administered by the Office of Foreign Disaster Assistance, are given "notwithstanding authority," which permits bypassing the usual contracting and procurement regulations in order to move funds rapidly. Not surprisingly disaster relief efforts tend to be better coordinated with other donors than are our typical assistance programs, for two reasons. The first is, of course, the waiving of cumbersome requirements, which allows for more flexibility and coordination. The second and perhaps more important reason is the sense of urgency and shared purpose in reconstruction situations, which provides an impetus to coordination and a clear sense of what needs to be done.[27] Under normal circumstances what needs to be done is less clear, and donors often disagree about priorities. In these instances the most positive examples of coordinated assistance are those where the host government has a clear vision of what it wants to do, such as Uganda taking ownership of its development strategy in the 1990s.

Donor coordination happens to a large extent in the field, where the greatest opportunities exist for collaboration but also for competition. Efficient allocation of resources depends on division of labor and avoiding redundancy. In the case of disaster relief and postconflict reconstruction, donors usually have a clear sense of shared purpose. While this consensus is critical, leadership is also important. Self-evaluations by donor agencies consistently call for a unified front led by a single actor. A leading donor helps focus the immediate objectives and simplifies coordination for the host government.

Many critics of poorly coordinated aid promote one or another multilateral institution as the ideal unifier of donor efforts and lobby for their own institution as the leader. In Afghanistan, for example, soon after the UN's Office for the Coordination of Humanitarian Affairs (OCHA) stepped in to provide an umbrella organization for disaster relief, the World Bank sought to administer a single trust fund in the postconflict reconstruction, and eventually took the leading role.[28] The first mover often, if not always, assumes de facto leadership. The United States led in East Timor because the Office of Transition Initiatives (OTI) established a presence most quickly. OTI's flexibility allowed it to begin disbursing funds and procuring goods before the UN or the World Bank could implement even their early response programs.[29] While other bilateral donors could offer only humanitarian assistance, the notwithstanding authority of OTI gave the United States the first mover's advantage. In the West Bank and Gaza, the World Bank praises early involvement and the actors' mutual understanding of one another's responsibilities.[30]

While many call for leadership in donor coordination, donors remain reluctant to relinquish control of funding. Due to disparate conditionality and earmarking requirements, donors often establish parallel or competing projects. Postdisaster assistance especially sees the problem of redundancy in the rush to send relief aid. In the wake of the El Salvador earthquake of 2001, the United States, Europe, and Japan sent four independent evaluation teams.[31] Unfortunately OCHA's reliance on voluntary contributions has limited its ability to lead. Still hoping to reduce unnecessary overlap, OCHA hosts a web-based information clearinghouse to facilitate the exchange of information among donors.[32] These disaster appeals do provide a model for detailing the tasks at hand and assigning responsibility. As mandated by UN Resolution 46/182, the secretary-general issues a consolidated appeal for assistance in emergencies requiring assistance.[33] This consolidated appeals process (CAP) attempts to promote joint programming, resource mobilization, and prioritization.[34] The CAP seeks to reduce redundant programming in disaster relief by clearly enumerating specific project needs and contributions. The Common Humanitarian Action Plan (CHAP) offers donors a menu of needed projects from which to choose.

Although the MCC will not be focusing on reconstruction or disaster situations, a number of lessons are relevant. The first is that limiting the conditions and requirements on MCC funds will be critical to rapid disbursement and therefore rapid results. In addition, leadership—often established via first response—is critical to donor coordination, and coordination and cooperation prevent redundancy. Coordination, meanwhile, is easier in countries that have a clear sense of their own poverty-reduction priorities. Ownership is key. The PRSP process, an important new tool for encouraging country ownership that either has been completed or is in process in many MCA qualifying countries, can play an important role in coordinating the efforts of the MCC with those of other major donors. This is particularly important for countries that receive large amounts of aid relative to the size of their economies, as will be the case for many MCA qualifying countries.

The disaster relief experience also suggests that leadership is often an important component of donor coordination. This suggests not an international-level "parceling up" of activities but rather that any new actor, like the MCC, be aware of areas where other actors have taken the lead and made headway—as have private sector donors in the public health arena, for example. Given the clear need for more resources to resolve any number of development challenges, avoiding redundancy should be a basic operating procedure for the MCC, even though the temptation is to establish leadership—and success—across a wide range of sectors and activities. This suggests that the MCC team develop a procedure for reviewing proposals that takes into account similar grants being made by other donors. This procedure could be at the country or the sector level.

Coordinating MCC Operations with Other Development Objectives

Another coordination issue that MCC managers must consider is how its efforts in a select group of low-income and lower-middle-income developing countries can complement and coordinate with the efforts of other donors and institutions in addressing similar problems in the remaining many countries with pressing poverty challenges. Poverty in lower-middle-income developing countries remains a pressing challenge, for example.[35] Because these countries tend to be more integrated in international financial markets, they are more vulnerable to volatility in international capital markets. Financial crises have high costs for the poor in lower-middle and middle-income developing countries. The number of people placed in poverty by the financial market crises in Mexico (1995), Thailand and Indonesia (1998), Brazil (1999), and Argentina and Turkey (2001) range from a low estimate of 40 million to a high estimate of 100 million—out of a combined population of 800 million.[36]

In the lower-middle-income developing countries (listed in table 2-1), the effects of foreign aid are usually secondary to those of other policies, such as trade and investment, on reducing poverty. Particularly as the MCC moves to countries with incomes between $1,435 and $2,975 in the third year, ensuring that its assistance policies are coordinated with other policies will be particularly important, as is described further in chapter 6. In these countries, coordination of aid, trade, and investment policies is as important as, if not more important than, coordinating aid efforts with other donors.

Summary of Recommendations

Donor coordination has been notoriously absent from the debate over the MCC, yet it is critical to most development success stories. The architects of the MCC should build from the international community's newly formed consensus on development objectives and utilize recently established mechanisms for donor coordination that reflect that consensus. This broad framework suggests a number of operating principles:

For the United States to present as its contribution to international efforts a Millennium Challenge Account that makes no reference to the millennium development goals will be seen as a bad case of unilateralism and, worse, bad policy. The MDGs have become the organizing principle for a host of mutually reinforcing international and bilateral poverty reduction efforts. The MCC should rely on the MDGs as broad organizing principles. It should coordinate with the international community's related efforts to identify the most pressing poverty needs within countries and regions and to monitor progress in achieving MDGs.

The MCC should coordinate with and build from the recently launched PRSP process for low-income and highly indebted poor countries. The PRSP relies on proposals from recipient countries, as the MCC intends to do, and is a means to foster country ownership and donor coordination. As the PRSP process goes forward, it provides valuable lessons about the promises and the pitfalls of incorporating local participation and about institutional capacity in poor countries. These lessons are directly relevant to the operations of the MCC. There may be economies of scale for the MCC, meanwhile, in collaborating with the monitoring and evaluation mechanisms established by the PRSP process.

The Global Fund provides valuable lessons as perhaps the most relevant operational model for the MCA. The Global Fund is pioneering precisely the sort of demand-driven, results-oriented grant-making approach that the MCA will adopt, based on competition among locally designed proposals. As such it provides useful comparisons on many operational issues, such as proposal review, participation by nongovernmental organizations, staffing, and monitoring and evaluation. It also provides informative contrasts. The Global Fund has a single-issue focus, unlike the MCA. And, lacking the strict selection criteria envisaged for the MCA, the Global Fund covers a vastly broader group of countries, which will provide valuable data for assessing whether the MCA's demand-driven approach could be compatible with broader coverage of poor countries over time.

HIPC may provide the most interesting parallel on selection criteria. HIPC differs from the MCA in that it has a narrow mandate, and the quantitative criteria select for unsustainable debt burdens, while judgments on policy performance are largely qualitative. Nonetheless HIPC is the best-known development program that determines eligibility strictly on the basis of quantitative indicators that are freely available, making possible a transparent and open selection process and creating valuable predictability for developing countries. It is noteworthy that, three years into the life of the HIPC program, public reactions to the outcomes led to a significant modification of the eligibility criteria.

Waiving standard regulations and conditions (earmarks) on assistance funds is key to the efficiency, coordination, and rapid disbursement that is typical of disaster relief efforts. As rapid disbursement and results are explicit objectives of the MCC, the same principles apply. In the case of disaster relief, clear and urgent objectives provide the impetus for donor coordination. In the absence of this clarity and urgency, country ownership of development policies and objectives plays a critical role, suggesting that fostering local ownership of policies, via the PRSP or proposals to the MCC, will be particularly important to coordinating the efforts of donors.

The programs supported by the MCC should complement other policies that affect development and poverty reduction, such as those concerning trade and foreign investment. This will be particularly important once the MCC begins to operate in lower-middle-income countries, where trade and investment opportunities and macroeconomic policies tend to be more important to growth and poverty reduction than are aid flows.

3

Who Should Qualify?

In his speech announcing the Millennium Challenge Account, President Bush proposed that funds from the new program go to low-income countries that are "ruling justly, investing in their people, and encouraging economic freedom."[1] The administration subsequently announced the procedure it proposes to follow in determining which countries are meeting these three broad criteria. The proposed methodology is one way to address several key issues central to the MCA, including:

—the income levels that will determine the set of eligible countries,

—the specific indicators that will be used to show commitment in the three broad areas,

—the passing grades on each indicator, and

—the method of aggregating across the indicators to determine the list of qualifying countries.

This chapter examines the administration's proposed methodology, exploring the judgments required and examining some

This chapter is from Steven Radelet, *Challenging Foreign Aid: A Policymaker's Guide to the Millennium Challenge Account* (Washington: Center for Global Development, 2003).

alternative methods. It then applies this methodology to determine which countries would qualify during the first three years, using the data available as of May 2003.

There are multiple ways to determine which countries meet the broad guidelines provided by the president.[2] The administration's proposal is a reasonable approach, but it could be improved by doing the following:

—dropping the third-year countries with per capita incomes between \$1,435 and \$2,975 from eligibility, since those countries have less pressing needs and more options for financing than the poorest countries;

—adjusting the list of sixteen indicators (over time) by dropping some of the weakest indicators, adding several new ones, and strengthening others;

—using an absolute standard as a passing grade on the indicators (where possible) rather than the median;

—reconsidering the requirement that all countries must pass the corruption hurdle; and

—considering creating an aggregate score for the sixteen indicators rather than using medians to determine qualification.

Section 1 briefly summarizes the debate about aid and country selectivity, providing the conceptual underpinnings of the qualification process. Section 2 reviews the main points of the administration's proposal. Section 3 examines the three country groups that the administration has proposed to be eligible to compete for MCA funding during the first three years. Section 4 explores each of the proposed sixteen indicators in depth, along with some alternative measures. Section 5 examines different methods of aggregating the sixteen indicators to determine which countries ultimately qualify. Sections 6 and 7 provide illustrative lists of the countries most likely to qualify using the administration's proposal and using an alternative aggregation system. The final sections offer concluding thoughts and recommendations to improve the selection process.

Conceptual Underpinnings: Aid and Country Selectivity

A central tenet of the MCA is that aid can be more effective in achieving development goals if it is focused on nations with governments that are committed to establishing policies and institutions conducive to economic growth and poverty reduction. At one level this idea seems to make common sense: Foreign assistance will go much further in countries where governments are dedicated to building better schools and clinics, creating good jobs, and rooting out corruption than it will in countries with dishonest or incompetent governments. Foreign assistance was more effective in Korea and Botswana, where governments placed a high priority on growth and development, than it was in the Philippines under Ferdinand Marcos or Liberia under Samuel Doe. This is not to argue that aid was a major determinant of growth in Korea or Botswana but that aid probably was a better investment there than in countries with weaker and more corrupt governments.

The idea of country selectivity, in which aid is in part conditioned on good policies and institutions, has gained much currency in aid programs in recent years. This idea is supported by the research of World Bank economists Craig Burnside, David Dollar, and Paul Collier, which shows that aid has a positive relationship to growth in countries with good policies and institutions and little or no effect in other countries.[3] This idea has influenced the policies of the World Bank, which claims that it has become more selective with its loans in recent years (although the evidence supporting this claim is far from convincing). Several bilateral aid agencies have also been influenced by these findings.

The research on the relationship between aid and economic growth, however, is hardly unanimous in its conclusions. Despite the findings of Burnside, Dollar, and Collier, the literature remains largely inconclusive. Some studies find a positive relationship between aid and growth in various circumstances (particularly studies focusing on microeconomic linkages), others find no relationship, while still others find that aid has had a negative impact on growth.[4] To some extent these ambiguous findings at the macroeconomic level should not be surprising, for several reasons. First, even under the best of circumstances, the impact of foreign aid on economic growth is probably small relative to other factors, making it difficult to detect a clear relationship. Second, the data underlying cross-country empirical growth studies are inherently weak, with data missing for many countries or for variables that may strongly influence the growth process. Third, as discussed in chapter 7, large portions of aid were historically given to countries for political and strategic reasons. Even when this aid was spent on development projects, it is hardly surprising that it had a limited impact on growth, since that was not its primary objective. Fourth, some types of aid should be expected to be negatively correlated with growth, especially humanitarian aid, disaster assistance, and aid provided in response to terms of trade shocks, since by definition all are aimed at countries suffering growth slowdowns.

The Burnside, Dollar, and Collier studies have come under attack from two directions in recent years. First, several studies challenge the finding that the positive aid-to-growth relationship depends on good policies, finding instead that aid is positively correlated with growth (with diminishing returns) regardless of the policy environment. These studies use differing sample sizes and specifications, cover different time periods, and control for a variety of other factors besides aid, making comparisons difficult. Second, a more recent study by William Easterly, Ross Levine, and David Roodman, built from the Burnside and Dollar data set, found that the initial results were not robust to new data points, different time frames, varying definitions of aid, and alternative definitions of policy, and found no clear relationship between aid and growth.[5]

Moreover the focus on the quality of policies in the recipient country, however important, only takes us so far in considering aid effectiveness. Other factors strongly influence the impact of aid, including the quality of the bureaucracy in the donor institutions, donor restrictions (such as aid earmarked for specific activities or tied to purchases in the donor country), reporting requirements, coordination across donors, and the capacity of the recipient country to manage aid money. Thus the country selectivity aspect of the MCA will not be enough. It must be coupled with changes in the way in which aid is delivered, as discussed in chapters 4, 5, and 6.

Thus the research remains inconclusive on the relationships between aid and growth. Much more research is needed on different kinds of aid interventions and the varying circumstances under which aid might be more or less effective. The Burnside, Dollar, and Collier results, while perhaps not statistically robust, nevertheless intuitively seem correct. The idea that aid works best in countries with governments committed to growth and development has caught on partly because of the research results but also because it resonates with development specialists from a variety of backgrounds and comports with the experience on the ground in many developing countries.

The Administration's Proposal

The proposed selection process has five key parts. First, the administration proposes rapidly expanding the group of countries eligible to compete for MCA funding during the program's first three years. Specifically, during the first year (fiscal year 2004), eligible countries will be those with per capita incomes below $1,435 that also are eligible to borrow from the World Bank's concessional lending window, the International Development Association (IDA). There are 74 such countries, which include all but 7 of the

81 IDA-eligible countries.[6] In the second year the IDA-eligible criteria will be dropped, increasing the group to include all 87 countries with per capita incomes below $1,435. In the third year the group of eligible countries will expand to include all 28 countries with per capita incomes between $1,435 and $2,975. Thus by the third year 115 countries will be eligible to compete for MCA funding. The increase in the number of eligible countries is designed to correspond with the proposed increase in available MCA funds, which the administration has proposed to ramp up to $5 billion between fiscal years 2004 and 2006.

Second, sixteen indicators will be used to assess country commitment to "ruling justly, investing in their people, and establishing economic freedom." Six indicators are used for ruling justly, four for investing in people, and six for establishing economic freedom. These sixteen indicators are examined in detail below.

Third, to aggregate scores across indicators, the administration proposes to use a "hurdles approach," in which a country must score higher than the median score (relative to other countries in its income group) to get credit on any indicator. To qualify for the MCA a country must score above the median on half the indicators in each of the three categories. That is, it must be above the median on three of the six indicators for ruling justly, two of the four indicators for investing in people, and three of the six indicators for establishing economic freedom. In addition, to qualify a country must score above the median on the corruption indicator.

Fourth, the list of countries eligible to compete will be split into two groups for scoring on the indicators. Countries with per capita incomes below $1,435 will compete against each other separately from those with incomes between $1,435 and $2,975. This step is meant to partially correct for the fact that, on almost any indicator, countries with higher incomes will score better than those with lower incomes. If the countries all competed against each other in a single pool, countries from the top income group would be more likely to score above the median on any indicator, which would effectively eliminate many poor countries.

Fifth, the quantitative process will not be the final determinant of country qualification. Rather, it will be the main input used by the MCC board of directors, which will determine the final list of qualifying countries. According to the administration's proposal, the board will be guided by the indicators, but in making final decisions it will be "empowered to take account of data gaps, lags, trends, or other material information, including leadership, related to economic growth and poverty reduction."[7] This last step introduces an element of subjectivity that probably is necessary, given the weaknesses in the data. However, care must be taken that this discretion is used carefully and in only a limited set of circumstances to guard against too much political influence in the selection process.

One implication of this proposed process is that the number of qualifying counties is likely to be small. To make an initial crude estimate, assume that country scores on any indicator are simply random, so that the odds of passing a minimum number of hurdles are the same as getting a minimum number of heads on a series of coin tosses. In this case, in turns out that approximately 18 percent of the countries would pass all four tests (control of corruption, two of the five other "ruling justly" indicators, two of the four "investing in people" indicators, and three of the six economic freedom indicators).[8] While this exercise is simplistic, it illustrates a basic point: Strictly using this system, the number of qualifying countries will not be large and will not change appreciably over time.

Income Levels for Broad Eligibility

There are several different ways to define *low income* and thus the universe of countries from which the MCA countries will be chosen. The administration has chosen three of the most common definitions, all drawn from the World Bank and based on the bank's definitions of IDA-eligibility, IDA's historical cutoff, and lower-middle-income countries. These choices have the important advantage of being internationally recognized categories; a disadvantage is that bank management's decisions about defining these categories could affect some countries' eligibility for the MCA.

In the first year of the MCA, eligible countries will be those with per capita incomes below $1,435 that are also eligible to borrow from the World Bank International Development Association (IDA).[9] There are seventy-four such countries (shown in table 3-1), seventy-one of which have incomes below the IDA operational income ceiling of $875. The remaining three countries are part of a group of "small island exceptions" that are eligible for IDA even though their incomes exceed the operational cutoff. This is a sensible starting point for the MCA, since they have the most extensive poverty and the greatest development needs. Including them is appropriate and generally noncontroversial.

In the second year the IDA-eligible criterion will be dropped, and all countries with average incomes of less than $1,435 will be eligible. This change adds thirteen countries to the competition. Adding these countries creates a trade-off. On one hand, as more countries are added, fewer funds will be available for the poorest countries. Of course, in the second year of the MCA, when these countries become eligible, funding will grow, so none

Table 3-1. *Countries Eligible to Compete for MCA Funding, First Three Years*

Year one: per capita income less than $1,435 and IDA-eligible			
Afghanistan	Congo,	Kyrgyz Republic	São Tomé and
Albania	Democratic	Lao PDR	Príncipe
Angola	Republic	Lesotho	Senegal
Armenia	Congo, Rep.	Liberia	Sierra Leone
Azerbaijan	Côte d'Ivoire	Madagascar	Solomon islands
Bangladesh	Djibouti	Malawi	Somalia
Benin	Eritrea	Mali	Sri Lanka
Bhutan	Ethiopia	Mauritania	Sudan
Bolivia	Gambia	Moldova	Tajikistan
Bosnia and	Georgia	Mongolia	Tanzania
Herzegovina	Ghana	Mozambique	Timor Leste
Burkina Faso	Guinea	Myanmar	Togo
Burundi	Guinea-Bissau	Nepal	Uganda
Cambodia	Guyana	Nicaragua	Uzbekistan
Cameroon	Haiti	Niger	Vanuatu
Cape Verde	Honduras	Nigeria	Vietnam
Central African	India	Pakistan	Yemen
Republic	Indonesia	Papua New	Yugoslavia
Chad	Kenya	Guinea	Zambia
Comoros	Kiribati	Rwanda	Zimbabwe
Year two: per capita income less than $1,435[a]			
Belarus	Equatorial	Paraguay	Turkmenistan
China	Guinea	Philippines	Ukraine
Ecuador	Kazakhstan	Swaziland	West Bank
	Morocco	Syria	
Year three: per capita income between $1,435 and $2,975[b]			
Algeria	Fiji	Micronesia	St. Vincent and
Belize	Guatemala	Namibia	the Grenadines
Bulgaria	Iran	Peru	Suriname
Colombia	Jamaica	Romania	Thailand
Dominican	Jordan	Russian	Tonga
Republic	Macedonia	Federation	Tunisia
Egypt	Maldives	Samoa	Turkey
El Salvador	Marshall Islands	South Africa	

Source: World Bank, World Development Indicators, 2002.

a. Thirteen countries added to seventy-four year-one countries.

b. These twenty-eight countries compose a second group added in year three.

of the original countries will necessarily receive less funding. Nevertheless fewer funds will be available to the first group than otherwise would have been the case if the second group (and later the third group) were not part of the MCA. Moreover the second-stage countries will tend to score higher on most indicators, pushing up the median scores and crowding out some of the first group that would have been above the median if they were judged only against other IDA-eligible countries. Thus, in all likelihood, by including the second group, fewer of the poorest countries will qualify, and fewer funds will be available for them to use. On the other hand, most of the second-stage countries have significant numbers of people living in poverty, and many have a sufficiently strong policy and institutional environment that they can put the MCA funds to good use. Moreover, since moving from stage one to stage two only increases the number of eligible countries from seventy-four to eighty-seven, concerns about the larger eligibility pool are not enormous.

In the third year, the administration proposes adding twenty-eight countries with per capita incomes between $1,435 and $2,975. These countries will compete separately from countries with incomes below $1,435, meaning that distinct median scores will be calculated for this group that they must surpass to qualify. All other qualification requirements will remain the same. Since they will be scored on the indicators separately, the third group will not affect the median scores of the first two groups and will not directly crowd out any of these countries by pushing them below the median. The main argument in favor of adding these countries is that, although their average incomes are higher than the poorest countries, they are by no means rich, and they include many people living in poverty.

However, adding this group of countries to the MCA raises significant concerns. Three strong arguments make a case against including these countries.

First, by adding these countries, fewer funds will be available for the poorest countries. Although these countries are poor, they are far better off than the poorest countries. The top half of table 3-2 compares several development indicators for the three groups. The countries with incomes between $1,435 and $2,975 are more than four times richer than the combined low-income group. They also have substantially lower illiteracy rates, higher life expectancy, and lower infant mortality. In each case the differences are large.

Second, these countries have significantly larger alternative sources of financing available to them than do the low-income countries. One purpose for the MCA is to help prepare poor countries to access private capital

Table 3-2. *Development Status and Resource Flows and Financing for Three MCA Country Groups (Medians)*

	IDA-eligible countries with incomes less than $1,435	*Countries with incomes less than $1,435*	*Countries with incomes between $1,435 and $2,975*
Development status			
GNI per capita, 2001 (dollars)	380	460	1,965
Adult illiteracy rate, 2000 (percent)	36	33	14
Life expectancy at birth, 2000 (years)	54	56	70
Mortality rate, infant, 2000 (per 1,000 live births)	75	69	27
Resource flows and financing (percent)			
Aid/GNI, 2000	10.8	8.5	1.4
Gross private capital flows/GDP	6.9	8.7	10.3
Tax revenue/GDP	11.7	12.6	21.8
Gross domestic savings/GDP, 2000	7.3	8.4	16.2
Number of countries	74	87	28

Source: World Bank, World Development Indicators, 2000.

markets and generate additional domestic resources, and most of these countries already have achieved progress in these areas. The bottom half of table 3-2 shows that while the third group of countries (appropriately) receive much less aid, they receive larger flows of international private capital, generate greater tax revenue, and have significantly higher domestic savings rates than the low-income countries. The U.S. Agency for International Development (USAID) currently does not have operations in twelve of these twenty-eight countries, in several cases (like Tunisia) because they were judged wealthy enough to no longer need aid and so graduated from USAID funding.

Third, and more subtly, adding these countries increases the risk that decisions about the allocation of MCA funds will be determined to a greater extent by political and strategic criteria than by the announced MCA criteria. Political considerations can never be separated totally from the MCA allocation process, but the third group contains several countries for which it will be especially difficult for the United States to override political and strategic concerns in favor of aid effectiveness. These countries include Colombia, Egypt, Jordan, Turkey, and Russia, among others. Strategic considerations could affect decisions on country qualification (especially for marginal cases), the amounts of money that qualifying countries receive, and funding reductions as a result of poor performance. One cannot help but wonder if the surprise decision to include these countries was at least partly motivated by a desire of some officials to have MCA funds available for strategic reasons when necessary. It is legitimate to use foreign assistance funds for strategic reasons, but it would be far better to use funds outside the MCA for these purposes and keep the MCA focused on increasing the effectiveness of U.S. assistance in supporting development.

Adding the countries with per capita incomes between $1,435 and $2,975 raises another issue. How will MCA funds be allocated between these countries and the lower-income group? There are two basic choices: Establish two pools of money, with a fixed amount of funding allocated to each group every year, or rely on a single pool of money, with the quality of proposals and country performance determining funding allocations. The second choice has merits. However, institutional capacity and human resource skills are so much greater in the top income group of countries that they would dominate the proposal process. The richer countries are more likely to show stronger results, since they face fewer constraints than the low-income countries (which is one reason they receive larger private capital flows). For these reasons, if the administration sticks with the proposal to include the countries with incomes between $1,435 and $2,975, it would be preferable to allocate some share of the MCA funds to these countries, with the remainder to be used in the lower-income group. As suggested by Radelet,[10] a reasonable amount would be $1 billion per year, 20 percent of the total. This amount is loosely based on population shares, since these 28 countries account for 19 percent of the population of the entire group of 115 countries eligible to compete for MCA funds.

Choosing the Indicators

This section describes the sixteen indicators proposed by the administration to select the qualifying countries with reference to the ideal characteristics described in box 3-1. It also briefly discusses other indicators that might be considered.

Box 3-1. *Ideal Characteristics of the Indicators*

Transforming the president's three broad criteria into specific indicators to determine qualification is far from straightforward. There are a large number of indicators from which to choose, each with particular advantages and disadvantages. In making these choices, certain attributes of the data should help guide the choice.[1] The indicators should be:

—simple, transparent, and publicly available, with good country coverage.

—moderate in number. Too many indicators can make the selection process overly cumbersome and opaque; too few could give a misleading perspective on a country's commitment to development. The administration has chosen sixteen indicators; one could consider adding a few more if they provided additional important information.

—measures of policies rather than outcomes. The indicators should focus on policy variables and institutional changes that are within the control of government officials, rather than outcomes that will change over time and may be influenced by exogenous factors.

—indicative of broader policies. Since they are moderate in number, the chosen indicators should capture related policies that are not directly measured. For example, the inflation rate gives a direct perspective on monetary policy but is also indicative of a country's overall macroeconomic management and is related to fiscal and exchange rate policies.

—associated with desired development outcomes The indicators should be demonstrably empirically related to critical outcomes, such as faster economic growth, decreased infant mortality, and increased literacy.

—accurate. All indicators are to some extent simply estimates of the true value, and the more accurate the estimate, the better. Indica-

Basic information on the sixteen indicators is summarized in table 3-3, including the number of countries covered by the indicator, the source of the data, and the frequency with which the indicator is updated. The table also shows the results of some simple statistical tests on the association between each of the indicators and three important development outcomes: per capita income growth, infant mortality, and literacy. All else being equal, indicators that have a demonstrated correlation with the targeted outcome

tors estimated with smaller margins of error (and with aggregation techniques that minimize rather than multiply those errors) should be preferred over those with larger measurement errors.

—updated frequently with short time lags.

—not easily subject to targeting or manipulation. Recipient governments will take great interest in the specific indicators used to determine MCA eligibility and will naturally try to make sure those indicators are as favorable as possible. Choosing indicators that are less easily manipulated, or choosing a larger set of indicators, would help reduce this problem.

—objective rather than subjective To the extent possible, indicators should be based on measurable quantities rather than personal judgments and should be measured in absolute terms rather than relative terms. However, many indicators, such as the level of corruption, cannot be measured in absolute terms.

In choosing the indicators, it will not be possible to meet all of these criteria. For example, it will be difficult to find indicators that are simultaneously simple, indicative of broader policies, and reliably accurate over time. As a result, some trade-offs are inevitable, and any indicator will be stronger on some attributes and weaker on others. The designers of the MCA need to be cognizant of these trade-offs and be willing to revise the methodology over time as data become more refined, problems in aggregation methods appear, or improved techniques and indicators are developed.

1. For a similar discussion, see Nancy Birdsall, Ruth Levine, Sarah Lucas, and Sonal Shah, "On Eligibility Criteria for the Millennium Challenge Account," Center for Global Development, September 12, 2002 (www.cgdev.org/nv/MCA_criteria.pdf [April 2003]).

(such as lower infant mortality) are preferable to indicators that have no such correlation. (It would be preferable to show causality between the indicators and the outcomes, a subject left for future research.) In each case, the results of correlation tests control for the initial level of income.[11] This procedure controls for the fact that many of the indicators simply improve with income levels. For example, richer countries tend to have higher

(*text continues on page 42*)

Table 3-3. *Characteristics of MCA Eligibility Indicators*

Indicator	*Countries covered*	*Source*	*Frequency*	*Correlation with*[a]		
				Growth, per capita income	*Log, infant mortality*	*Log, literacy*
Ruling justly						
Control of corruption	115	World Bank Institute[b]	Annual	√***	√*	√
Rule of law	115	World Bank Institute	Annual	√**	√*	√
Voice and accountability	115	World Bank Institute	Annual	√	√*	√*
Government effectiveness	115	World Bank Institute	Annual	√***	√*	√
Civil liberties	115	Freedom House[c]	Annual	√	√*	√*
Political rights	115	Freedom House	Annual	√	√*	√*
Investing in people						
Immunization rate: DPT and measles	112	World Health Organization[d]	Annual	√***	√*	√*
Primary education completion rate	99	World Bank[e]	Periodic	√	√*	√*
Public primary education spending, of GDP	83	World Bank[d]	Annual		√	√
Public expenditure on health, of GDP	88	World Bank[d]	Annual		√*	√*
Economic freedom						
Country credit rating	85	Institutional Investor[f]	Semiannual	√**	√*	√
Inflation	97	IMF[g]	Monthly	√*	**	*
Regulatory quality	115	World Bank Institute	Annual	√***	√*	√*
3-Year budget deficit	103	World Bank	Annual	√*	√	

Trade policy	92	Heritage Foundation[h]	Annual	√	√*	√
Days to start a business	63	World Bank			√	√
Other possible indicators						
Political stability	98	World Bank Institute	Annual	√**	√*	√***
Access to essential drugs	106	World Health Organization		√	√**	√
Net enrollment rates	82	World Bank	Annual	√	√**	√*
Access to improved water	96	World Bank	Decade	√	√**	√
Girls' participation in primary education	85	World Bank	Annual	√	√	√*

a. Correlations control for initial level of income. A √ indicates the correlation has the "correct" sign—whether a better score on an indicator is positively associated with economic growth, negatively associated with infant mortality, and positively associated with higher literacy. (Direction of sign, positive or negative, is not shown, since for some indicators a higher score is a better outcome, while for others a higher score is a worse outcome.) Statistical significance, if any, is shown as: *less than 1 percent (highly statistically significant), **between 1 percent and 5 percent, and ***between 5 percent and 10 percent.

b. D. Kaufmann, A. Kraay, and M. Mastruzzi, "Governance Matters III: Governance Indicators for 1996–2002," World Bank Policy Research Working Paper (www.worldbank.org/wbi/governance/govdata2002.htm).

c. Freedom House, "Freedom in the World, 2001–02" (www.freedomhouse.org/research/freeworld/FHSCORES.xls).

d. World Development Indicators 2002, World Bank.

e. Barbara Bruns, Alain Mingat, and Ramahatra Rakotomalala, *Achieving Universal Primary Education by 2015: A Chance for Every Child* (Washington: World Bank, 2003).

f. Institutional Investor, Country Credit Rankings, March 2003.

g. International Financial Statistics 2002, International Monetary Fund.

h. Heritage Foundation, 2002 Index of Economic Freedom.

immunization rates, and they also have lower infant mortality rates. A simple correlation between immunization rates and infant mortality rates may simply be picking up the effect of income on both variables. By controlling for the level of income, we can determine whether or not, for two countries with the same income level, if one with a higher immunization rate also has a lower infant mortality rate. These basic tests are not meant to be deterministic models or tests of causality but simply controlled correlations.

Ruling Justly

The administration has proposed using six indicators to measure the extent to which countries are ruling justly: control of corruption, rule of law, voice and accountability, the quality and effectiveness of government, civil liberties, and political rights.

CONTROL OF CORRUPTION. Corruption is the exercise of public power for private gain. It undermines the rules that govern interactions between public servants and the citizenry, adversely affects business decisions, and can be especially detrimental to the poor. Many different surveys measure various aspects of corruption, including those from DRI/McGraw-Hill, Transparency International, the Economist Intelligence Unit, and the Political Risk Services Group. These surveys draw on specialists in individual countries and experts with knowledge across many countries. They explore many dimensions of corruption, including the frequency of paying bribes, the effectiveness of anticorruption measures, and the impact of corruption on foreign investment.

The administration draws its corruption indicator from a governance database compiled by Dani Kaufmann and Aart Kraay at the World Bank Institute (hereafter KK).[12] The methodology and sources used for this database are described in box 3-2. Although the KK indicators are subjective and more complex than most other indicators, they show a strong causal relationship with key development outcomes, they are based on a wide range of sources, they cover all the potential MCA countries, and they are updated fairly regularly. They are the best set of governance indicators currently available.

In creating their indexes, the KK authors draw on 275 indicators from twenty different sources to construct six aggregate indicators of different dimensions of governance. The KK indicator for control of corruption draws on surveys by DRI/McGraw-Hill, the Economist Intelligence Unit, the World Bank's business surveys, Political Risk Services, and others. It does not draw directly on Transparency International's (TI) well-known corruption indicator, because TI is itself a compilation of other surveys rather than an original source. The KK indicator is preferable to TI, because KK draws on all the surveys contained in the TI index plus several others. The KK index contains data for all 115 countries in the world with incomes below $2,975 in 2002.

The KK index on control of corruption is scaled so that the worldwide mean score is 0, and values that are one standard deviation above or below the mean are reassigned values of 1 and −1, respectively. We use a recalibrated version of the data in which each country's score is shown as a percentile rank. As shown in table 3-3, this index performs fairly well statistically. It shows a modestly strong correlation (controlling for initial income) with faster economic growth and a very strong relationship with reduced infant mortality. It is also correlated with improved literacy, although the controlled correlation is not statistically significant at conventional levels.

RULE OF LAW. For economic development to proceed, societies need fair and predictable rules to govern economic and social interactions. Ideally these rules should govern the enforceability of contracts, dispute settlement, criminal behavior, procedures for the judiciary, the protection of property rights (including intellectual property rights), tax evasion, and black market activity as an impediment to business development. Several sources touch on these issues, including DRI/McGraw-Hill, the Economist Intelligence Unit, the Heritage Foundation/Wall Street Journal Index, and others. The administration uses the KK index on rule of law, which compiles information from each of these sources and includes coverage for all 115 countries in 2002. As shown in table 3-3, this index shows a strong and statistically significant correlation with faster economic growth and lower infant mortality in the 1990s. It is positively associated with higher literacy, but the controlled correlation is not statistically significant.

VOICE AND ACCOUNTABILITY. Ruling justly requires institutions that protect civil liberties, ensure that governments are held accountable for their actions, and allow citizens to participate in the political process, choose and replace their leaders, and freely voice their opinions. Countries with free and fair elections, representative legislatures, fair legal systems, a free press, and a small role for the military in elections are more likely to be responsive and accountable to their people. Similarly governments must respect basic freedoms of speech, assembly, and religion. Several surveys focus on these issues, most importantly by Freedom House. In addition the Economist Intelligence Unit and Political Risk Services include questions that touch on these topics, as do several other surveys. The KK indicator on voice and accountability incorporates measures from all these sources, with coverage for all 115 MCA countries in 2002. This measure is

Box 3-2. *The KK Governance Indicators*

To create the KK database, the authors compile 275 governance indicators from twenty sources, including Freedom House, Gallup International, the Economist Intelligence Unit, DRI/McGraw-Hill, the Heritage Foundation, the World Bank, and others. They then construct the most comprehensive composite measures of governance available, which they organize into six separate indicators. Note that these data are not World Bank data per se but are compiled by bank staff from other independent sources. The administration uses four of these measures as "ruling justly" indicators (control of corruption, rule of law, voice and accountability, and government effectiveness) and one as an indicator of economic freedom (regulatory quality). It does not use the KK "political stability" variable as an indicator.

Since the KK database draws from so many sources, it covers a much larger set of countries than any individual source. Country coverage is complete, with data on all 115 countries with per capita income below $2,975. Research with these indicators shows more than just an association with development indicators; it shows a strong causal relationship from these indicators to higher levels of income, lower rates of infant mortality, and higher rates of literacy. Moreover the method of aggregation provides measures of the precision of the estimates, so users know the margin of error associated with any indicator. Most other survey sources do not even discuss the sampling error associated with their estimates, giving users a false sense of precision. The authors have written a paper focused on the use of their indicators for the MCA in which they discuss the issue of margins of error at some length, including expressing reservations about using a "hard hurdle" for corruption. In the aggregation process the KK methodology gives greater weight to survey results with a smaller

positively correlated with economic growth, although the correlation is not statistically significant. The relationships with infant mortality and literacy are both strong and highly statistically significant.

QUALITY AND EFFECTIVENESS OF GOVERNMENT INSTITUTIONS. Good governance requires effective public institutions. A poor-quality civil service, red tape, ineffective bureaucracies, and weak management all impede the ability of the government to deliver basic public services. Drawing from a

measurement error and less weight to survey results with greater uncertainty.

The KK database has some drawbacks. As with most databases on corruption and other governance concepts, the KK database is primarily based on subjective perceptions of governance. As a result a country's score is measured relative to other countries in an individual year.[1] When a country improves from one year to the next, it is impossible to tell the extent to which the country improved or other countries got worse (this is a weakness of most governance-related indicators). Also, the database has a short history, with data available for 1997–1998, 2000, and 2002. Henceforth it will be compiled on an annual basis. In addition the authors are in the process of compiling data from the mid-1990s to produce earlier baseline values for each indicator. Finally the statistical methods used to combine various surveys to create the KK database are more complicated than the methodology for any individual survey, making the final scores somewhat more complex and less transparent than other measures. The gain from this method, however, is far more information from many data sources, with a better idea of the precision of the estimates. This accuracy and increased amount of information is well worth the price of some additional complexity. All in all, this is the most comprehensive and best-quality database on governance indicators available.

1. Specifically, the scores are scaled so that the mean value is set to equal zero, and the scores that are one standard deviation above and below the mean are set equal to +1 and −1, respectively. Thus each variable is reported on a scale from approximately −2.3 to +2.3 (corresponding to 2.3 standard deviations below and above the mean, respectively).

similar set of sources, the KK indicator on government effectiveness compiles data on these and related issues for all 115 MCA countries in 2002. This measure shows a moderately significant relationship with economic growth and a strong relationship with reduced infant mortality. It is also positively associated with literacy, but the relationship is not statistically significant.

CIVIL LIBERTIES. The Freedom House civil liberties and political rights indexes evaluate the rights and freedoms enjoyed by individuals in countries and territories around the world. Freedom House does not rate governments per se but rather the extent to which citizens enjoy basic rights. The civil liberties index focuses on the freedoms for citizens to develop independent views, institutions, and personal autonomy apart from the state. It is a subjective index, ultimately based on the judgments of the Freedom House survey team, with the ratings subject to several layers of review. The ratings review process involves about thirty outside regional experts, consultants, and in-house staff. Scores are based on a relatively narrow range of one to seven (whole numbers only), although underlying these numbers is a confidential Freedom House index in which countries are given a score between 1 and 100.

While this scoring system is appropriate for Freedom House's objectives, the small number of possible scores raises a statistical problem for the MCA. Since many countries are assigned the same score, they are bunched together around the median score, which is where the administration draws the line between passing or failing on a particular indicator. In this case there is a big difference between the administration's proposal that scores greater than the median be given a passing grade and the alternative, in which a score greater than or equal to the median is given a passing grade. For example, of the eighty-seven countries eligible for the MCA in the second year, nineteen have the median score of five on the civil liberties index. An index with a more differentiated scale would be preferable. The decision as to whether these countries should be given a passing grade on this indicator could make a significant difference in the final list of eligible countries. We return to this issue later in the chapter.

The 2001–2002 Freedom House survey contains information on 192 countries, including all of the 115 MCA countries.[13] This information is also included in the KK indicator on voice and accountability, so the Freedom House information is actually counted twice in the MCA process. Using our simple statistical analysis, better civil liberties scores are associated with faster growth, although the correlation is not statistically significant. Better scores are strongly associated with both lower infant mortality and higher literacy.

POLITICAL RIGHTS. According to Freedom House, political rights "enable people to participate freely in the political process, which is the system by which the polity chooses authoritative policy makers and attempts to make binding decisions affecting the national, regional, or local community." These rights allow all adults to vote and run for elected office and elected officials to have decisive votes on public policies. As with the civil liberties index, political rights are measured on a scale of one to seven, which raises the same issue about median scores. As with the civil liberties indicator, the political rights indicator has a positive but insignificant correlation with growth and a strong relationship to reduced infant mortality and higher rates of literacy.

Investing in People

The administration uses four indicators to gauge whether a country is investing in people: the immunization rate, primary school completion rate, public spending on primary education, and public spending on health.

IMMUNIZATION RATE. Immunizations are among the most effective means to prevent the spread of infectious diseases and ensure the basic health of the population. Countries with higher immunization rates against diphtheria, pertussis (whooping cough), tetanus (DPT), and measles tend to have lower rates of infant mortality and longer life expectancy. Moreover, although immunization rates are not a policy per se, they are within the control of the government and can be increased in most countries where governments make the commitment to do so. They also are a good indication of broader health policies and strategies. Governments that establish systems to provide broad-based immunizations tend to also take other steps to improve basic health. The United Nations has adopted the measles immunization rate as one indicator of progress toward achieving the millennium development goal of reducing under-age-five mortality rates by two-thirds between 1990 and 2015.[14] The World Health Organization (WHO) provides data on the share of children under one year of age that received immunizations for DPT (three doses) and measles (one dose). The administration uses the average of the two for its indicator. The data are a little uneven, at times varying from year to year within one country by wide margins. Data are available for 112 of the 115 MCA countries, although in some cases they are three or even four years old. As shown in table 3-3, this variable is strongly related to lower infant mortality (not surprisingly) and has an equally strong relationship with increased literacy rates. It also shows a moderately positive association with economic growth.

PRIMARY SCHOOL COMPLETION RATE. Primary school enrollment rates have long been used as a basic indicator of education policy. However, enrollment rates provide little information on achievement of basic standards of competence. Attending just a year or two of school reaps little benefit. A growing body of evidence suggests that students must complete five or six years of school in order to achieve basic competencies in literacy and numeration.[15] Thus completion rates for primary school are a stronger indicator of student achievement of minimum skill levels than are enrollment rates. As described in chapter 2, one of the thirteen MDGs adopted by the United Nations is to "ensure that, by 2015, children everywhere, boys and girls alike, will be able to complete a full course of primary schooling."

The World Bank defines the primary completion rate as "the total number of students successfully completing (or graduating from) the last year of primary school in a given year, divided by the total number of children of official graduation age in the population."[16] The best source of primary school completion rates is the database compiled by World Bank researchers Barbara Bruns, Alain Mingat, and Ramahatra Rakotomalala.[17] This database is relatively new, as completion rates have only recently been a focus of attention, and so it provides an excellent foundation for a stronger education database. However, this indicator has several drawbacks. First, completion rates tend to increase noticeably only several years after governments initiate a firm commitment to improving primary education. Second, this indicator is either missing or is several years old for many countries. Only about half the countries have data for 1999 or subsequent years. The authors are planning to strengthen this indicator in the future by expanding the number of countries covered and updating it on an annual basis. The school completion rate is strongly correlated with lower infant mortality and higher literacy. It also is positively correlated with economic growth, but the relationship is not statistically significant at conventional levels.

PUBLIC SPENDING ON PRIMARY EDUCATION AS PERCENT OF GDP. Public sector spending on education is a policy variable that is very much in the government's control. For most of the poorest countries, primary schools are the appropriate focus for government expenditure. At face value, public spending should be indicative of a broader government commitment to improving education. However, greater spending generally does not translate into better schools or better outcomes if it is spent inefficiently or is poorly targeted, so this variable is probably a weak indicator of effective government policies on education. The pattern of expenditure (on books, salaries, building maintenance) is just as important, as is a focus on curriculum development and other aspects of the quality of education.

One problem with this indicator is that it is not directly available: it must be constructed using other variables. The World Bank publishes data on overall spending on education and on primary school spending per student. The data on primary school spending as a share of GDP were constructed from data on spending per student, the number of students, and GDP. Unfortunately these data are missing for many countries (data are available for just 83 of the 115 MCA countries) and are several years old in other countries. Moreover the indicator is weakly correlated with development outcomes. Higher primary education spending is correlated with lower infant mortality and higher literacy, but neither relationship is statistically significant. It has a slight negative association with economic growth, although the relationship is not statistically significant. Statistically speaking, this variable is one of the weakest of the sixteen indicators. This fact, combined with the need to construct this indicator, makes it a prime candidate for improvement if it is to be used for the MCA in the future.

PUBLIC SPENDING ON HEALTH AS PERCENT OF GDP. Public spending on health has many of the same characteristics as spending on primary education. It is a policy variable clearly in the government's control and is likely to be indicative of broader health policies. However, more spending generally is not associated with better health outcomes for the poor, for instance, if spending is focused on urban cancer hospitals rather than rural clinics. This indicator is drawn from the World Bank's World Development Indicators database, which defines public health expenditure as "recurrent and capital spending from government (central and local) budgets, external borrowings and grants (including donations from international agencies and nongovernmental organizations), and social (or compulsory) health insurance funds."[18] It is available for 88 of the 115 MCA countries, slightly more than the education spending indicator. Public expenditure on health (after controlling for income levels) is strongly correlated with lower infant mortality and higher literacy. However, more sophisticated econometric analyses that control for a larger set of variables find little or no relationship between health spending and these outcomes.[19] As with public spending on primary education, its correlation with economic growth is of the wrong sign and is not statistically significant. Along with spending on primary education, this indicator should be strengthened or replaced over time for MCA selection purposes.

Other Possible Indicators

Several other variables could be used as indicators for health and education policies. It is somewhat surprising that the administration proposed only four indicators for investing in people—two each for health and education—while they proposed six each for ruling justly and economic freedom. Although adding more indicators may not change appreciably the final list of countries, it would make it more difficult for recipient countries to focus too narrowly and target one indictor rather than broader health and education policies. Following are other health and education indicators.

RATIO OF GIRLS TO BOYS IN PRIMARY SCHOOL. This measure is indicative of both education policies and gender discrimination. It is widely available for most countries and is updated regularly. This ratio is used as an indicator by the United Nations toward achieving the MDG of "promoting gender equality and empowering women." It is strongly correlated with literacy rates but not strongly correlated with other outcome variables. Nonetheless substantial research highlights primary education of girls as a high-payoff development investment with beneficial effects on family size and children's health as well as through the more direct channels.

PRIMARY SCHOOL ENROLLMENT RATES. This indicator measures the ratio of the number of children of primary school age who are enrolled in school to the corresponding population. It is similar to school completion rates but is more widely available and is easier for governments to influence in a short time period than completion rates. Focusing on enrollment rates alone would be a mistake, as discussed earlier, since enrollment in school does not ensure a quality education. The combination of enrollment and completion rates would provide more complete information about government policies than either indicator alone. However, net enrollment rates are available for just 82 of the 115 MCA countries. This indicator is strongly correlated with lower infant mortality and higher literacy but is not strongly associated with economic growth.

ACCESS TO IMPROVED WATER SOURCES. This variable measures the share of the population that has reasonable access to water from an improved source, such as a household connection, public standpipe, borehole, protected well or spring, or rainwater collection. Access to clean water can improve a wide variety of health indicators. Moreover government policy can directly impact the share of the population with access to water. The UN uses access to improved water sources as an indicator of progress toward one of the MDGs. The obstacle to using this variable is that it is recorded just once every ten years in the World Bank database, and even then it is missing for many countries. Access to water is strongly correlated with lower infant mortality but is not strongly associated with literacy or economic growth.

ACCESS TO ESSENTIAL DRUGS. Every year the WHO Action Program on Essential Drugs interviews relevant experts in each country about access by the population to essential drugs. The interviewees can choose from four levels: less than 50 percent of the population, between 50 and 80 percent, 80 to 95 percent, and above 95 percent. This variable appears to be too subjective for use in the MCA, as it would be relatively easy for recipient governments to influence its measurement.

Establishing Economic Freedom

The administration uses six indicators to measure the extent to which countries are establishing economic freedom: country credit ratings, inflation rates, regulatory policies, budget deficits, trade policies, and days to start a business.

COUNTRY CREDIT RATINGS. A large number of credit ratings and investor guides exist for many countries around the world. These ratings usually measure the risk of default on government or private sector debts and, as such, give a broad indication of the opinion of private creditors on the economic environment in a country. However, relatively few of these ratings agencies report regularly on the poorest countries in the world. One exception is Institutional Investor, which provides credit ratings based on the perceived risk of government default every six months for 145 countries around the world, including 85 of the MCA countries.[20] Countries are ranked on a scale from 1 to 100, based on information provided by economists and sovereign risk analysts from banks and money management and securities firms. This indicator is strongly correlated with faster economic growth and strongly correlated with lower infant mortality. It is positively associated with higher literacy, but the relationship is not statistically significant.

INFLATION RATES. Higher rates of inflation make the environment for new investment more risky and tend to reduce the profitability of most businesses. High rates of inflation are especially harmful to the poor, who are least able to protect themselves from inflation. The administration measures inflation on a year-on-year basis from the most recent twelve months available, based on data drawn from the International Monetary Fund's monthly publication *International Financial Statistics.* For inflation, the administration determines the passing grade differently than it does for any other indicator. Whereas the passing score for the other indicators is the median, the passing grade for inflation is a rate lower than 20 percent. Since the median rates of inflation are under 8 percent for each of the three country groups, the 20 percent standard is much easier to pass than the median. Presumably this approach is taken because strong evidence indicates that inflation rates greater than 20 percent are harmful, but not much evidence indicates that an 8 percent rate is necessarily superior to a 10 percent rate in developing countries. Eighty-seven of the 115 MCA-eligible countries pass this hurdle, making it by far the easiest hurdle to pass. Lower inflation has a strong and positive relationship with economic growth. However, lower inflation is also strongly correlated with higher infant mortality and lower rates of literacy, the opposite of what might be expected.

REGULATORY POLICIES. While a certain amount of regulation is necessary to make some markets (such as financial markets) work better, too much regulation, intervention, and government control can undermine the incentives for investment and job creation. Common types of burdensome regulations include wage and price controls; inadequate bank supervision; excessive controls on trade, investment, and business start-up; excessive restrictions on international capital flows; ponderous legal restrictions on ownership and equity positions by nonresidents; and other restrictions and red tape. For its indicator on these issues, the administration uses the "regulatory quality" measure from the KK database, which is probably the most comprehensive measure available of these policies. Other major sources of data on regulatory quality are the Heritage Foundation/Wall Street Journal Index and the DRI/McGraw-Hill data set. Each of these is incorporated into the KK data set, but individually each has less country coverage and larger standard errors in measurement than the KK composite index. Like the other KK measures, this indicator is a composite of the leading surveys and other data on regulatory issues. The KK indicator covers all 115 MCA countries. It has a modestly strong positive correlation with economic growth and very strong and significant correlations with both lower infant mortality and high literacy.

BUDGET DEFICITS. The budget deficit is a key indicator for overall macroeconomic policy, with larger deficits tending to be associated with macroeconomic instability, inflation, and exchange rate depreciation. It is also the basic measure of a government's propensity to spend beyond its means. Of course a lower budget deficit is not always better; sometimes running a slightly larger budget deficit is appropriate, especially as a countercyclical policy tool. Moreover donor assistance to fund particular programs can increase the budget deficit (as conventionally measured) because of associated government spending, with donor funds entering the accounting as a below-the-line financing item. Problems can arise, however, when deficits become large, are not funded by grants or highly concessional loans, and persist over time.

Budget deficits can be measured in several different ways. In this context, perhaps the most appropriate measure would be the deficit remaining after donor receipts (grants and concessional loans), averaged over three years. In essence this measure would capture the extent of government spending that is not financed by tax or aid receipts and must be financed by resort to central bank financing or borrowing from domestic or international commercial markets. The biggest problem with this indicator is that budget data are surprisingly incomplete for most countries, with data missing for many countries for concessional loans that finance the budget.

Thus the administration uses the budget deficit after receipt of grants but not concessional loans. It measures the average over three years in order to allow for variation in the year-to-year deficit for economic management purposes. The main public source for budget data is the International Monetary Fund's *Government Financial Statistics,* as reported in the World Bank's World Development Indicators.[21] The IMF also keeps a confidential database for a number of countries where the data cannot be made public. The administration is using this confidential database for this indicator, the only indicator that is not publicly available. Thus the public data used here are different from those used by the administration. The budget deficit data are available for 103 of the 115 MCA countries. Lower budget deficits are strongly and positively associated with economic growth. Lower deficits are associated with lower rates of infant mortality, although the relationship is not statistically significant. There is no correlation between deficits and literacy rates.

TRADE POLICY. Most economists would agree that, at least at a broad level, trade openness is good for growth. Controversy abounds, however, on exactly what kind of trade policy is best for developing countries and how to measure it. Many economists argue that lower tariff rates and quota coverage are essential to open trade and growth; others believe that modest and time-bound import substitution in selected industries can be conducive to long-term growth. Overall tariff averages can be misleading because the composition of the items protected can matter a great deal. Moreover other institutions and policies, such as export processing zones and directed credit to exporters, make statutory tariff rates less meaningful, so it is difficult to summarize overall trade policy in a single index. Also data on average tariffs and quota coverage are surprisingly sparse for most countries. If the data were available, perhaps the most appropriate indicators would be the average tariffs and quota coverage for capital and intermediate goods (and not consumer goods).

As a substitute, some surveys include a trade policy component in an attempt to capture business and expert opinions on overall trade policy. The administration uses one of these as its indicator: the trade component of the Heritage Foundation/Wall Street Journal Index of Economic Freedom.[22] The 2003 index includes information gathered during the last half of 2001 and the first half of 2002. This index is subjective, with the authors assigning countries a rating from one to five, basing their judgments primarily on tariff and quota rates, where available. Missing entries are filled in with data that, in some cases, unfortunately may not be indicative of trade openness. For example, the authors use government tariff revenues as a share of imports as a substitute for tariffs. However, in many low-income countries, low tariff collections are more indicative of corruption in the customs department than of open trade policy.

Partly because of these issues, this indicator is only weakly correlated with development outcomes. A better score is positively associated with economic growth and higher literacy, but the relationships are weak and not statistically significant. The index is strongly correlated with lower rates of infant mortality. This index also suffers from the same problem as the Freedom House indexes when working around the median. Since there are only five possible scores, many countries receive the median score. Very few low-income countries receive a score of one or two; of the ninety-two MCA-eligible countries with available data, eighty-two receive a score of three, four, or five. In effect it becomes a three-point scale, with countries either passing, at the median, or failing. This makes the judgment on whether a passing grade is greater than the median or greater than or equal to the median an important one, since thirty-three of the ninety-two countries receive the median score of four. It would be preferable to have greater differentiation among countries in the scores. The administration should work toward identifying or creating a stronger index for the future based on actual tariff and quota rates.

DAYS TO START A BUSINESS. The procedures, time, and costs of starting a new business can be serious detriments to entrepreneurial energies in many countries. The administration's indicator draws on data on the number of days to start a business as compiled by Simeon Djankov and his coauthors.[23] This database counts the number of days required for companies to complete all procedures necessary to legally start a new business. The time required is high in most countries, especially low-income countries. The average number of days required in low-income countries is sixty-six, compared with two days in Canada. The authors find that heavy start-up regulations are not correlated with better social outcomes (such as lower pollution or fewer accidental deaths) but are correlated with higher levels of corruption (a relationship that is not statistically significant in low-income countries).

The major difficulty with this database is that it is available for only 110 countries worldwide and only 63 of the MCA countries. This implies that 52 countries fail this hurdle because of missing data. Another 32 will score at or below the median, and only 31 will pass the hurdle. Also, since this database is relatively new, it has not been thoroughly tested over time, and there is not yet a process in place to update it annually. Using our simple correlation controlling for level of income, no statistically significant relationship exists between this variable and economic growth, infant mortality, or literacy in the 1990s. Although this indicator has merit in principle, and the authors have done a commendable job of creating it, more work is necessary to improve the coverage of the indicator and its relationship to growth. One possibility (suggested by the authors) is to combine this indicator with other measures of costs and procedures necessary to start a business (which are available in their database) to build a more comprehensive measure of barriers to new business. In the near future the authors also hope to expand the scope of their database to include bureaucratic harassment, protection of property rights, quality of infrastructure services, and other related issues.

Aggregating the Indicators

Once the indicators are chosen, several alternatives can be used to determine the standards that countries are expected to meet on each indictor, how much weight to give each indicator in the final determination of eligibility, and how to aggregate the indicators into a final ranking of countries. In turn, the answers to these questions are related partly to the question of how many countries should qualify, since the final number will depend directly on how high or low the standards are set for each indicator. Does the United States want the MCA to focus on the top ten countries according to the president's criteria? The top twenty? Or the top thirty? Analytically no precise right answer exists for how many countries should be chosen, since there is no precise empirical evidence of the exact point at which policy and institutions become so weak that aid is not effective.[24] I describe two broad methodologies for setting standards, aggregating the data, and choosing the final set of qualifying countries: establishing specific hurdles for each indicator or adding together the scores (appropriately rescaled) for each indicator.

Hurdles Approach

In the hurdles approach, countries are expected to meet a specific standard on each indicator. The administration's proposal uses this approach. It requires that countries score above the median (the hurdle) on half the indicators in each of the three groups of criteria. In addition the administration adopted a "hard" hurdle for corruption: A country must be above the median on corruption to qualify, regardless of how well it does on the other indicators. The special treatment of this indicator has no basis in economic research. (Apparently the president insisted on it.)

The hurdles approach has several advantages. First and foremost, countries do not have to do well on every indicator to qualify. For example, those who are concerned that the administration is insisting on a litmus test for free trade can rest easy. A country can have the highest tariff rates in the world and still qualify for the MCA as long as it makes enough of the other hurdles. Indeed a country can have both high trade barriers and a large budget deficit and still qualify, as long as it makes three of the remaining four economic freedom indicators. Second, the system is transparent and easy to understand. All one needs to know about a country are its score on an indicator and the median. Third, it helps countries to quickly identify where they need to improve if they want to qualify, since it is clear which indicators they have missed. Fourth, it helps partially alleviate the missing data problem. Presumably missing data counts as a missed hurdle, but since a country needs to make only half the hurdles, it can still qualify even if it is missing some data (yet incentives remain for countries to collect more data).

There is no magic to the administration's choices of using the median as the hurdle, or the requirement that a country must pass half the hurdles in each area, or the insistence that countries make the corruption hurdle. The hurdles could have been set at lower or higher levels (for example, at the 40th or 60th percentile) or at specific numbers, such as a 70 percent immunization rate. The required number of hurdles could have differed as well. These decisions come with clear trade-offs. The higher the standard on each indicator or the more hurdles required, the fewer countries will qualify. Thus these three variables must be decided jointly: the standard on each indicator, the number of hurdles required, and the approximate number of desired qualifying countries.

Implicit in the hurdles approach is the view that a country must surpass critical values on each indicator in order to achieve growth and development or at least to make foreign aid effective. But whereas evidence indicates that lower corruption or higher immunization rates are associated with better development outcomes, little evidence points to specific minimum levels that must be achieved for better outcomes. Perhaps the one exception is inflation, where strong evidence indicates that inflation rates over 20 percent are particularly detrimental. Consistent with this finding, the administration has adopted 20 percent as the inflation hurdle.

One weakness of the hurdles approach is that it limits the incentives for countries to continue to improve on the indicators once they have passed the hurdle. A country either meets the hurdle or not; it does not receive additional credit for making the hurdle by a large margin, nor does it receive an extra penalty for missing by a large margin. Thus, once a country is above the hurdle, it does not need to improve to continue to be eligible (unless the hurdle rises over time). Moreover, countries with scores well below the hurdle receive no credit until they pass it; there is no benefit for improving from, say, the 10th percentile to the 40th. For countries starting from a poor, resource-constrained situation (like Mozambique or Rwanda), it may be many years before they are able to pass some of the hurdles, especially the "investing in people" indicators.

The choice of using the median as the hurdle raises two major concerns. First, the median will change over time. Countries with an immunization rate that is too low in one year could pass in the next year with the same immunization rate if the median falls. Conversely a country that meets the standard in one year could find that it does not meet it in the next year if the median rises. Moreover countries that nearly qualify in one year and work to raise their scores may be disappointed to find that their improved scores fall below new, higher medians. This problem would occur if any percentile score is used, not just the 50th percentile (the median). Moving scores are inconsistent with the idea of choosing countries that meet a minimum standard of policy quality, which should not change arbitrarily from year to year (although it could be gradually increased by a preannounced amount over time).

Second, using medians as benchmarks severely limits the potential for the number of MCA countries to expand over time. As near-miss countries raise their scores to try to qualify, the medians will rise, so other countries will be bumped off the list. Under the methodology proposed by the administration, it is highly unlikely that the number of MCA countries will expand much beyond twenty, even if over time dozens of countries improve their scores above the first-year medians.

The best way to address these concerns is to set absolute standards for hurdles where possible (as the administration has done with inflation), perhaps determined by the median in the first year. Thus, if the median immunization rate in the first year is 70 percent, the hurdle in each subsequent year would be 70 percent (or, as a variant, the hurdle could gradually increase over time). While this approach has appeal for many of the indicators, it cannot be used for the subjective indicators that are always measured on a relative scale, such as corruption (at least as those indicators are currently measured). Nevertheless using absolute instead of relative hurdles where possible would improve the system.

Missing data poses a different issue for the hurdles approach. The administration counts missing data as below the hurdle in determining scores, which makes sense. But how should missing data be treated in calculating the median? Omitting these data assumes that the missing entries are normally distributed about the median—that is, that the median would be the same whether the missing entries were included or not. However, missing data tend to come from either very small countries where surveys are not completed or from poorly performing countries. To the extent that most missing data come from poor performers (which is probably the case), omitting their low scores tends to increase the median. Thus it is quite possible that a country with a score just above the true median would end up below the observed median when data from some countries are omitted. In effect this country is penalized (and could miss qualifying) because of missing data from other countries.

A final and important concern with the hurdles approach is errors in the data. Margins of error in estimating the indicators can be a significant problem, as highlighted in a recent paper by Daniel Kaufmann and Aart Kraay.[25] Many indicators are based on survey data, including all six of the indicators for ruling justly and several of the indicators for economic freedom (regulatory quality, credit risk, and even inflation, which is based on price surveys). Survey results are always estimated with margins of error. Indeed even the nonsurvey-based indicators are estimated with margins of error, albeit from different sources (for instance, immunization rates are estimated by vials of vaccine distributed, which is at best an imperfect gauge of actual immunizations). The problem is that for a country with an observed score just below the median on any indicator, we cannot have a high degree of confidence that the true level is below the median. Margins of error in the estimation could be the difference between making a hurdle or not. By contrast some countries that have observed scores above the hurdle may have true levels below the hurdle and thus receive passing grades when they are not warranted.

The administration reduces the potential problems stemming from measurement errors by requiring that countries make only half the hurdles. Thus, even if a country misses a hurdle because of bad data, it can still qualify for the MCA (and might even benefit from bad data in its favor on a different hurdle).

In one indicator, however, measurement errors remain a major concern: corruption. A country that scores below the median on corruption is eliminated from qualifying for the MCA, regardless of its scores on other indicators, so a country could be eliminated from the MCA simply because of bad data on corruption. Kaufmann and Kraay express reservations about using a hard hurdle for corruption. They point out that for many of the countries with estimated levels of corruption near the median, we can be only 90 percent certain that the actual level is somewhere between the 40th and 60th percentile. They examine the corruption indicator for the sixty-one countries with available data from the pool of seventy-four countries eligible for the MCA in the first year. For twenty-one of these countries the probability is 75 percent or higher that the actual score is above the median, and for seventeen countries the probability is 75 percent or higher that the actual score is below the median. But in twenty-three intermediate cases there is much less certainty about whether they fall above or below the median. Thirteen of these countries have estimated scores that fall below the observed median and are therefore eliminated from the MCA, despite this uncertainty.[26]

Although there is merit to a high standard on corruption, the make-or-break requirement may unnecessarily eliminate some countries. One alternative would be to fully eliminate only the seventeen countries with a 75 percent or higher probability of a corruption score below the median. Other countries would remain eligible for the competition, following the other rules as set out by the administration. Thus, if a country was not one of the seventeen eliminated but scored just below the median on corruption, it would not get credit for the corruption hurdle but could qualify for the MCA so long as it passed half the hurdles in each of the three categories. Changing this approach, however, is bound to be difficult, as no one will want to appear to be soft on corruption because of what may appear to be an arcane statistical problem.

Aggregate Ranking Approach

An alternative to the hurdles approach is to rescale each indicator and then add the scores together to create a final tally. Countries can then be ranked from highest to lowest score, and the administration can choose, say, the top fifteen or twenty to qualify for the MCA. The simplest way to do this is to rescale each indicator so that the mean score is reassigned a value of zero, and the values that are one standard deviation above or below the mean are reassigned values of 1 and −1, respectively. All other scores are converted accordingly. This is a common statistical approach in aggregating numbers with different scales. It is used, for example, in compiling the KK measures that are used for five of the sixteen MCA indicators. Once the sixteen indicators are rescaled, they can be added together, giving each country an aggregate score. Different weights can be assigned to different indicators or to groups of indicators. Countries can then be ranked from best to worst scores.

One advantage of this approach is that it avoids the need to establish (rather arbitrary) hurdles that a country either passes or fails. Also countries are given more credit for a higher score on any indicator, so they continually have an incentive to improve, even if they are above the hurdle. Moreover all the information available for a country's score on each indicator is used in calculating the final score, not just whether it passed a particular hurdle or not. This method eliminates questions about whether a score exactly equal to the median passes or not. It also significantly reduces (although it does not eliminate) the issues surrounding margins of error discussed previously, as it is of no concern if a country barely misses one or more hurdles. This method could be combined with the hard hurdle for corruption, if desired. That is, a country's final ranking would determine its MCA qualification, but if it scored too low on the corruption index, it could be eliminated, regardless of its overall ranking.

One drawback is that a particularly high or low score could significantly alter a country's overall score. Moreover, missing data are a concern in this approach, as it is not clear what value to add to a country's score. One approach would be to add the lowest score achieved by any other country. Another would be to give the country its average on other indicators, so that the missing value does not affect its overall score. Both these approaches, however, are problematic.

Once an overall ranking is tabulated, the administration would have to choose where to draw the line between the qualifiers and the nonqualifiers. This choice would be arbitrary, similar to the arbitrary choice of standards on each indicator in the hurdles approach. This approach requires only one line to be drawn, but it is an important line and will be seen as obviously arbitrary. Thus, while this approach has the advantage of allowing a country to see exactly where it ranks vis-à-vis other countries, it could create diplomatic pressures on those administering the MCA. For example, if the top fifteen countries were chosen to qualify, there would be immense pressure from the governments of the next several countries to include them and draw the line at eighteen or twenty countries. It would be difficult for the administration to defend the choice of fifteen countries rather than eighteen or twenty on analytic or technical grounds.

Moreover, this approach makes it difficult to compare country performance over time. By combining as described, this approach only measures a country's performance relative to its peers. It cannot show if all countries are getting better or worse over time. In other words, if a country moves up from twenty-first to nineteenth, is it because it is getting better or because the others got worse? This is a difficult issue for both the aggregate ranking and the hurdles approach (since the latter uses relative scores like medians as hurdles). When scores are measured relative to other countries, it is difficult to observe all scores rising so that more countries can qualify over time.

In sum, there is no perfect way to aggregate across indicators. Either method requires arbitrary judgments and raises some difficulties with measurement errors, relative rankings, and other issues. Either method will lead to some surprises, both in terms of countries that miss qualifying and some that qualify. The imperfections inherent in the underlying data are magnified when combined across such different indicators. The administration should continue to examine the data with both methodologies and improve them over time, even if only one method is the official procedure.

Possible Qualifying Countries under the Proposed Methodology

Although the administration has described in detail the methodology it proposes to use for choosing the MCA countries, it has not yet selected the countries. Nevertheless, based on the proposed methodology, Radelet has determined which countries would qualify for the MCA during each of the first three years using the most recent data available today.[27] It is important to emphasize that this is a best estimate of the list of qualifying countries. It probably differs slightly from the official list that the administration ultimately will announce. There are several reasons for these possible differences.

First, the underlying data may differ slightly. While data have been obtained from the public sources the administration named, some slight differences probably remain. For example, I may have filled in missing data from secondary sources in a slightly different way than the administration. For example, my understanding is that the administration is filling in some missing data from secondary sources that are not publicly available. On one indicator, the budget deficit, the administration uses confidential data from the IMF to which I do not have access, so I use public IMF data, which may differ slightly.

Second, the first round of MCA countries will not be chosen until just before fiscal year 2004 begins. Some of the indicators will be revised before then, which will change both the medians and the qualifying countries. The process of choosing countries for the second and third round from the expanded set of countries is even further in the future, so the underlying data are likely to change significantly.

Third, the MCA Board will have the power to adjust the list under certain circumstances, as discussed previously.

Possible Qualifying Countries in Year One

Table 3-4 lists the countries that are most likely to qualify for the MCA in the first year, based on data available today. The table shows the score for each of the sixteen indicators for each country, along with the median score for each indicator. The eleven countries qualifying in the first year meet the criterion of having scores above the median in half the indicators in each of the three broad areas as well as on corruption. Of these eleven, three are from Africa (Ghana, Lesotho, and Senegal), five are from Asia (Armenia, Bhutan, Mongolia, Sri Lanka, and Vietnam), and three are from Latin America (Bolivia, Honduras, and Nicaragua).

Many of these countries seem to be sensible choices, including Ghana, Lesotho, Senegal, Bolivia, and Honduras. Others are more questionable, particularly Bhutan and Vietnam. Bhutan misses all three democracy indicators (civil liberties, political rights, and voice and accountability) but passes most of the other indicators where data are available. Vietnam also misses the three democracy indicators, yet it barely qualifies by making the minimum number of hurdles in each category.

The table shows that three more countries (Cape Verde, Guyana, and Nepal) would qualify if the administration changed its criteria slightly so that a score equal to the median counted as passing a hurdle.[28] Cape Verde's and Guyana's trade policy scores are equal to the median, as is Nepal's primary education spending score. Each country needs to pass these hurdles to qualify. These countries are cases in which missing data in other countries, or adding or deleting countries from the sample, could change the median score and the country's qualification status. In my opinion, given the uncertainties in the data, median scores should count as passing grades.

Guyana is worth closer inspection. It passes eleven of the thirteen indicators for which it has data and achieves a median score on a twelfth indicator, yet it fails to qualify. It passes all six indicators for ruling justly and three of four indicators for investing in people (it has no data on public primary education spending). Of the six economic freedom indicators, it is missing data on two through no fault of its own (days to start a business and credit rating). Of the four remaining variables it misses one (the budget deficit) and scores at the median on another (trade), so that it passes only inflation and regulatory quality indicators. Cape Verde follows a similar story, except that it also misses (barely) the public health spending indicator. These two countries would seem to be prime candidates to be elevated to qualification status by the board of directors of the new corporation, which would bring the number of qualifiers to thirteen.

The table also shows five countries that score above the median on half the indicators in each area but do not score above the median on control of corruption and therefore are eliminated. Albania scores just below the median on the corruption indicator, and Malawi and Moldova are also fairly close to the mark. These three countries would qualify if the corruption rule were modified to eliminate only those countries with at least a 75 percent probability that the actual corruption score is below the median, as discussed previously. Malawi's and Mozambique's corruption scores were significantly lower in 2002 than in 2001, moving both countries off the list of potential qualifiers. Malawi suffered much from a scandal surrounding the disappearance of food stocks prior to the current drought, which led to the firing of the minister of poverty alleviation. Mozambique's reputation suffered from the murder of a journalist who was investigating a scandal in the banking system.

Finally table 3-4 also shows eight countries that did not qualify because they missed one more hurdle than allowed by the proposed procedure. Five of the eight (Benin, Burkina Faso, India, Mali, and Mauritania) fall short in the category of investing in people, where they each make one out of four hurdles. Georgia and Togo fall short on ruling justly, where they each pass two of the six hurdles. São Tomé and Príncipe passes eleven of the twelve indicators for which it has data, including all six indicators for ruling justly and three of four for investing in people. It is missing three of the six indicators for establishing economic freedom and passes two of the three remaining ones—one short of the requisite number. Like Cape Verde and Guyana, São Tomé and Príncipe would be a strong candidate for the board to add to the list of qualifiers. If all three were added to the qualification list—and in my opinion they should be—fourteen countries would qualify in the first year. Benin, India, and Mali also should be given strong consideration, which could bring the number of qualifiers to seventeen. Each is a strong democracy that scores well on other indicators but falls one short on investing in people.

Possible Qualifying Countries in Year Two

Table 3-5 displays the same information for countries likely to qualify in fiscal year 2005, when the pool of eligible countries is expanded to include all eighty-seven countries with per capita incomes under $1,435. The number of qualifying countries increases from eleven to twelve. Two new countries

(*text continues on page 68*)

Table 3-4. *Possible Qualifying Countries, Year One (IDA-eligible with per capita incomes below $1,435)*[a]

Counties	*Civil liberties*	*Political rights*	*Voice and account-ability*	*Govern-ment effective-ness*	*Rule of law*	*Control of corrup-tion*	*Public primary education spending (percent) of GDP)*	*Primary education completion rate (percent)*	*Immuni-zation rate: DPT and measles (percent)*
	(1 to 7, 1 = best)		*(0 to 1, 1 = best)*						
Qualify									
Armenia	**4**	**4**	0.36	0.41	0.41	0.30	**1.20**	82	93.5
Bhutan	**5**	**6**	**0.12**	0.81	0.58	0.81	**NA**	**59**	83
Bolivia	3	2	0.53	0.34	0.32	0.25	2.30	72	80
Ghana	3	2	0.52	0.59	0.53	0.42	1.40	64	80.5
Honduras	3	3	0.48	0.27	**0.23**	0.27	**1.20**	67	95
Lesotho	3	2	0.49	0.49	0.54	0.48	3.20	69	81
Mongolia	2	2	0.63	0.51	0.65	0.54	2.40	82	95
Nicaragua	3	3	0.53	**0.17**	0.32	0.39	2.10	65	95.5
Senegal	3	2	0.54	0.52	0.52	0.53	1.50	**41**	**50**
Sri Lanka	**4**	3	0.45	0.59	0.61	0.54	**NA**	111	99
Vietnam	**6**	**7**	**0.08**	0.48	0.45	0.33	**1.10**	101	97.5
Qualify if median score counts to pass a hurdle									
Cape Verde	2	1	0.68	0.50	0.60	0.66	**NA**	117	75
Guyana	2	2	0.69	0.47	0.42	0.38	**NA**	89	88.5
Nepal	4	4	0.34	0.36	0.37	0.46	1.20	65	**71.5**
Eliminated by corruption									
Albania	3	3	0.46	0.38	**0.17**	**0.23**	**1.00**	89	96
Bangladesh	**4**	**4**	0.32	0.35	0.26	**0.08**	**0.90**	70	79.5
Malawi	**4**	**4**	0.36	0.28	0.46	**0.19**	1.80	**50**	86
Moldova	**4**	3	0.42	0.30	0.39	**0.21**	1.40	79	85.5
Mozambique	**4**	3	0.44	0.42	0.30	**0.15**	**1.00**	**36**	86
Missed by one indicator									
Benin	2	3	0.55	0.31	0.43	0.34	1.60	**39**	**70.5**
Burkina Faso	**4**	**4**	0.43	0.28	0.34	0.57	1.60	**25**	**43.5**
Georgia	**4**	**4**	0.40	0.25	**0.10**	**0.12**	**0.30**	82	79.5
India	3	2	0.58	0.54	0.57	0.49	**1.00**	76	**60**
Mali	3	2	0.58	**0.19**	0.34	0.46	**1.00**	**23**	**44**
Mauritania	**5**	**5**	**0.26**	0.52	0.48	0.64	1.80	**46**	**59.5**
São Tomé and Príncipe	2	1	0.70	0.29	0.40	0.50	1.90	81	75.5
Togo	**5**	**5**	**0.16**	**0.09**	0.29	0.32	1.80	63	**61**
Median	**4**	**4**	**0.31**	**0.24**	**0.25**	**0.24**	**1.2**	**59.3**	**72.5**

Source: Steven Radelet, *Challenging Foreign Aid: A Policymaker's Guide to the Millennium Challenge Account* (Washington: Center for Global Development, 2003).

a. Bold indicates missed hurdles.

Public expenditure on health (percent of GDP)	*Country credit rating (1 to 100, 100 = best)*	*Inflation (percent)*	*3-year budget deficit (percent)*	*Trade policy (1 to 5, 1 = best)*	*Regulatory quality (0 to 1, 1 = best)*	*Days to start a business*	*Number of passed hurdles*		
							Ruling justly	*Investing in people*	*Economic freedom*
4.02	**NA**	0.9	**-4.6**	1	0.59	**79**	4	3	3
3.22	**NA**	2.7	-2.7	**NA**	0.31	**NA**	3	2	3
4.12	30.7	2.4	-4.1	3	0.51	**104**	6	4	5
1.66	25.2	13.1	**-9.6**	**4**	0.44	**126**	6	3	3
3.92	25.9	8.1	**-7.5**	3	0.41	**146**	5	3	4
NA	26.5	7.1	**-5.5**	3	0.36	**NA**	6	3	4
NA	21.5	3.1	**-9.5**	2	0.48	31	6	3	5
8.50	**18.2**	7.4	**-7.6**	2	0.39	**69**	5	4	3
2.62	27.6	1.1	-3.9	**4**	0.46	58	6	2	5
1.74	34.8	11.3	**-9.0**	3	0.59	**73**	5	2	4
0.79	33.5	4.6	-2.4	**5**	**0.25**	**68**	3	2	3
1.81	**NA**	1.2	**-16.6**	4	0.47	**NA**	6	2	3
4.54	**NA**	1.5	**-8.1**	4	0.40	**NA**	6	3	3
1.28	23.3	3.0	-3.9	**5**	0.35	25	6	2	5
2.00	**15.7**	4.1	**-8.5**	**5**	0.41	62	4	3	3
1.71	28.2	3.5	-4.3	**5**	**0.14**	29	3	2	4
2.77	19.4	16.5	**-14.2**	**4**	0.42	56	3	3	4
2.88	**17.4**	6.4	-2.1	2	0.49	41	4	4	5
2.81	19.8	9.0	**-11.9**	**4**	0.27	**214**	4	2	3
1.61	21.3	1.6	-3.2	**4**	0.31	**63**	6	1	4
1.50	19.5	3.9	**-11.5**	**4**	0.47	39	4	1	4
0.75	**16.9**	5.8	-3.0	**4**	**0.21**	62	2	2	3
NA	49.4	5.2	**-7.5**	**5**	0.43	**95**	6	1	3
2.09	18.9	3.8	**-8.8**	3	0.36	61	5	1	5
1.38	**NA**	0.6	-0.4	**4**	0.55	**NA**	3	1	3
NA	**NA**	9.8	**-44.9**	**NA**	0.43	**NA**	6	3	2
1.29	**17.1**	1.3	-4.3	3	0.27	**NA**	2	2	4
1.86	**18.2**	**20.0**	**-4.6**	**4**	**0.26**	**63**			

Table 3-5. *Possible Qualifying Countries, Year Two (per capita incomes below $1,435)*[a]

Counties	Civil liberties	Political rights	Voice and account-ability	Govern-ment effective-ness	Rule of law	Control of corrup-tion	Public primary education spending (percent) of GDP)	Primary education completion rate (percent)	Immuni-zation rate: DPT and measles (percent)
	(1 to 7, 1 = best)		(0 to 1, 1 = best)						
Qualify									
Armenia	**4**	4	0.36	0.41	0.41	0.30	**1.20**	82	93.5
Bhutan	**5**	**6**	**0.12**	0.81	0.58	0.81	**NA**	**59**	83
Bolivia	3	2	0.53	0.34	0.32	0.25	2.30	72	80
Honduras	3	3	0.48	0.27	**0.23**	0.27	**1.20**	67	95
Lesotho	3	2	0.49	0.49	0.54	0.48	3.20	69	81
Mongolia	2	2	0.63	0.51	0.65	0.54	2.40	82	95
Nicaragua	3	3	0.53	**0.17**	0.32	0.39	2.10	65	95.5
Philippines	3	2	0.55	0.55	0.38	0.37	1.6	92	**72.5**
Senegal	3	2	0.54	0.52	0.52	0.53	1.50	**41**	**50**
Sri Lanka	**4**	3	0.45	0.59	0.61	0.54	**NA**	111	99
Swaziland	**5**	**6**	**0.14**	0.40	0.29	0.48	1.8	81	**74.5**
Vietnam	**6**	**7**	**0.08**	0.48	0.45	0.33	**1.10**	101	97.5
Qualify if median score counts to pass a hurdle									
Cape Verde	2	1	0.68	0.50	0.60	0.66	**NA**	117	75
Gambia	**5**	5	**0.20**	**0.21**	0.37	0.24	1.60	70	93
Ghana	3	2	0.52	0.59	0.53	0.42	1.40	**64**	80.5
Guyana	2	2	0.69	0.47	0.42	0.38	**NA**	89	88.5
Eliminated by corruption									
Bangladesh	**4**	4	0.32	0.35	0.26	**0.08**	**0.90**	70	79.5
Ecuador	3	3	0.48	**0.13**	0.33	**0.14**	**NA**	96	94.5
Malawi	**4**	4	0.36	0.28	0.46	**0.19**	1.80	**50**	86
Moldova	**4**	3	0.42	0.30	0.39	**0.21**	**1.40**	79	85.5
Paraguay	3	4	0.40	**0.07**	**0.12**	**0.04**	2	78	**71.5**
Ukraine	**4**	4	0.31	0.26	**0.24**	**0.17**	2.4	94	99
Eliminated from receiving U.S. foreign assistance for statutory reasons									
China	**6**	**7**	**0.06**	0.63	0.51	0.42	**0.7**	108	79
Syria	**7**	**7**	**0.05**	0.33	0.43	0.47	**NA**	90	92.5
Missed by one indicator									
Benin	2	3	0.55	0.31	0.43	0.34	1.60	**39**	**70.5**
Burkina Faso	**4**	4	0.43	0.28	0.34	0.57	1.60	**25**	**43.5**
India	3	2	0.58	0.54	0.57	0.49	**1.00**	76	**60**
Mali	3	2	0.58	**0.19**	0.34	0.46	**1.00**	**23**	**44**
Mauritania	**5**	**5**	**0.26**	0.52	0.48	0.64	1.80	**46**	**59.5**
Morocco	**5**	**5**	0.35	0.61	0.59	0.58	**NA**	**55**	96
São Tomé and Príncipe	2	1	0.70	0.29	0.40	0.50	1.9	81	75.5
Median	**4**	**5**	**0.30**	**0.24**	**0.26**	**0.24**	**1.4**	**64.6**	**75.0**

Source: Steven Radelet, *Challenging Foreign Aid: A Policymaker's Guide to the Millennium Challenge Account* (Washington: Center for Global Development, 2003).

a. Bold indicates missed hurdle.

Public expenditure on health (percent of GDP)	*Country credit rating (1 to 100, 100 = best)*	*Inflation (percent)*	*3-year budget deficit (percent)*	*Trade policy (1 to 5, 1 = best)*	*Regulatory quality (0 to 1, 1 = best)*	*Days to start a business*	*Number of passed hurdles*		
							Ruling justly	*Investing in people*	*Economic freedom*
4.02	**NA**	0.9	**–4.6**	1	0.59	**79**	5	3	3
3.22	**NA**	2.7	–2.7	**NA**	0.31	**NA**	3	2	3
4.12	30.7	2.4	**–4.1**	3	0.51	**104**	6	4	4
3.92	25.9	8.1	**–7.5**	3	0.41	**146**	5	3	4
NA	26.5	7.1	**–5.5**	3	0.36	**NA**	6	3	4
NA	21.5	3.1	**–9.5**	2	0.48	31	6	3	5
8.50	**18.2**	7.4	**–7.6**	2	0.39	**69**	5	4	3
1.56	43.4	2.7	–3.9	2	0.58	**62**	6	2	5
2.62	27.6	1.1	–3.9	**4**	0.46	58	6	2	5
1.74	34.8	11.3	**–9.0**	3	0.59	**73**	5	2	4
2.49	28.9	12.2	–2.3	2	0.45	**NA**	3	3	5
0.79	33.5	4.6	–2.4	**5**	**0.25**	**68**	3	2	3
1.81	**NA**	1.2	**–16.6**	4	0.47	**NA**	6	2	3
2.27	**NA**	4.0	**–4.0**	4	0.33	**NA**	3	4	3
1.66	25.2	13.1	**–9.6**	4	0.44	**126**	6	2	4
4.54	**NA**	1.5	**–8.1**	4	0.40	**NA**	6	3	3
1.71	28.2	3.5	**–4.3**	**5**	**0.14**	29	4	2	3
1.67	23.2	10.1	0.3	**4**	0.30	**90**	4	2	4
2.77	**19.4**	16.5	**–14.2**	**4**	0.42	56	4	3	3
2.88	**17.4**	6.4	–2.1	2	0.49	41	4	3	5
1.68	28.6	18.2	–1.6	3	0.32	**NA**	3	2	5
2.92	25.5	10.9	–1.4	3	0.28	42	3	4	6
2.08	60	–3.6	–3.2	**5**	0.40	55	3	3	5
0.89	25.2	–0.6	–0.5	**4**	**0.16**	42	3	2	4
1.61	21.3	1.6	–3.2	**4**	0.31	**63**	6	1	4
1.50	**19.5**	3.9	**–11.5**	**4**	0.47	39	5	1	3
NA	49.4	5.2	**–7.5**	**5**	0.43	**95**	6	1	3
2.09	**18.9**	3.8	**–8.8**	3	0.36	61	5	1	4
1.38	**NA**	0.6	–0.4	**4**	0.55	**NA**	3	1	3
1.20	46.1	2.2	–3.2	**5**	0.55	**62**	4	1	4
NA	**NA**	9.8	**–44.9**	**NA**	0.43	**NA**	6	3	2
1.9	**19.9**	**20.0**	**–4.0**	**4.0**	**0.26**	**62**			

qualify in the second year: the Philippines and Swaziland. However, Ghana, one of the original qualifiers, drops out in the second year. The basic reason is that the addition of the thirteen new countries, which tend to be better off than the original seventy-four, raises the median score on many of the indicators. Ghana's level of public sector spending on primary education (1.4 percent) surpasses the median in the first year, but is exactly equal to the median in the second year, so technically it would not pass that hurdle and would not pass enough hurdles to qualify. Obviously Ghana would qualify if median scores are counted as passing grades.

How should countries be treated that qualify in year one but not in year two? In my opinion, these countries should remain eligible in year two. It would make no sense for them to drop off the list simply because the medians moved slightly. This raises a larger issue: Once a country becomes eligible for the MCA, how long should it remain eligible? As discussed in chapter 5, once a country qualifies, under the administration's plan it would negotiate one or more contracts with the U.S. government to fund specified activities over a multiyear period (probably three to four years). The country would continue to receive funding during the life of the contract, as long as it continues to meet specified benchmarks and there are no major negative events (such as a coup d'état), even if it dips below the strict qualification requirements during the life of the contract. At the end of the contract, the country would have to requalify for the MCA to seek funding for a follow-on proposal.

The fact that a country can drop off the list between the first and second years reveals a quirky characteristic of using median scores rather than absolute scores to determine qualification. Scores that are good enough to make the grade in one year (with the implication that the economic and institutional environment is of sufficiently high quality that foreign aid can be used effectively) might not make it in a different year. Conversely, scores that are not high enough in one year could be a passing grade in another if the medians fall. Ghana's case illustrates the importance of shifting the hurdles from a relative score (the median) to an absolute score, at least for the indicators in which this change is possible. While Ghana can be accommodated by a multiyear funding process, the fact remains that, for other countries that did not qualify in year one, the bar effectively will be raised in year two, making qualification more difficult.

Four additional countries would qualify in the second year if median scores count as passing a hurdle: Cape Verde, Guyana (the same as in the first year), Ghana (as discussed), and Gambia. Gambia has the median score on three indicators: political rights, corruption, and trade policy. Six other countries miss qualifying because they score below the median on corruption. These include three countries that were in the same status the first year (Bangladesh, Malawi, and Moldova), joined by Ecuador, Paraguay, and Ukraine. Two other countries—China and Syria—are eliminated from the MCA because they are precluded from receiving foreign assistance from the United States for statutory reasons. Syria is on the State Department's list of state sponsors of terrorism. China is treated as though it is on the list of countries statutorily prohibited from receiving aid for human rights reasons, even though officially China is not on it. China scores well on indicators for both investing in people and establishing economic freedom. It also passes three of six of the criteria for ruling justly, each by reasonably comfortable margins, including corruption, rule of law, and government effectiveness. Not surprisingly, it does not pass civil liberties, political rights, and voice and accountability indicators. These overall high scores reflect China's strong performance over the past twenty years on economic growth and poverty reduction, which has been among the best in the world.

In year two, seven countries fall one hurdle short of qualifying. Six of the seven (Benin, Burkina Faso, India, Mali, Mauritania, and Morocco) fail to pass sufficient hurdles in the investing in people category. As in the first year, São Tomé and Príncipe passes eleven of the twelve indicators for which it has data, but fails to pass sufficient hurdles in establishing economic freedom.

Table 3-6 is an indicator scorecard for all eighty-seven countries that are eligible to compete for the MCA during the first two years. For each of these countries the table indicates which indicators the country passes and which it fails to pass, using current data.

Possible Qualifying Countries in Year Three

In the administration's current proposal, countries with per capita incomes between $1,435 and $2,975 will become eligible to compete for funding in the third year (fiscal year 2006). This group of twenty-eight countries would compete separately from countries with incomes less than $1,435, with different medians calculated independently for the two groups. Table 3-7 shows the six countries that would qualify from this group if the administration's proposal to include these countries is ultimately adopted: Belize, Bulgaria, Jordan, Namibia, South Africa, and St. Vincent and the Grena-

(*text continues on page 75*)

Table 3-6. *Indicator Scorecard, MCA Countries with Incomes below $1,435*[a]

Country	*Civil liberties*	*Political rights*	*Voice and accountability*	*Government effectiveness*	*Rule of law*	*Control of corruption*	*Education spending as percent of GDP*	*Primary education completion rate*	*Immunization rate*	*Health spending as percent of GDP*	*Country credit rating*	*Inflation*	*3-year budget deficit*	*Trade policy*	*Regulatory quality*	*Days to start a business*
Afghanistan	X	X	X	X	X	X	X	X	X	X	X	X	X	X	X	X
Albania	■	■	■	■	X	X	X	■	■	■	X	■	X	X	■	■
Angola	X	X	X	X	X	X	X	X	X	X	X	X	X	X	X	X
Armenia	X	X	■	■	■	■	X	■	■	■	X	■	X	■	■	X
Azerbaijan	X	X	X	X	X	X	X	■	■	X	■	■	■	■	X	X
Bangladesh	X	X	■	■	■	X	X	■	■	X	■	■	■	X	X	■
Belarus	X	X	X	X	X	■	■	■	■	■	X	X	■	X	X	X
Benin	■	■	■	■	■	■	■	X	X	X	■	■	■	X	■	X
Bhutan	X	X	X	■	■	■	X	X	■	■	X	■	■	X	■	X
Bolivia	■	■	■	■	■	■	■	■	■	■	■	■	■	■	■	X
Bosnia and Herzegovina	X	X	■	X	X	■	X	■	■	■	X	X	X	■	X	X
Burkina Faso	X	X	■	■	■	■	■	X	X	X	■	■	X	X	■	■
Burundi	X	X	X	X	X	X	■	X	■	X	X	■	■	X	X	X
Cambodia	X	X	X	■	X	X	X	■	X	X	X	■	X	■	■	X
Cameroon	X	X	X	■	X	X	X	X	X	X	■	■	■	X	X	■
Cape Verde	■	■	■	■	■	■	X	■	■	X	X	■	X	X	■	X

Central African Republic	X	X	X	X	X	X	X	X	X	■	X	■	X	X	X	X
Chad	X	X	X	■	X	X	X	X	X	■	X	■	X	X	X	X
China	X	X	X	■	■	■	X	■	■	■	■	■	■	X	■	■
Comoros	X	X	■	X	X	■	X	X	X	X	X	X	■	X	X	X
Congo, Dem. Rep.	X	X	X	X	X	X	X	X	X	X	X	X	■	X	X	X
Congo, Rep.	X	X	X	X	X	X	X	X	X	■	X	■	■	X	X	X
Côte d'Ivoire	X	X	X	X	X	X	■	X	X	X	X	■	■	X	■	X
Djibouti	X	X	X	X	■	■	■	X	X	■	X	X	■	X	X	X
Ecuador	■	■	■	X	■	X	X	■	■	X	■	■	■	X	■	X
Equatorial Guinea	X	X	X	X	X	X	X	X	X	X	X	X	■	X	X	■
Eritrea	X	X	X	■	■	■	■	X	■	X	X	X	X	X	X	X
Ethiopia	X	X	X	X	■	■	X	X	X	X	X	■	X	X	X	■
Gambia	X	X	X	X	■	X	■	■	■	■	X	■	■	X	■	X
Georgia	X	X	■	■	X	X	X	■	■	X	X	■	■	X	X	■
Ghana	■	■	■	■	■	■	■	■	■	X	■	■	X	X	■	X
Guinea	X	X	X	■	■	■	X	X	X	■	X	X	X	X	X	X
Guinea-Bissau	X	X	X	X	X	■	X	X	X	X	X	■	X	X	X	X
Guyana	■	■	■	■	■	■	X	■	■	■	X	■	X	X	■	X
Haiti	X	X	X	X	X	X	X	X	X	X	X	■	■	■	X	X
Honduras	■	■	■	■	X	■	X	■	■	■	■	■	X	■	■	X
India	■	■	■	■	■	■	X	■	X	X	■	■	X	X	■	X
Indonesia	X	■	■	■	X	X	X	■	X	X	■	■	■	■	■	X
Kazakhstan	X	X	X	X	X	X	X	X	■	■	■	■	■	X	X	■
Kenya	X	X	X	X	X	X	■	X	■	■	■	■	■	X	■	X
Kiribati	■	■	■	■	■	■	X	X	■	X	X	X	X	X	X	■

(*continued*)

Table 3-6. (*Continued*)

Country	*Civil liberties*	*Political rights*	*Voice and accountability*	*Government effectiveness*	*Rule of law*	*Control of corruption*	*Education spending as percent of GDP*	*Primary education completion rate*	*Immunization rate*	*Health spending as percent of GDP*	*Country credit rating*	*Inflation*	*3-year budget deficit*	*Trade policy*	*Regulatory quality*	*Days to start a business*
Kyrgyz Republic	X	X	X	X	X	X	■	X	■	■	X	■	■	X	■	■
Lao PDR	X	X	X	X	X	X	X	■	X	X	X	■	X	X	X	X
Lesotho	■	■	■	■	■	■	■	■	■	X	■	■	X	■	■	X
Liberia	X	X	X	X	X	X	X	X	X	X	X	X	X	X	X	X
Madagascar	X	■	■	■	■	■	X	X	X	X	X	■	■	■	■	X
Malawi	X	X	■	■	■	X	■	X	■	■	■	■	X	X	■	■
Mali	■	■	■	X	■	■	X	X	X	■	■	■	X	■	■	■
Mauritania	X	X	X	■	■	■	■	X	X	X	X	■	■	X	■	X
Moldova	X	■	■	■	■	X	■	■	■	■	X	■	■	■	■	■
Mongolia	■	■	■	■	■	■	■	■	■	X	■	■	X	■	■	■
Morocco	X	X	■	■	■	■	X	X	■	X	■	■	■	X	■	X
Mozambique	X	■	■	■	■	X	X	X	■	■	■	■	X	X	■	X
Myanmar	X	X	X	X	X	X	X	X	X	X	X	X	■	X	X	X
Nepal	X	X	■	■	■	■	X	■	X	X	■	■	■	X	■	■
Nicaragua	■	■	■	X	■	■	■	■	■	■	X	■	X	■	■	X
Niger	X	X	■	X	■	X	■	X	X	X	X	■	X	X	X	■
Nigeria	X	X	X	X	X	X	■	■	X	X	■	■	■	X	X	■

Pakistan	X	X	X	■	■	■	X	X	X	X	■	■	X	X	X	X
Papua New Guinea	■	■	■	X	X	X	X	X	X	■	■	■	X	X	■	X
Paraguay	■	■	■	X	X	X	■	■	X	X	■	■	■	■	■	X
Philippines	■	■	■	■	■	■	■	■	X	X	■	■	■	■	■	X
Rwanda	X	X	X	X	X	■	■	X	■	■	X	■	■	X	X	X
São Tomé and Príncipe	■	■	■	■	■	■	■	■	■	X	X	■	X	X	■	X
Senegal	■	■	■	■	■	■	■	X	X	■	■	■	■	X	■	■
Sierra Leone	X	X	■	X	X	■	■	X	X	X	X	■	X	X	X	X
Solomon Islands	■	■	■	X	■	X	■	■	■	X	X	X	X	X	X	X
Somalia	X	X	X	X	X	X	X	X	X	X	X	X	X	X	X	X
Sri Lanka	X	■	■	■	■	■	X	■	■	X	■	■	X	■	■	X
Sudan	X	X	X	X	X	X	X	X	X	X	X	X	■	X	X	X
Swaziland	X	X	X	■	■	■	■	■	X	■	■	■	■	■	■	X
Syrian Arab Republic	X	X	X	■	■	■	X	■	■	X	■	■	■	X	X	■
Tajikistan	X	X	X	X	X	X	X	■	■	■	X	■	■	■	X	X
Tanzania	■	X	■	■	■	X	X	X	■	X	■	■	X	X	■	■
Timor Leste	■	■	■	X	X	■	X	X	X	X	X	X	X	X	X	X
Togo	X	X	X	X	■	■	■	■	X	X	X	■	■	■	■	X
Turkmenistan	X	X	X	X	X	X	X	X	■	■	■	■	■	X	X	X
Uganda	X	X	X	■	X	X	■	■	X	X	■	■	X	■	■	■
Ukraine	X	■	■	■	X	X	■	■	■	■	■	■	■	■	■	■
Uzbekistan	X	X	X	X	X	X	■	X	■	■	■	X	■	X	X	■
Vanuatu	■	■	■	■	■	■	■	■	■	X	X	X	X	X	X	X

(*continued*)

Table 3-6. (*Continued*)

Country	*Civil liberties*	*Political rights*	*Voice and accountability*	*Government effectiveness*	*Rule of law*	*Control of corruption*	*Education spending as percent of GDP*	*Primary education completion rate*	*Immunization rate*	*Health spending as percent of GDP*	*Country credit rating*	*Inflation*	*3-year budget deficit*	*Trade policy*	*Regulatory quality*	*Days to start a business*
Vietnam	X	X	X	■	■	■	X	■	■	X	■	■	■	X	X	X
West Bank	X	X	X	X	■	X	X	X	X	X	X	X	X	X	X	X
Yemen, Rep.	X	X	X	X	X	■	■	X	■	X	X	■	■	■	■	X
Yugoslavia, Fed. Rep.	■	■	■	■	X	■	X	X	■	X	X	X	■	X	■	X
Zambia	X	X	■	X	■	X	X	■	■	■	X	X	X	X	■	■
Zimbabwe	X	X	X	X	X	X	■	■	X	■	X	X	X	X	X	X

Source: Steven Radelet, *Challenging Foreign Aid: A Policymaker's Guide to the Millennium Challenge Account* (Washington: Center for Global Development, 2003).

a. ■ = above median; **X** = below median.

dines. Their median scores are much higher than those of the first two groups on almost every indicator, reflecting their higher development status. For example, the median primary school completion rate is 92 percent, compared with 65 percent for the countries with incomes below $1,435. Similarly the immunization rate is 92 percent, compared with 75 percent for the second-year countries. The Freedom House political rights median score is 2 (on a scale of 1 to 7, with 1 the top score), compared with 5 for the other group.

Romania is the only country from this group to fail solely because of its corruption score. The Maldives, Thailand, and Tunisia miss qualification by one hurdle. The Maldives misses qualification essentially because it is missing data for three of the six indicators for establishing economic freedom. Table 3-8 contains an indicator scorecard for all twenty-eight lower-middle-income countries eligible to compete for the MCA under the administration's proposal.

Each of these countries is a reasonable qualifier, including the three countries that miss by one indicator, with the possible exception of Jordan. Although Jordan has had a decent economic record in recent years, it already receives substantial bilateral flows from the United States, so in a sense it is already receiving many of the benefits that the MCA might confer. Moreover, including Jordan in the MCA could politicize allocation decisions. It would be best if Jordan remained out of the MCA and continued to receive funding through the State Department's economic support funds. The other countries seem plausible on economic grounds, but most are rich enough that they can access private capital markets and have less need of aid flows than the poorest countries (South Africa may be an exception, given the extent of the HIV/AIDS crises there). For example, Tunisia graduated from USAID funding several years ago, so, while its policy record is sufficient, its need for large sums of foreign aid is questionable.

As mentioned earlier, it would be best if this group of countries were dropped from the MCA. Although these countries include many people living in poverty, overall their standards of living are substantially higher than those in low-income countries, and they have access to several other sources of financing that are out of reach of the poorest countries.

Changing the Emphasis Placed on Indicators

Some observers have suggested giving greater prominence to various indicators in the country selection process, including economic competitive-

Table 3-7. *Possible Qualifying Countries, Year Three, with Per Capita Incomes between $1,435 and $2,975*[a]

Counties	Civil liberties (1 to 7, 1 = best)	Political rights (1 to 7, 1 = best)	Voice and account-ability (0 to 1, 1 = best)	Govern-ment effective-ness (0 to 1, 1 = best)	Rule of law (0 to 1, 1 = best)	Control of corrup-tion (0 to 1, 1 = best)	Public primary education spending (percent of GDP)	Primary education completion rate (percent)	Immuni-zation rate: DPT and measles (percent)
Qualify									
Belize	2	1	0.72	0.55	0.56	0.50	3	**82**	92.5
Bulgaria	2	1	0.64	0.56	0.57	0.52	1.6	**91.8**	**92**
Jordan	**5**	**6**	**0.32**	0.66	0.64	0.59	2.2	104	99
Namibia	**3**	**2**	0.61	0.63	0.67	0.63	4.9	**90**	**60.5**
South Africa	2	1	0.70	0.69	0.60	0.67	**NA**	98	**76.5**
St. Vincent and the Grenadines	1	**2**	0.79	0.57	0.70	0.70	3	**84**	98.5
Eliminated by corruption									
Romania	2	**2**	0.62	**0.46**	0.54	**0.45**	**1.3**	98	98.5
Missed by one indicator									
Maldives	**5**	**6**	**0.24**	0.76	0.66	0.60	4.1	112	98.5
Thailand	**3**	2	0.56	0.64	0.62	0.53	**1.2**	**90**	95
Tunisia	**5**	**6**	**0.19**	0.71	0.62	0.67	**NA**	**91**	94
Median	**3.0**	**2.0**	**0.55**	**0.49**	**0.48**	**0.49**	**1.5**	**91.9**	**92.0**

Source: Steven Radelet, *Challenging Foreign Aid: A Policymaker's Guide to the Millennium Challenge Account* (Washington: Center for Global Development, 2003).

a. Bold indicates missed hurdles. No countries were eliminated because of corruption.

ness, trade, and democracy. The question is finding the right balance, since giving one indicator more weight automatically gives others less. For example, Pasicolan and Fitzgerald recommend that the MCA rely exclusively on economic competitiveness criteria, and not include criteria for ruling justly or investing in people. They argue that improved health and education and improved governance are the result of rapid economic growth, rather than inputs to the growth process.[29] This argument, however, differs from a large body of research showing better health, education, and governance as causal factors of growth, as well as benefiting from growth in the long term.[30] The administration's proposal is more consistent with both economic theory and empirical research.

Other observers suggest giving more prominence to trade policy since trade is central to the growth process. This argument is more consistent with empirical evidence. However, as discussed earlier, strong trade policy

Public expenditure on health (percent of GDP)	Country credit rating (1 to 100, 100 = best)	Inflation (percent)	3-year budget deficit (percent)	Trade policy (1 to 5, 1 = best)	Regulatory quality (0 to 1, 1 = best)	Days to start a business	Number of passed hurdles		
							Ruling justly	Investing in people	Economic freedom
2.27	38.8	1.2	**−10.7**	**4**	0.60	**NA**	6	2	3
3.89	39.6	3.8	1.4	**4**	0.69	30	6	2	5
3.62	38.6	0.9	**−2.7**	**5**	0.58	**89**	3	4	3
3.33	39.6	13.6	**−3.9**	3	0.64	**NA**	4	2	4
3.33	52.4	8.4	−2.0	3	0.69	32	6	2	6
4.16	**NA**	−0.8	−2.3	**NA**	0.61	**NA**	5	3	3
3.77	**33.9**	17.8	**−3.0**	4	0.56	46	3	3	3
3.67	**NA**	−2.1	**−4.7**	**NA**	0.74	**NA**	3	4	2
1.87	52.2	2.2	**−5.4**	**4**	0.65	45	4	1	4
2.21	50.7	1.5	**−2.5**	**5**	0.54	47	3	1	4
3.2	**38.1**	**20.0**	**−2.4**	**4.0**	**0.53**	**48.5**			

indicators are surprisingly scarce, and the immediate emphasis should be on developing more accurate indicators.

Still others suggest giving more weight to democracy. Although most of the potential MCA qualifiers are democracies, the possibility that Bhutan, Swaziland, and Vietnam could qualify under the proposed methodology raises red flags. Including these countries, critics argue, would undermine the credibility of the MCA and contradict U.S. efforts to advocate democracy worldwide.[31] However, to come extent, the administration's proposal takes this viewpoint into account: it gives democracy greater prominence in the selection process than any other area except corruption by including three democracy indicators (political rights, voice and accountability, and civil liberties). As mentioned previously, both of the Freedom House indicators (political rights and civil liberties) are components of the World Bank Institute's voice and accountability indicator, so they are counted twice in the selection process. Giving additional weight to democracy would mean

(*text continues on page 80*)

Table 3-8. *Indicator Scorecard, MCA Countries with Incomes between $1,435 and $2,975*[a]

Country	*Civil liberties*	*Political rights*	*Voice and accountability*	*Government effectiveness*	*Rule of law*	*Control of corruption*	*Education spending as percent of GDP*	*Primary education completion rate*	*Immunization rate*	*Health spending as percent of GDP*	*Country credit rating*	*Inflation*	*3-year budget deficit*	*Trade policy*	*Regulatory quality*	*Days to start a business*
Algeria	X	X	X	X	X	X	X	X	X	X	X	■	■	X	X	■
Belize	■	■	■	■	■	■	■	X	■	X	■	■	X	X	■	X
Bulgaria	■	■	■	■	■	■	■	X	X	■	■	■	■	X	■	■
Colombia	X	X	X	X	X	X	X	X	X	■	X	■	X	X	X	X
Dominican Republic	■	X	■	X	X	X	X	X	X	X	X	■	■	X	X	X
Egypt	X	X	X	X	■	X	X	■	■	X	■	■	X	X	X	X
El Salvador	X	X	X	X	X	X	X	X	■	X	■	■	■	■	■	X
Fiji	X	X	X	■	X	■	X	■	X	X	X	■	■	X	X	X
Guatemala	X	X	X	X	X	X	X	X	X	X	X	■	X	■	X	■
Iran	X	X	X	X	X	X	X	■	■	X	X	■	■	■	X	X
Jamaica	X	X	■	■	X	X	■	■	X	X	X	■	X	X	■	■
Jordan	X	X	X	■	■	■	■	■	■	■	■	■	X	X	■	X

Macedonia	X	X	X	X	X	X	X	X	X	■	X	■	X	X	X	X
Maldives	X	X	X	■	■	■	■	■	■	■	X	■	X	X	■	X
Marshall Islands	■	■	■	X	X	■	X	X	X	X	X	X	X	X	X	X
Micronesia	■	■	■	X	X	X	X	X	X	X	X	X	X	X	X	X
Namibia	X	X	■	■	■	■	■	X	X	■	■	■	X	■	■	X
Peru	X	X	■	X	X	■	X	■	X	X	X	■	■	X	■	X
Romania	■	X	■	X	■	X	X	■	■	■	X	■	X	X	■	■
Russian Federation	X	X	X	X	X	X	X	■	■	X	■	■	■	X	X	X
Samoa	■	X	■	■	■	■	X	■	■	■	X	■	X	X	X	X
South Africa	■	■	■	■	■	■	X	■	X	■	■	■	■	■	■	■
St. Vincent and the Grenadines	■	X	■	■	■	■	■	X	■	■	X	■	■	X	■	X
Suriname	■	■	■	■	■	■	■	X	X	X	X	X	■	X	X	X
Thailand	X	X	■	■	■	■	X	X	■	X	■	■	X	X	■	■
Tonga	X	X	X	X	X	X	X	X	■	X	X	■	X	X	X	X
Tunisia	X	X	X	■	■	■	X	X	■	X	■	■	X	X	■	■
Turkey	X	X	X	■	■	X	X	■	X	■	X	X	X	■	■	X

Source: Steven Radelet, *Challenging Foreign Aid: A Policymaker's Guide to the Millennium Challenge Account* (Washington: Center for Global Development, 2003).

a. ■ = above median; **X** = below median.

giving less weight to health, education, and other indicators. In addition, the precise empirical relationship between democracy and economic development and poverty reduction remains unclear, as summarized by the United Nations Development Program's 2002 *Human Development Report,* which found that "the literature finds no causal relationship between democracy and economic performance, in either direction."[32] Probably the best way to give more weight to democracy in the few cases where it is necessary is by using the procedure by which the MCC board can adjust the list of qualifying countries. The administration should use the discretion afforded by this process to eliminate the most egregious nondemocracies (such as China) rather than reorganizing the indicators in a way that might inadvertently deemphasize other important aspects of the qualification process.

The administration's weighting of the sixteen indicators is arbitrary and should be recognized as such. Different weighting systems might be more consistent with identifying countries where aid can be effective in supporting economic growth and poverty reduction. Deeper research is necessary on alternative weighting systems to consider moving in that direction.

An Alternative Ranking System: How Would the List Change?

The analysis earlier in this chapter suggests an alternative way to aggregate the same sixteen indicators to determine the set of qualifying countries. Briefly, each indicator is rescaled so that the mean score is reassigned a value of zero, and values that are one standard deviation above or below the mean are reassigned values of 1 and –1, respectively. All other scores are converted by a proportional scale. To account for the problem of missing data, they are (arbitrarily) assigned the score equal to the 25th percentile—that is, halfway between the worst score and the median score. This produces scores ranging from about –2.5 to +2.5. The rescaled indicators are then added together within each of the three broad criteria, to calculate one score for each country for each of the three areas. Finally the three scores are added together to determine a single aggregate score for each country. This score is used to rank countries from best to worst.

Table 3-9 shows the top twenty-five countries in each of the first two years and the top ten in the third year, using this ranking system. Under this system the administration would have to decide how many countries would qualify—say, the top fifteen or twenty. This would be an arbitrary decision, replacing the arbitrary decision to use medians in the other system.

Table 3-9. *Countries That Qualify for MCA Using Aggregate Ranking Method*

Ranking	*Year one: IDA-eligible with per capita incomes less than $1,435*	*Year two: All countries with per capita incomes less than $1,435*	*Year three: Per capita incomes between $1,435 and $2,975*
1	Mongolia*	Mongolia*	St. Vincent and the Grenadines*
2	Sri Lanka*	Philippines*	Bulgaria*
3	Nicaragua*	Nicaragua*	South Africa*
4	Lesotho*	Sri Lanka*	Samoa
5	Bolivia*	Lesotho*	Maldives
6	Cape Verde	Bolivia*	Thailand
7	Guyana	Cape Verde	Romania
8	Armenia*	Guyana	Jordan*
9	Vanuatu	Armenia*	Namibia*
10	India	Vanuatu	Jamaica
11	Moldova	Moldova	
12	Senegal*	Ukraine	
13	Bosnia and Herzegovina	Morocco	
14	Ghana*	Senegal*	
15	Honduras*	India	
16	São Tomé and Príncipe	Bosnia and Herzegovina	
17	Bhutan*	China@	
18	Benin	Ghana	
19	Kiribati	Swaziland*	
20	Mauritania	São Tomé and Príncipe	
21	Albania	Honduras*	
22	Madagascar	Bhutan*	
23	Nepal	Benin	
24	Uganda	Kiribati	
25	Vietnam*	Ecuador	

Source: Steven Radelet, *Challenging Foreign Aid: A Policymaker's Guide to the Millennium Challenge Account* (Washington: Center for Global Development, 2003).

* Countries that also qualify using the administration's methodology.

@ Ineligible to receive U.S. foreign assistance due to statutory reasons.

Notes about other countries that possibly qualify using the administration's methodology:

In Year 2, Vietnam ranks number 33.

In Year 3, Belize ranks number 11.

This list and the original list of qualifiers (shown in tables 3-3 to 3-5) overlap by a fair amount. For example, in year one, ten of the eleven original qualifiers are in the top seventeen. The eleventh, Vietnam, ranks twenty-fifth. In the second year, Honduras (twenty-one), Bhutan (number twenty-two), and Vietnam (thirty-three) all score outside the top twenty. In the third year, three of the original qualifiers rank one through three (St. Vincent and the Grenadines, Bulgaria, and South Africa). Several other countries not on the original list score highly in the new ranking, including Cape Verde, Guyana, and India, each of which would seem to be reasonable choices for the MCA. Most of the more controversial qualifiers under the current administration's system score relatively poorly in this system, including Bhutan, Vietnam, Swaziland, and Jordan. Indeed, with the exception of Bosnia and Herzegovina, the top sixteen countries in each of the first two years and the top six in the third year are all reasonable qualifiers in this system.

One concern with this system is that extreme scores on one indicator can heavily influence the rankings. A high score drives Nicaragua's ranking on health spending (8.5 percent of GDP) far higher than other countries. Bosnia and Herzegovina, which does not qualify under the administration's system because of poor scores on ruling justly, climbs to number thirteen because of high health spending (8 percent of GDP). But Honduras tumbles to number twenty-one, largely because of a poor score of 146 on days to start a business.

Overall, this is a reasonable alternative aggregation method, and in some ways it is superior to the administration's system. The biggest single issue is deciding how many countries should qualify. This method creates difficulties for countries not qualifying, as it is less clear exactly what standards they must attain to qualify. Nevertheless this system should be used at least as a cross-check on the other system, to guide decisions about modifying the original list, if it does not become the basic system to determine qualification. With certain modifications and refinements, this system could be made superior to the original.

Conclusion

Using the administration's proposed system, eleven countries will qualify in the first year. Two additional countries will qualify in the second year, and six more in the third. Thus, using data available today, nineteen countries could qualify for the MCA in the first three years. Six of these countries are in sub-Saharan Africa (SSA), five are in south and east Asia, two are in Eastern Europe and Central Asia, five are in Latin America and the Caribbean, and one is in the Middle East. In addition, twenty-five other countries miss qualifying by one indicator (including corruption). Several of these countries, including Cape Verde, Guyana, and São Tomé and Príncipe, fail to qualify only because they are missing data on several indicators (through no fault of their own). These countries should be added in the first year. Several other countries that miss qualifying by one indicator would also make strong candidates. Conceivably several of these countries could improve their scores and attain qualification within a few years. However, even if they do, under the administration's proposal the total number of countries qualifying for the MCA is unlikely to expand much beyond the original size, because the use of the median as the hurdle dictates that, as some countries improve their scores to qualify, the medians will rise, and other countries will fall below the qualifying standard.

Africa has been a special focus of attention in the MCA. The six SSA countries most likely to qualify constitute 12 percent of the population of the region. Excluding Nigeria from the equation, which accounts for one-fifth of the population of SSA and is far from qualifying for the MCA, the qualifiers account for 14 percent of SSA's population. The countries that miss by just one hurdle account for an additional 8 percent of the region's population (excluding Nigeria), so a total of 22 percent of SSA's population outside Nigeria is likely to qualify or be close to qualifying for the MCA during the first three years. This is a fairly small share. This outcome raises the important issue of what the U.S. strategy is for working with countries that do not qualify for the MCA. Many African countries (along with low-income countries from other regions) are far from qualifying for the MCA, and no clear strategy exists to help them qualify. This issue is addressed in the context of the overall U.S. foreign assistance strategy discussed in chapter 7.

The administration's proposed methodology to select MCA countries is a reasonable initial approach, by and large. Most countries that appear on the qualification list are sensible choices (with some exceptions). The system has some weaknesses, but fortunately it can be improved. Some of these changes can be implemented immediately; others will take more time.

The biggest single concern is the inclusion of countries with incomes between \$1,435 and \$2,975 in the group of eligible countries. Although some of these countries have many people living in poverty, their overall development status is much more advanced than the lower-income countries, and they have access to a wider array of financial resources to address these problems. These countries should not be eligible for the MCA and should continue to access traditional forms of U.S. assistance, as appropriate. Instead the MCA-eligible countries should be split into two groups in a different way. The first group would include all countries with per capita incomes of $875 or less (the World Bank's current operational cut-off for IDA eligibility). This group would include the 68 poorest countries in the world. The second group would be composed of 19 additional countries, with per capita incomes between $875 and $1,435. In this system the 87 poorest countries in the world would be eligible for the MCA, rather than the 115 in the current formulation, eliminating the 28 wealthiest from the original group. The two groups would compete separately for funding, as in the current proposal, with the vast majority of funds going to the lower-income group. Alternatively, if the current income groups are retained, a limit should be adopted (up to a maximum of $1 billion a year) which would be available to the richer country group, consistent with its population share.

The use of the median as the hurdle raises three concerns. First, medians change from year to year, so countries will be aiming at moving targets. Second, using medians as benchmarks severely restricts the potential for the number of MCA countries to expand over time. Because of these first two concerns, the administration should move quickly to adopt absolute hurdles for as many indicators as possible, perhaps using the medians from the first year as a guide. This step could be taken immediately for the four indicators for investing in people, inflation (already using an absolute standard of 20 percent), the budget deficit, and days to start a business. This step will be more difficult for the other indicators, but the administration could work with the suppliers of those data to explore ways in which these indicators could be adjusted to an absolute scale that could be compared over time. Third, the administration should try to refine some of the indicators that use narrow scales that result in many countries bunched together at or near the median. The Heritage Foundation/Wall Street Journal trade policy index is the weakest indicator in this area, but the Freedom House civil liberties and political rights indexes are also of concern. Once this step is taken, median scores can be a passing grade on each hurdle.

The proposal to eliminate all countries with corruption scores below the median regardless of their performance in other areas should be reexamined. The data used for this indicator (along with most other indicators) are not robust enough to produce a high degree of confidence about the true level of corruption for countries with scores near the median. As an alternative, the worst corruption offenders, where the data indicate a 75 percent chance or greater that the true score is below the median, could be eliminated immediately. Alternatively, countries with corruption scores in the bottom quartile could be eliminated. Other countries would remain eligible and could qualify if they meet half the hurdles in each of the three categories, even if they miss on the corruption indicator.

The chosen indicators, while far from perfect, probably are the best available at the moment to help choose countries for the MCA. The indicators can be improved over time, and the administration should consider exploring other indicators that could be used either in place of or in addition to existing indicators. Although the proposed system is a reasonable starting point, it has some clear weaknesses.

For example, the list of qualifying countries is a good start but is less than ideal. Many countries that would qualify are reasonable choices to receive funding from the MCA, including Bolivia, Honduras, Ghana, Lesotho, and Senegal. However, several other countries are surprising qualifiers, including Bhutan, Honduras, and Vietnam. A few others are surprising for not making the list of qualifiers, such as Guyana and Thailand. The proposal to allow the board of directors of the new corporation to modify the list of qualifying countries could help remove some of these anomalies. But the outcomes indicate some weaknesses in the chosen indicators, as well.

The economic freedom indicators give heavy weight to several standard macroeconomic variables, so countries with a reasonable macroeconomic environment but weaker microeconomic policies still pass these hurdles. One striking result is that Nigeria, Cameroon, Haiti, Syria, Turkmenistan, and Ukraine all pass three or more of the economic freedom indicators. This suggests that greater attention should be given to the microeconomic foundations of sustained economic growth, such as licensing and regulatory burdens, agriculture pricing distortions, financial market operations, and state ownership of productive assets. In a different direction, the indicators for investing in people are particularly difficult for poor, highly indebted countries to pass, since two of the indicators relate to public spending on health and education. Expanding this set of indicators, or exploring ways to take account of significant improvements in health and education (which still may fall short of the qualifying level), could strengthen the process.

Summary of Recommendations

The administration should consider the following changes to the indicators:

—Countries should be urged to make data available on tariff and nontariff barriers to trade, with a breakdown for capital and intermediate goods. These data could replace the current trade indicator, which is among the weakest of the indicators, because of both its subjectivity and its narrow range of scores.

—Budget data should be improved to refine the measure of the budget deficit and the most appropriate spending items for health and education.

—Data on days to start a business should be expanded to include information on other barriers to starting new businesses.

—An indicator should be added to measure the extent of state ownership of productive assets. It should be limited to measuring state ownership in manufacturing, retail trade, and financial services, where the benefits of privatization are clearer and less controversial. It should exclude measures of state ownership of infrastructure and utilities (including water), where the results of privatization have been less clear. This indicator would take a year or two to develop.

—The indicators for investing in people should be expanded to include the ratio of girls to boys in primary schools, perhaps the primary school enrollment ratio, plus one other health indicator.

—The indicators on spending on aggregate primary education and health should be replaced over time by indicators that measure spending n the most important areas of education and health.

In general the MCA should be used to stimulate broader and deeper data collection efforts that will help guide effective development policies and foreign assistance programs in the future.

Countries should be ranked by their aggregate score as well as by the original system to double-check the list of qualifiers. Both ranking systems should continue to be modified and refined to determine which can evolve into the stronger and more accurate method.

Ultimately these kinds of refinements would change the list of qualifying countries marginally, adding some countries and dropping others. They would not change the fundamental character of the qualification process, which is designed to select a small number of countries for the MCA.

Improving the selection methodology will take time, energy, and technical skill. The administration and Congress should commission a team of independent technical experts to review the selection process on an annual basis and make recommendations for improvement. These experts could review the choice of indicators, weighting and aggregation methods, and data quality and report their findings publicly. This would ensure a stronger selection process so that MCA funds are allocated to the countries that are most committed to supporting economic growth and poverty reduction.

4

Policy Framework for the Millennium Challenge Account

In contrast to the sprawling mission and multiple objectives of the U.S. Agency for International Development (USAID), the Millennium Challenge Account will achieve greatest effectiveness by having a narrowly defined mission and developing a core competence in limited areas related to it. The mission of the MCA should be to support growth and sustainable development and combat poverty in poor nations with a demonstrated record of sound policy, social investment, and good governance, by underwriting meritorious strategies designed and implemented by recipients. This chapter sets out a simple set of criteria to determine the priority program areas for the MCA. Chapter 5 elaborates a new approach for delivering aid more effectively.

Keeping the Program Focus Narrow

A narrow focus is critical to protect the MCA from political interference. But it is also critical to ensure the MCA is effective, bringing to bear the expertise needed to effectively evaluate proposals and monitor and evaluate ongoing activities. As discussed in later chapters, by taking on too many objectives, USAID has at times lost its focus, and in some areas expertise is spread too thin. In contrast, the MCA should restrict its focus to a limited set of activities that are directly related to its core mission. It can shape its staff around these areas, building expertise in proposal review, monitoring, evaluation, and learning from results. Moreover, for its part, the MCA will achieve greatest effectiveness while still remaining lean only if it establishes depth in a few areas of expertise.

It could be argued that the MCA should fund good proposals in any area deemed a priority by recipients, in keeping with the country ownership approach. But that is misguided for two reasons. First, it would ignore decades of experience and research suggesting that some types of programs and investments have much greater impact than others and are more suitable to public intervention and foreign support in particular. Second, for the MCA to achieve expertise that is both deep enough and broad enough to evaluate proposals effectively and negotiate workable contracts across twenty to twenty-five countries and all sectors is inconsistent with maintaining a relatively lean organization. Inevitably, either the MCA would fall prey to the functional sprawl that undermines USAID, or it would fall short on its proposal assessment and oversight role. Moreover, recipients should be able to tap a combination of other donors, possibly private sector financing and budget resources (possibly freed up by MCA budget support in MCA priority areas) for areas not covered by the MCA. Finally, as described further in the next chapter, the MCA could provide program-wide budget support. Thus, for instance, funding for primary education could include not only direct elements (teacher salaries, books, curriculum design) but also critical indirect elements (transportation infrastructure to ensure access).

The Millennium Challenge Corporation (MCC) should focus its grant making on a core set of sectors that meet four criteria:

—evidence that the sector is an important determinant of growth and poverty reduction;

—inclusion of the sector in the millennium development goals (MDGs), whose importance to poverty reduction is a matter of international consensus;

—evidence that public intervention is needed in the sector to address areas where private investment falls short of the socially desirable level; and

—an established track record of foreign aid delivering results in the sector and evidence that the U.S. has particular expertise and experience there.

The compatibility between a program area and the recipient-led, lean approach of the MCA should also be considered.

These criteria strongly support the proposed emphasis on primary education, agricultural development, and basic health and sanitation. But the criteria would suggest focusing on the policy environment, rather than directly financing private sector development, and building capacity more broadly than the administration's narrow focus on capacity in trade and investment only. It is important that the criteria also include environmental and energy policy. Although support for good governance and democracy meet several of the criteria, because of uncertainty about the level of demand and the small size of the MCA staff, we suggest that governance proposals be subcontracted to USAID for review and monitoring, at least initially.

The core focus of the MCA should thus encompass five areas, with a sixth area reserved for further study (see table 4-1):

—basic health (including family planning and sanitation),
—primary education,
—agricultural development,
—strengthening the policy environment for private sector development, and
—environment and energy.

The MCA might also expand its program focus to include governance, but we recommend that proposals in this area be subcontracted out to USAID initially in order to assess the demand and fit with the MCA model.

These are areas in which USAID has long experience and expertise and has financed many successful projects. They are key to the development process and are high-priority investment areas in almost every low-income country. They are consistent with the selection criteria for the MCA as well as for most countries' poverty-reduction strategy papers (PRSPs) and the international MDGs. They are consistent with stated U.S. government priorities for foreign assistance to developing countries. And they are areas in which the private sector has underinvested and is likely to continue doing so.

Basic Health

Basic health should be a priority focus of the MCA, as it is for three of the eight MDGs. The evidence linking improved health to growth and standards of living is compelling.[1] Substantial research suggests that increases in child survival and life expectancy and reductions in morbidity have important developmental benefits, including improvements in productivity, savings and investment patterns, and educational investments, as well as more

Table 4-1. *Principles for Selection of MCA Program Areas*

	Demonstrated contribution to development	*Millennium development goal target*	*Private sector under-investment*	*Good track record for aid*	*Compatible with MCA recipient-led approach*	*MCA role*
Basic health, family planning, and sanitation	✓	✓	✓	✓	✓	Core program
Primary education	✓	✓	✓	✓	✓	Core program
Agricultural development	✓	X	✓	✓	✓	Core program
Environment and clean energy	Complex relationship	✓	✓	✓	✓	Core program
Policy environment for private sector development	✓	X	✓	✓	✓	Core program
Microfinance	✓	X	✓	✓	✓	Core program
Enterprise fund (venture capital)	✓	X	X	X	X	None
Democracy	Complex relationship	X	✓	Mixed	X	None
Governance	✓	X	✓	Mixed	?	Subcontract to USAID

✓ = relationship exists.
X = no relationship.
? = relationship unclear.

sustainable population growth patterns.[2] The market on its own yields socially suboptimal health outcomes in developing countries, since health exhibits many of the characteristics of public goods.[3] Official international efforts have an impressive record in health—in areas like vaccines and oral rehydration therapy—which have led to measurable and highly cost-effective improvements. USAID has considerable strength in the health field, particularly in family planning and HIV/AIDS.

Primary Education

Targeting primary education for all girls and boys should be a core focus of the MCA, as it is for two of the eight MDGs. Primary education has obvious direct economic benefits but also important indirect benefits. Improving girls' educational attainments has been linked to better health and education outcomes for families and more sustainable fertility patterns. The evidence on the relationship between education and economic growth is relatively weak, partly because of data deficiencies and partly because education programs in low-income countries have sometimes created poor incentives by focusing on the quantity of students rather than the quality of education. Some research finds a relationship between education and growth, and some does not, but few would argue with the notions that quality education is an important goal in itself and is central to the broader development process.[4] Education at the primary level also has many of the characteristics of public goods. And while foreign aid's record on education is mixed, well-designed programs suggest substantial potential for good outcomes.

Environment and Clean Energy

The Bush administration's proposal for the MCA is strangely silent on environment and energy, even though this area is an important focus of both international development efforts and existing U.S. foreign assistance programs. The analysis here would argue for placing considerations of sustainable development more squarely in the central mandate of the MCA.

The environment differs from most of the other proposed program areas in that it is not included in the set of selection criteria proposed by the Bush administration. The administration is right to go slowly on this issue. Although in principle it would be attractive to include environmental selection criteria for the purposes of providing incentives for improving environmental protection, in practice finding objective and generally applicable environmental parameters is a work-in-progress. (See box 4-1.) The MCA would do well to study the work underway on developing solid environmental indicators for possible future consideration.

Should the MCA make grants on renewable energy and environmental stewardship? A strong case can be made for private sector underprovision. Environmental stewardship is one of the classic examples of a public good—a situation where the costs to individual market actors do not adequately reflect the costs to society as a whole. In many environmental areas, such as climate change, ozone depletion, fishery depletion, transboundary air pollution, and highly migratory chemical toxins (like PCBs and DDT), the case for foreign official assistance is bolstered by the presence of international spillovers. Foreign aid has a relatively strong record in this area, and both the U.S. government and multilateral development banks have extensive experience with it. Also, stewardship of natural resources and sustainable development are considered priority goals in the international development agenda, as reflected in the MDGs and elsewhere.[5] The link between environment and development was the central theme of the 2002 World Summit on Sustainable Development in Johannesburg, South Africa.[6]

Box 4-1. *Environmental Indicators: A Work-in-Progress*

Over the past decade, the Environmental Protection Agency, the World Bank, the United Nations Environment Program, and others have developed a variety of environmental indicators. To date these indicators are proving more useful in gauging a country's performance over time than in comparing its environmental performance to other nations. Further work is needed on environmental indicators before they should be considered proxies for good environmental policy.

Environmental conditions differ enormously from country to country. Environmental policies that make sense for China may not prove appropriate in Egypt or Malaysia. Environmental performance is a function not only of government policies but of geography. Air pollution, for example, depends greatly on factors that governments cannot control easily (such as climate and urbanization). Even seemingly generally applicable indicators, such as per capita environmental spending, are difficult to quantify and do not appear to correlate precisely with environmental excellence.

Some might argue for focusing the MCA exclusively on growth, which in turn would result in greater environmental protection.[7] Economic growth and progress on some environmental indicators have gone hand in hand in recent decades.[8] But the relationship between wealth and environmental stewardship is complicated; poorly managed economic growth tends to exacerbate some environmental problems.[9] Some environmental problems get worse rather than better as a society becomes wealthier. In some cases poor environmental choices are temporary, but the effect is permanent. The path to wealth pursued by many poor countries includes a period of unsustainable export of natural resources. Indonesia's forests were once among the most expansive and biologically rich in the world. Over 40 percent of the country's forests were cleared in the past fifty years, with half the loss occurring in the last decade.[10] The Congo and other central African nations with tropical forest resources are following suit. Other environmental problems are directly connected to wealth. The consumption patterns of the rich produce more carbon dioxide than those of the poor. Per capita greenhouse gas emissions in highly energy-efficient Japan still exceed by a factor of nine those of energy-inefficient India.[11]

Many poor countries necessarily prioritize economic needs above environmental stewardship and lack the regulatory and governance capacity to formulate and enforce suitable environmental regulation. These choices have direct economic and health costs for current generations in terms of unhealthy air and water quality. Environmental factors, such as waterborne diseases, are the largest cause of infant mortality in developing countries.[12] In other cases regrettable and irreversible trade-offs are made between the interests of current and future generations, and these can have consequences for people living outside the borders. The case for foreign aid to rebalance the equation is strong.

At the Monterrey conference and elsewhere, developing nations have emphatically sounded the call for more environmental funding.[13] Many poor nations are the most vulnerable to environmental threats like climate change. No doubt many of them would welcome MCA support for environmental proposals. Developing countries also increasingly understand the economic, ecological, and cultural importance of preserving wilderness. The MCA should use grants to help poor nations make better environmental decisions that have consequences now and in the future.

Developing countries are also eager to obtain the most modern, environmentally friendly technologies available. This was one of the loudest messages from the Monterrey conference in March 2002 and the World Summit on Sustainable Development in September 2002.[14] After decades of research, a range of renewable energy technologies—including solar, wind, and wave energy applications—is bearing fruit. Yet developing countries lag behind in the adoption of modern clean energy technologies. The carbon dioxide intensity of China's energy production is five times higher than that of the United States.[15] China and other developing countries seek international help to close that gap.

The environment must also be taken into account in the assessment of grant proposals in other program areas. The MCC should be required to adopt procedural safeguards to ensure that activities funded by its grants do no environmental harm. The United States has led the world in ensuring that the government makes decisions with full knowledge of possible environmental consequences at home and abroad, including through long-standing bipartisan efforts to convince other countries and multilateral institutions to conduct their own environmental assessments. By statute U.S. international development agencies, including USAID, the Export-Import Bank (Ex-Im), and the Overseas Private Investment Corporation (OPIC), must screen projects for environmental sensitivity, conduct rigorous assessments of possible environmental consequences, and monitor environmental results. Executive orders extend similar requirements to some commercial agencies, such as the U.S. trade representative.[16] The MCA should be no exception, in contrast to other areas (discussed in chapter 6), where the logic of the MCA approach demands greater operational flexibility than is accorded other U.S. foreign assistance programs.

Indeed the MCA should place emphasis on building the capacity of local organizations over time to conduct environmental assessments, as well as on ensuring a transparent process. By way of illustration, OPIC's environmental assessment process is discussed in the appendix. This process includes prompt and full disclosure of relevant project information as well as opportunities for public comment.

Agricultural Development

Agriculture is centrally important to the economies of many developing countries. It is the sector that often employs the majority of the work force and is the initial driver of productivity and growth. Although the share of agricultural output normally declines as incomes rise, a strong and vibrant agricultural sector is a prerequisite for sustained growth throughout the economy. Raising agricultural productivity is instrumental for achieving the MDG targets on eradicating extreme poverty and hunger. However, it is important to avoid competing with the private sector, which should be the primary investor and actor. Instead the MCA should target those collective goods that are underprovided by the market and where foreign aid is most effective, such as rural roads and other infrastructure, applied research tailored to local conditions, and collective marketing arrangements.

Agriculture has received diminished focus in recent years from both donors and recipient governments, with donor funding for agriculture falling sharply in the late 1980s and 1990s. While donor programs in agriculture have a mixed record, there have been major successes, from the green revolution to building rural roads in Indonesia and other countries. At one point USAID had strong expertise in agriculture, but that has diminished in recent years.

Strengthening the Policy Environment for Private Sector Development

Clearly a strong and vibrant private sector is critical to economic growth. But many aspects of private sector development are better left to the market, especially areas where the track record of foreign aid is not strong. The four criteria would argue for strengthening the environment for entrepreneurship, financial intermediation, private investment, and trade generally, rather than the administration's singular focus on trade and foreign investment and financing private sector activities directly.

Policy and regulatory reform is a role appropriate to the public sector, and U.S. assistance has had some successes in this arena. Moreover although the administration is correct to propose support for strengthening the policy climate for trade and foreign investment, other areas are similarly important to a dynamic and vibrant private sector, such as financial market regulation, a predictable bankruptcy regime, competition policy, and policies affecting small business creation.

The remaining question is whether the MCA should fund private businesses more directly. The criteria above would rule out enterprise funds or other direct financing to business—with the possible exception of microfinance. The grant-making focus of the MCA is ill-suited to the role of financial intermediary, the record of U.S. government enterprise funds is mixed, and the MCA should not duplicate the work of existing U.S. and multilateral institutions dedicated to financing trade and foreign investment.

There is some support for using MCA funds to finance either equity funds or enterprise funds in recipient countries. In effect the MCA could endow a fund that could be used to make equity investments, loans to for-profit companies that could be repaid and used again, or to issue guarantees for loans. Proponents usually point to the successful Polish Enterprise Fund as an example of how this system could work.[17] However, enterprise funds have been tried in many countries, and their record is mixed, raising questions about whether this is an appropriate role for the public sector.

The administration has discussed modeling the work of the MCC on the Overseas Private Investment Corporation (OPIC), the U.S. Export-Import Bank (Ex-Im), and the enterprise funds previously established by the U.S. government. These are attractive models on governance structures, staff composition, and statutory provisions, but they are and should remain fundamentally different from the MCA in terms of their mission and program.

OPIC contributes to economic and political stability, especially in emerging democracies, but it does so primarily through facilitating U.S. business opportunities in these countries.[18] By providing political risk insurance, project finance, and financing through private investment funds, OPIC encourages U.S. private sector investment on favorable terms in regions characterized by high levels of political risk. OPIC was designed to bridge the gap between the interests of American business and some capital-scarce developing nations by facilitating risk transfer. It presupposes and exploits the relevance to economic development of projects appropriate to American investors. However, it cannot affect the fundamentals that determine overall investment climate, such as a healthy and educated work force. In addition OPIC's purview is limited to facilitating linkages with American business interests and business advancement, irrespective of whether such linkages are the most efficient or promising or address the elemental economic needs of the country in question. The MCA simultaneously aims to reach further than OPIC into the dilemmas of development, beyond situations that can attract private foreign capital, even on terms of shared risk, and to do so with a degree of flexibility that eschews the encumbrance of competing interests and objectives.

Ex-Im depends on a strategic concept similar to that of OPIC but one even more geared to the interests of American business and less calculated to meet the criteria of success set forth by the MCA. Ex-Im was created to help establish a more level playing field for U.S. firms competing in international markets against foreign firms supported by credit subsidies provided by their home governments.[19] It provides working capital, loan guarantees to foreign purchasers, and credit insurance to protect U.S. sellers. The common thread is assumption of risk, a central strategic concept it shares with OPIC. But by adopting an agenda dependent on the priorities of U.S. business interests, Ex-Im as a model for the MCC is subject to objections similar to those that arise with OPIC. The problems are, if anything, even greater, because Ex-Im imposes U.S. content requirements for goods purchased and stipulates that eligible transactions not adversely affect the U.S. economy.[20]

With the exception of microfinance and perhaps some small-enterprise activities, the MCA should not be used to directly finance for-profit activities. Although it is true that the private sector is the key to long-term growth and poverty reduction, it is far from clear that foreign aid is most effective at stimulating it. The U.S. government need not get into the commercial banking and investment banking business in low-income countries. The U.S. agencies described above and international agencies (such as the International Finance Corporation and the Multilateral Investment Guarantee Agency) already play this role to some extent, and it would be wasteful for the MCA to duplicate their activities.

The MCA should focus on helping countries improve the policy environment for private sector investment rather than on supplying financing directly. Microfinance and in some cases support for small enterprises are exceptions, since financial markets often undersupply these markets even when profitable opportunities exist.

Democracy and Governance

Governance meets many but not all the criteria established above for the core grant-making mandate of the MCA. There is evidence linking good governance to poverty reduction and growth outcomes, which is reflected in the emphasis on governance in the MCA selection criteria. This is an area where the market will not yield the desired outcomes on its own. But two considerations weigh against making this area a core competence of the MCA. First, foreign aid in general and USAID in particular have an uneven record of interventions on governance reforms. Second, it is unclear to what degree eligible countries will put forward grant proposals, because governance has traditionally been characterized as a donor-driven priority.

Defined more broadly than the "good governance" programs usually coupled with democracy assistance, governance programs might include a central government proposal to undertake judicial reform, with obvious benefits to the population and long-term development. But they also might extend to reorganizing key functional ministries, such as finance, agriculture, or trade, to better reflect domestic and international realities, or to establishing other programs aimed at increasing the capacity of the government to fulfill functions critical to national development. In these cases MCA assistance could be relevant and would be much more likely to be applied to large-scale programs. Moreover, governance is an area where preserving space for independently submitted civil society proposals might be particularly valuable.

Weighing the obvious benefits of promoting governance reforms against the uncertainty surrounding the likely demand for governance funding and the desire to keep the MCA as lean and narrowly focused as possible leads to a phased recommendation. The MCA should include governance as one of its core grant-making mandates. However, for the first several years, while there is an assessment of likely demand and whether recipient-designed programs achieve better outcomes, the MCA should not build in-house expertise in this program area but should subcontract the proposal review and monitoring and evaluation processes to USAID (on a reimbursable basis). If, over time, the MCA receives strong demand for governance reform and the results are good in particular areas, it could deepen its in-house expertise at that time.

In principle it would be appealing to integrate democracy programs with development aid to demonstrate that the two domains can be complementary and to reinforce the importance of democratization in its own right. Including democracy as a grant-making area of the MCA would reinforce its primacy and allow for experimentation among the approaches of the multiple sources of U.S. democracy aid. However, the MCA emphasis on funding eligible country proposals primarily through large-scale grants managed by a small staff does not lend itself to supporting democracy programs. Democracy aid is most effective in the form of small grants, which are by definition oversight-intensive, to civil society organizations or relatively small government institutions, such as national election boards, rather than directly to recipient governments.[21] To the extent that the MCA receives such proposals, it could simply pass them along to the many alternative organizations that have made democracy a core focus, such as USAID, the State Department, the National Endowment for Democracy, the Asia Foundation, and the Eurasia Foundation.

When Priorities Diverge

An important question is whether particular amounts should be set aside for each program area, or if other mechanisms should steer MCA funds toward investments that the United States considers high priorities within a beneficiary country. Clearly it would be more in keeping with the recipient-driven approach for MCA funding to be allocated strictly on the strength of recipient priorities. But then what happens if a country that the U.S. government, through the auspices of USAID, has deemed to be a high priority for primary education programs applies to the MCA only for infrastructure financing, for instance, to develop industrial capacity?

This discussion highlights the tension between recipient government ownership of development projects and donor priorities. On the one hand, most development practitioners today recognize the importance of donor-funded activities being consistent with recipient government priorities and ensuring that those governments are committed to success. Countless donor programs, including many by the World Bank, regional development banks, and bilateral donors, have foundered because recipients were interested only in receiving funds and were not committed to achieving successful development results. On the other hand, donors have specific priorities that they (and the taxpaying populations they represent) are most interested in. Nevertheless at times views differ on these priorities, with recipients wanting funding for activities in which donors are not interested, and donors offering financing for projects that recipients may not see as important. The MCA, as planned, will build in several safeguards (the country selection process, narrow list of program areas, proposal review, and monitoring and evaluation) to ensure that it will not fund anything that is contrary to U.S. interests. Nevertheless, differences may still emerge on the priority activities within qualifying countries.

Although the United States rarely funds activities that recipient governments are actively against, it often funds projects that are of low interest to host governments. For example, many governments are not interested in funding judicial or electoral reforms, even though these issues may be important priorities for the United States. Some environmental protection projects funded by the United States do not enjoy strong support by recipient governments. This tension can be minimized, especially in countries (like MCA countries) that are showing results and have generated more confidence from the donors, because both donors and recipients are more willing to work together and trust each other's views. It is probably worth continuing to push some areas that are donor priorities, at least as a signal to recipient governments of U.S. values and concerns. However, donors should recognize that without strong government commitment, the activities are likely to show weak results, even if the idea behind the project is sound.

Summary of Recommendations

The Millennium Challenge Account will achieve greatest effectiveness by having a narrowly defined mission and developing a core competence in limited areas related to it. The MCA mission should be to support growth and sustainable development and combat poverty in poor nations with a demonstrated record of sound policy, social investment, and good governance, by underwriting meritorious strategies designed and implemented by recipients.

The MCA should focus on sectors that are known to contribute significantly to poverty reduction and growth, as reflected in the MDGs and elsewhere, where the private sector is least likely to invest, and where foreign assistance (and U.S. aid in particular) has a track record of delivering results. There is broad agreement that the MCA should focus on primary education, basic health, water and sanitation, agricultural development, and strengthening the policy environment for private sector development. But in contrast to the administration's proposal, these criteria would suggest direct financing for the private sector for only limited purposes, such as microfinance, while expanding the mandate to include environment and clean energy. While governance reform and democracy support meet several of the criteria, it would be wise to subcontract governance proposals out to USAID for review and monitoring, until the level of demand can be determined. The small staff of the MCA would make it a poor home for democracy activities, which demand intensive staff supervision and involvement.

5

A New Approach to Aid

Once countries qualify for the Millennium Challenge Account, how should funds be delivered to ensure that they are as effective as possible in supporting growth, poverty reduction, and human development in recipient countries? This chapter examines the core elements of the policy framework for the MCA, including the responsibility for proposing and designing activities funded by the MCA, the types of activities that should be funded, the question of funding projects versus programs, monitoring and evaluation, and coordination with other donors. Each element of the MCA value chain (sketched in figure 5-1) is discussed in turn.

The Donor-Driven Approach

Currently U.S. foreign assistance is delivered mainly through a "country programming" approach, in which the U.S. Agency for

This chapter draws heavily from Steven Radelet, *Challenging Foreign Aid: A Policymaker's Guide to the Millennium Challenge Account* (Washington: Center for Global Development, 2003), as well as contributions from Ann Florini of Brookings, Bob Cavey of the Carnegie Endowment for International Peace, and several other authors.

Figure 5-1. *Millennium Challenge Corporation Value Chain*

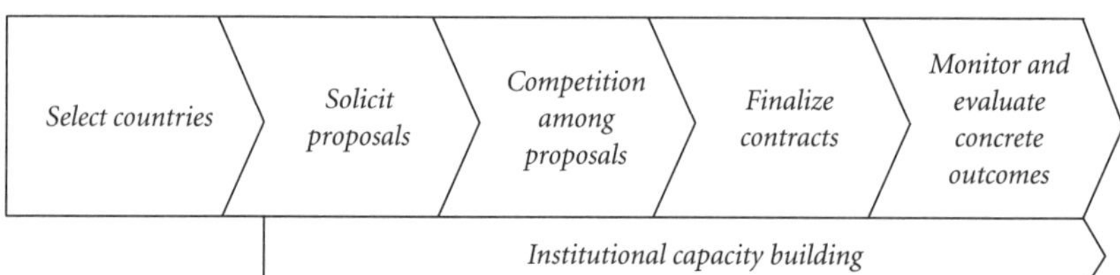

International Development (USAID) has responsibility for assessing the economic and social situation in the recipient country, developing an overall country strategy, designing and implementing specific interventions, and evaluating the outcomes.[1] This top-down approach became popular with donors around the world beginning in the 1960s and 1970s. In effect, there has been a great reluctance to give recipient governments much voice or responsibility in determining how U.S. assistance funds are spent. Congress reinforced this approach by enacting legislation that specifically directed how and where funds should be spent. Over the years the proportion of aid earmarked to particular institutions or programs and countries has risen sharply.

This approach has advantages and shortcomings. The biggest advantage is that it allows the U.S. government to maintain control in establishing priorities and determining how funds are spent. U.S. foreign assistance is taxpayer money, and Congress has both the right and obligation to spend monies carefully and to ensure that they reflect American priorities. This system can help reduce graft and ensure that funds are spent in areas that the United States believes are important. It also makes it easier to connect funds to specific outcomes, allowing the United States to "plant a flag" on activities that it funds, which in turn may help garner more support for aid (at least in the short run).

However, the top-down, donor-driven approach has important shortcomings that would be fundamentally inconsistent with the logic of the MCA. When the U.S. government has the lead in design, the recipient country often lacks ownership in and commitment to specific interventions. Of course, in designing projects and programs, USAID staff members work with recipient governments (to varying degrees in different settings), but in the end USAID plays the lead role, with projects reflecting U.S. priorities and interests. In most cases this weaker recipient commitment to projects reduces the chances of success. U.S.-designed projects and programs often are only partially coordinated with a recipient government's overall development strategy. This might be a virtue in a country with an incompetent government with no development strategy or a destructive one (like Zimbabwe), but it makes little sense for MCA countries.

In addition a donor-led process undermines recipient government capacity to design and implement effective development programs. There is no way that governments can build that capacity when donors take on these roles themselves. Moreover, with donors designing all the projects, there is little opportunity to introduce new, innovative ideas from on-the-ground sources, so projects are not tailored to the particular circumstances of each country and evolve only slowly across countries and over time. Finally top-down programming requires a significant commitment of staff, adding to the costs and bureaucracy associated with foreign aid.

The traditional donor-driven approach (or parts of it) might make sense in countries with weak or unaccountable governments that show little commitment to development. However, it makes little sense for countries eligible for the MCA. The MCA provides the opportunity for the United States to improve the way it delivers aid by using different approaches in countries with different circumstances, strengths, and weaknesses.

A New Approach: Country Ownership

Since the MCA focuses on a small set of countries with a demonstrated commitment to good development policy and transparent and accountable governments, the United States can approach the aid process fundamentally differently than in countries with weaker or less accountable governments. A new approach would help achieve better development outcomes in MCA countries. This builds on the broader global trends described in chapter 2 that place greater emphasis on donors supporting strategies and programs designed and implemented by the recipient nation. Similar to the Global Fund to Fight AIDS, Tuberculosis, and Malaria (Global Fund), and as proposed earlier by Birdsall and coauthors, Radelet, and others, the MCA program should shift much of the responsibility for designing projects and programs to the recipients.[2] In this approach, country eligibility for the MCA would be a necessary but not sufficient condition for receiving funds. Eligibility would need to be followed by the submission of grant proposals based on compelling goals, a well-thought-out strategy for effective implementation, and concrete, measurable outcomes.

For example, the government of an MCA-recipient country could write a proposal to fund a significant portion of its education program. To write a good proposal, the government would first have to develop a strong education program—something many developing countries lack. It would need to give careful consideration to budgets, costs, trade-offs, and the various steps necessary over time to achieve success. The proposal would have to be based on a broad consultative process with citizens' groups, nongovernmental organizations (NGOs), and other parties, especially those that represent the poor. Proposals would be expected to spell out the specific actions that the recipient would take and the benchmarks by which success would be measured, pushing recipients at the outset to establish concrete goals for measuring success over a specific timeline. The proposals would also spell out the contributions that the recipient would make to the project, including financing, personnel, and materials. To ensure strong commitment to the proposed activities, recipients should be expected to provide a significant share of the funding, with the MCA or other donors providing other funds.

The MCA would concentrate on soliciting and selecting the best proposals in a demand-driven competition rather than designing and overseeing projects itself. This approach is similar to the process used by the Global Fund. Potential recipients are expected to write detailed proposals to fund specific interventions containing all the elements listed above. Although it is too early to evaluate fully the Global Fund's experience, it is clear so far that organizations within recipient countries—national government, subnational government, NGOs, and other organizations—have responded well to the opportunity to write proposals and have made many high-quality submissions.

An integral part of giving recipients greater responsibility and ownership is that there should be an explicit emphasis on building local institutional capacity at each stage of the process, from developing goals and plans to overseeing implementation to monitoring results. If the process works well, MCA recipients should build greater institutional capacity and assume greater responsibility for each stage of the process, rather than becoming more dependent on outside consultants and donor expertise over time, as discussed further in chapter 6.

The administration's initial proposal for designing MCA activities, as contained in the draft legislation submitted by the president to Congress on February 4, 2003, is broadly consistent with this approach.[3] It calls for a "contract" between the MCC and the recipient country that would propose the activities to be undertaken, the time frames involved, and specific goals and benchmarks, both in terms of substance and in terms of strengthening institutions and administration. It squarely places responsibility for designing the program, establishing priorities, and setting benchmarks and goals with the recipient country. In conjunction with the increased flexibility given to the recipient, it would hold the recipients accountable for achieving the specified benchmarks and results.

What Kinds of Organizations Can Submit Proposals?

It is clear that nongovernmental actors, including both private sector entities and nonprofit bodies such as NGOs, will play important roles in the MCA process, as they do in other donor-funded development efforts.[4] At a minimum, governments will need to consult with these groups in developing their MCA proposals, much as governments are supposed to do in developing their poverty-reduction strategy papers (PRSPs). Much of the actual service delivery and external evaluations will most likely be carried out by NGOs and private firms, as described in chapter 6. But beyond these roles, an important strategic question is whether to allow nongovernmental groups to submit to the MCA their own proposals for funding. There is a significant difference between requiring that governments consult with nongovernmental groups and directly providing those groups with resources to implement specific development activities.

Several options are possible in defining the types of organizations eligible to write proposals, including:

—the central government, including individual ministries;
—subnational governments, including provincial, state, local, and municipal governments;
—public-private partnerships, in which government agencies would team with nongovernmental actors, such as domestic and international private voluntary organizations, charities, nonprofit organizations, private hospitals, and schools;
—NGOs independently of any government agency; or
—private, for-profit companies independently.

All these approaches have been tried in other development efforts. The two most controversial are funding to the private sector through enterprise or equity funds, which was discussed in the last chapter, and the increasing practice of providing funds directly to NGOs. At present nearly a third of U.S. official development assistance (ODA) goes to American and foreign NGOs rather than to governments.[5] This expanding role for NGOs has come about for compelling reasons in many cases, as donors found that governments either were too corrupt or did not have the capacity to use the funds effectively. Donors were also looking for ways to promote the development of civil society as a worthy goal in itself, and many NGOs were carrying out effective projects.

Much good has come from this increased NGO role. It has strengthened the ability of civil society to hold governments accountable. It has enabled development efforts to expand into some of the poorest (often rural) areas not reached by governments and to mobilize an increased level of popular participation. And it has made it possible to tap the considerable creative energies of both indigenous groups and international NGOs.

But there have been drawbacks, as well. Concern is growing that in some circumstances, and especially in some African nations, the bypassing of governments in favor of NGOs has contributed to a hollowing out of government capacity. In some cases direct funding of NGOs has led to disaggregated sectoral development interventions, characterized by collections of individual projects rather than by more comprehensive and therefore strategic interventions. Moreover, although many NGOs have proven to be effective, efficient, and accountable in their use of development funds, others have not.

In receiving proposals from NGOs, adequate screening mechanisms are important but difficult to develop. Indigenous nongovernmental organizations and grass-roots organizations are not necessarily more accountable, responsive, legitimate, or competent than government authorities. If many different NGOs submit proposals, sorting the bad from the good is a time-consuming process requiring substantial knowledge of individual countries. It can be done—international foundations, like the Ford and Rockefeller foundations, meet this challenge—but it requires a strong field presence, a commitment to fund the best proposals possible, and a tolerance for some failures to accompany the successes.

In addition some developing country governments have expressed increasingly vociferous objections to donors' growing reliance on NGOs. They argue that governments that have come to power through free and fair elections are the legitimate national representatives who should be determining their country's development strategies and priorities. Sometimes these objections reflect legitimate concerns about strategies and priorities, and sometimes they indicate a government's desire to centralize control and power over financial flows.

Nonetheless there are good reasons to make provision for the consideration of NGO proposals. National governments certainly do not have a monopoly on good development ideas, and the quality of MCA proposals and funded activities could be improved by competition with outside players, including subnational governments and NGOs.

Further, most national governments do not have the capacity to implement the full range of investments possible to support development. The MCA is based on the premise that governments must establish a strong policy and institutional environment for public and private investments to be effective and development to proceed—not that national governments by themselves are responsible for development and must be the focal point for all investments. Opening the proposal process to subnational governments and NGOs will allow a larger set of actors to implement MCA-funded activities, potentially increasing its effectiveness. Moreover, since most MCA funding will go through the central government, providing a smaller amount of funding to NGOs is unlikely to hollow out government capacity.

In addition, governments may have adversarial relationships with specific NGOs that are effective agents of development. Because national governments may not engage these outside actors in the process of determining a development strategy and delivering MCA money, allowing a small portion of the MCA funds to be channeled directly to NGOs may help to ensure broad public engagement in the development process.

The challenge for the MCA is to design processes that help to promote strong, capable, accountable governments, while maintaining the appropriate space for civil society. Several competing ideas suggest how this might be done.

National Governments as Sole Implementers

The MCA could provide all funding through governments but require national governments to consult with subnational governments, NGOs, and civil society, such as in the current poverty-reduction strategy papers (PRSP) process described in chapter 2. The World Bank follows something like this model, funding national and subnational governments but not NGOs.

However, prohibiting independent NGO proposals altogether goes too far. It could seriously undermine the independence of the NGOs from the government. If all proposals must go through the central government, some NGOs will become beholden to the government in order to receive MCA funding, and others may be shut out of the process for political reasons unrelated to the merit of their work. Second, the process will enlarge the government bureaucracy on the recipient end—hardly the intended outcome.

The MCA almost certainly will increase the size of the recipient government, no matter how it is managed. Recipient governments will need additional staff to oversee and monitor activities, account for finances, and do other related activities. Establishing a system in which all funds go through a government-controlled process could lead to a larger public sector than would be the case if some money were channeled directly to NGOs.

National Government Coordinating Mechanism

The Bush administration's legislative proposal for the MCA suggests that there be a single contract with recipient countries, but that many actors could carry out the activities subsumed by that contract. The administration's background document accompanying the legislation states that "MCA programs will be implemented by nongovernmental organizations and the private sector, in addition to public sector agencies, and the MCA will strive to achieve within recipient countries a broad coalition around development investments. The recipient country's MCA program should reflect an open consultative process, integrating official interests with those of the private sector, civil society, and other donor partners, and bringing an inclusive perspective to discussions between the country and the MCA."[6] Although the details are far from clear, the administration seems to intend that national governments consult with subnational governments and nongovernmental actors and provide a role for them to carry out some related activities. This suggests that the national government would establish a coordination process to combine the best ideas and proposals from a variety of actors, including NGOs and the private sector, into a single contract with the MCC. According to the draft legislation, the contract would specify "the role and contribution of the business community, private and voluntary organizations, and other members of civil society in designing that plan and achieving objectives."

As described in chapter 2, the Global Fund provides a similar model. It strongly encourages all recipient countries to establish a country coordinating mechanism (CCM). The CCM is a committee including a wide range of local stakeholders: government, NGOs, the private sector, religious groups, academic institutions, and people afflicted with AIDS, tuberculosis, or malaria. The Global Fund requires that the CCMs integrate proposals from all local actors into a single national proposal, which is either accepted as is or revised through a consultative process. But the administration's proposed design for the MCA differs in important ways. First, the Global Fund accepts up to three proposals per year from a CCM (one per disease), whereas the administration proposes combining all activities into a single contract. Second, the Global Fund allows for the direct submission of proposals outside of a CCM, albeit only when governments are dysfunctional or NGOs can show that they were unfairly shut out of the CCM process. Third, and most important, the Global Fund accepts proposals from any country; there is no country selection process that screens for accountable or strongly performing governments.

A CCM-style body makes it possible to create a larger role for NGOs, even if each country submits just one broad proposal (encapsulated into one contract) rather than multiple proposals from different entities within a given country. The recipient government would establish a local committee composed of government officials (national and subnational), members of parliament, private sector representatives, academics, NGO representatives, local communities, and others. This group would accept and review proposals from around the country, accepting some and rejecting others, and combining the best ones into a single proposal to the MCC. In this system the national government would almost always hold the central role and would chair the committee.

This model could work well and has been successful in many countries in its initial stages at the Global Fund, but experience is still in the early stages. Central control of the process by the national government has caused difficulties in some cases. For example, the South African Ministry of Health has objected strenuously to direct funding from the Global Fund to KwaZulu Natal province and has threatened to not allow the funds to be delivered unless they go through the national Ministry of Health. The reasons are at least partly political, as the national and provincial governments are controlled by two different political parties (the African National Congress and Inkatha, respectively).

Foundation Model

To avoid such difficulties, the MCA could instead be designed like a private foundation to accept proposals directly from a wide range of interested parties, including national government ministries, subnational government entities, NGOs, and certain private sector entities to submit proposals.[7] Even with this approach, the bulk of the funding would go to governments, as they would be the actors in a position to make the large programmatic (as opposed to project) proposals that should dominate the MCA's agenda. The foundation model would encourage the greatest possible competition among public and private actors within the recipient countries. It would take advantage of a wide array of entities implementing good projects and programs in developing countries and avoid the problem of giving the national government too much central control.

The MCA proposal process could strike the right balance between improving government capacity and ensuring space for civil society by including elements from the second and third models in different proportions, depending on the circumstances of each country. The emphasis in the administration's bilateral-contract model on the leading role of the recipient government is appropriate, given that the process will select accountable and reform-oriented governments capable of carrying out that role, but the process should also include actors beyond governments. The Global Fund's insistence on institutionalized consultation via the CCM provides a formal mechanism to ensure widespread public engagement in the process. But it may not be necessary in many cases to insist on the establishment of a new formal mechanism such as a CCM as long as the principal recipient can demonstrate substantial involvement by appropriate subnational, nongovernmental, and private organizations in proposal design and implementation. In general the MCC should emphasize government-NGO cooperation in its grant-making criteria and review and during the negotiations over the contract(s).

The foundation model should be applied on a limited scale, to create a mechanism to provide funding directly to subnational governments and NGOs doing high-quality work in low-income countries. Opening the process for this limited degree of competition will foster creativity, innovation, and entrepreneurship, which should lead to higher-quality proposals, better projects, and stronger results, without unduly fracturing the development process. It will also help to ensure that governments engage civil society in the contract-preparation process, knowing that NGOs who are unfairly excluded will have an opportunity to make their case directly (as they do under the Global Fund's rules). But because the majority of funds would flow through the government, the much smaller amounts provided to NGOs would not draw significant staff from the government, nor would they exacerbate tensions between the government and the NGO community in a significant way.

Even with these restrictions, evaluating the sometimes bewildering variety of NGOs of varying legitimacy, quality, and political orientation will be a challenge for the MCC, as it has proven to be for other donors. There is no litmus test. Donors typically ask applicant NGOs to prove their credibility in proposals by describing their past work, to show that they have a record of effective aid delivery, a current practice within parts of USAID. Proposals also often detail the personal qualifications of NGO leaders and the links between the NGO and the community in which it works. Donors often augment this information by consulting with outsiders with expertise in the relevant country, either formally or informally. Sometimes those experts are from international NGOs. Another approach is to rely on a support NGO, which is an NGO established for the purpose of channeling money from international donors to local NGOs. Philippine NGO Support Program distributes aid from donors such as the International HIV/AIDS Alliance, the European Commission, and the Packard Foundation to Philippine NGOs dealing with AIDS. To the degree that MCA funds go to NGOs, the MCC should draw on expertise available elsewhere in the donor community. A related possibility would be for the MCA to fund a local foundation or foundations—the equivalent of a local Ford Foundation—that would fund smaller NGO projects throughout the country. Finally, the volume of proposals could be reduced by establishing a minimum size requirement to eliminate very small proposals.

This more open process would provide a check on excessive central government direct control and ensure that funds go to agencies that have creative ideas, write the best proposals, and can best use the funds. Governments should be asked to participate in the process by commenting on subnational and NGO proposals, including how the proposed activities might fit into the government's broader development strategy. However, governments should not be given veto power over NGO proposals and should not be empowered to choose which NGOs would be eligible for funding. In most cases the difficulty of determining the legitimacy and standing of NGOs would not apply to subnational governments.

At this early stage it is difficult to tell whether it would be better for the MCA to work through a single or multiple contracts with recipients in qualifying countries. The best way forward would be to encourage the MCC to explore different approaches during its early years. The enabling legislation should not restrict the corporation to establish only one contract with a recipient country and instead should leave open the possibility of accepting multiple contracts for different program areas.

Contract or Compact?

The administration strongly emphasizes creating a "genuine partnership" with recipient countries. The language is consistent with President Bush's call for "a new compact for development" in his speech originally proposing the MCA. It envisions the recipient country as responsible for ensuring wide involvement by the private sector and civil society in developing the contract, managing coordination with other donors, publicizing the terms of the contract, holding accountable the different parties responsible for implementing parts of the program, and monitoring progress toward specified goals. It sees the MCC as responsible for providing technical assistance as needed, disbursing the funds as quickly and efficiently as possible, and monitoring progress toward benchmarks and goals.

Senior administration officials debated whether to refer to the agreement as a *contract* or a *compact.* They ultimately decided that *compact* was insufficiently binding, with unclear expectations and obligations. *Contract* implies a legally enforceable agreement, with clear expectations on both sides and definable outcomes. This terminology is consistent with the approach of a focus on results and an emphasis on monitoring and evaluating outcomes.

However, it raises a question: To what extent can contingency clauses be built in or the understandings be modified, if either side does not fulfill the precise terms of the contract? There will always be tension between specifying clear, serious benchmarks and adjusting to the complexities of the situation on the ground. It is probably true that donors have erred on the side of too much discretion in the past, continuing to disburse funds even when basic conditions clearly had not been met.[8] It remains to be seen whether the contract is an appropriate adjustment in this balance or is a push too far in the opposite direction.

The risk, of course, is that a contract may be too tight a bind for either side. In part this will depend on whether the divergence owes to external events or to deliberate actions on the part of the recipient. A further distinction can be made between violating the precise terms of the contract and the spirit of the broader MCA approach. To illustrate, imagine a country that fulfills its contractual obligations but at the same time brutally cracks down on an opposition party, shuts down a feisty newspaper, or buys a fleet of new limousines for the personal use of the president's family. The United States might want to reduce MCA funding, a step that could undermine the contractual nature of the agreement and have the unfortunate effect of reversing critical achievements on health or education—the original goals of the grant. Conversely, consider a situation in which the country makes a great effort to achieve the specified benchmarks but does not make them, through no fault of its own—because of a drought or a delay in another donor's financing. The United States might want to continue funding, even though benchmarks were missed. Some of these issues could be handled through contingency clauses written into the contracts but, as donors have learned through experience, it is difficult to predict in advance all the possible contingencies that might influence fulfillment of the contract.

On the recipient's side, the contract would propose the specific activities to be undertaken; would specify the goals, benchmarks, and timetables for progress; would demonstrate that an open and inclusive process was used to establish the program details; and would clarify the roles of various actors in carrying out the program. It would in many ways be similar to proposals that are written to foundations for funding, or business plans that investors might evaluate before taking an equity stake in a business start-up. It would specify the funding required from the MCA to carry out the activity, the amount of funding supplied by the recipient, and possible contributions from other donors. On the MCA side, the contract would specify the amount of funding to be delivered, to whom, when, and how. It would provide for technical assistance, as necessary, to strengthen data collection, improve public sector management and financial accountability, and undertake other activities. It would also clarify the U.S. government's role in monitoring and evaluation.

Regardless of the terminology, it is important that two types of goals be specified in each contract, as suggested in Radelet.[9] Substantive goals would focus on the core sectoral elements of the program (health, education, and so on). These goals might include, for example, increasing the immunization rate, improving access to essential medicines, raising test scores, or increasing the number of trained teachers. Administrative and institutional goals would focus on the quality and timeliness of financial oversight systems, legal frameworks, administrative systems, implementation capacity, hiring and training of key personnel, delivery systems, and related capacities. Both kinds of goals should be tied to specific intermediate benchmarks with clear time frames during the life of the contract.

The contracts should clearly specify the recipient's plans for implementing the proposed activities. To carry out this work, recipients should be able to use a mix of their own staff, local or international consultants, or local or international subcontractors, as they see fit, to reach the established benchmarks. Consultants or subcontractors, to the extent that they are used for either design or implementation, would work directly with the grant recipient rather than the donor to carry out specified activities. International consulting firms therefore would be eligible to carry out the same kinds of activities in which they are now involved, but they would be working with the grant recipients rather than the donor. Instead of these firms competing against each other in response to USAID's requests for proposals, it is important that they would compete to provide their services to the in-country organization that writes the proposal. Thus recipients would need to judge that international consultants were worth the higher fees they charge relative to local expertise. Consultants and recipients would work out their own contractual agreements and payment mechanisms, and some might complain that this would make their job more difficult. But the MCA must move toward putting the responsibility for managing development programs with the recipient.

Choosing the Best Proposals

The MCA should be able to select the best proposals from eligible countries in a genuinely open competition without exogenously established set-asides for particular countries, regions, or program areas (although separate pools should be created for different income classes, as discussed in chapter 3). All proposals must be vetted by a strong but streamlined interagency review process. At the same time it would be difficult (and ultimately ineffective) to establish one review panel with the expertise to vet every proposal. Staff with expertise on Mozambique should not be vetting proposals from Bolivia, and health experts should not be reviewing education proposals. The challenge is to ensure the selection of the most promising proposals through in-depth expert review, without creating a large bureaucratic process, with layer upon layer of reviews.

USAID experience in this area is only partially relevant to the MCA, because USAID country and regional offices present grant proposals in the context of their own programs and priorities rather than selecting them on the basis of an open competition. However, some elements of the USAID process are relevant, in particular the emphasis on integrating country expertise with sectoral expertise and assessing proposals for budgetary soundness and technical feasibility. The processes used by private foundations likewise are only relevant in part, since they too tend to consider grant proposals in the context of their field office programs and budgets rather than as an overall competition. The Global Fund's emphasis on competitive grant proposals may represent the closest analogy.

The MCA assessment process must be structured to permit an open grant competition across countries and program areas. This can best be accomplished by establishing a set schedule so that each pool of proposals can be considered against each other—perhaps twice a year, following the Global Fund time frame. Each proposal would be assessed in a central competition with a sector and country crosscut, and recommendations would be sent to the board for final review.

To ensure that the best proposals are funded from each pool of submissions, a central review process should reflect a country and sectoral crosscut and draw from all relevant parts of the U.S. government as well as from outside expertise, including research institutions, NGOs, and the private sector. As with the Global Fund, review teams would recommend that some proposals be approved, possibly with modest modifications, that others be sent back for revisions and resubmission, and that others be rejected.

As in Radelet, the administration's proposal calls for contracts to be reviewed by both a sector team (with expertise in the substantive area of the proposal) and a country team (with expertise in the recipient country).[10] Review teams would differ across contracts and could even differ in assessing different components of an overall contract. For example, a Ghanaian education proposal should be reviewed by a team consisting of Ghana experts (who would judge the proposal against all other proposals from Ghana) and education specialists (who would judge it against other education proposals). A Ghanaian health proposal would be reviewed by a slightly different group, involving the same Ghana specialists, this time working with health experts. Some of the expertise needed to assess contracts is available from existing U.S. agencies, including the Departments of State and Treasury, USAID, the U.S. trade representative, the Departments of Education, Agriculture, and Health and Human Services, and other agencies, where appropriate. Since the administration plans to staff the MCC with personnel on detail from these agencies, most of the participants in the proposal review would be working for the MCC, although some staff not working directly for the MCC could be called upon in this process where necessary.

In addition it is important that outside expertise be employed on every proposal, without exception, both on the substance and on the country, including both Americans and experts from the recipient country. The quality of the contracts and the specific proposals embedded in them will be markedly enhanced by including independent, technically skilled experts from outside government in the review process. It would also make the proposal review process more transparent. The United States insisted on this structure for the Global Fund, and it should implement this idea in the MCC.

As an input into the central review, proposals should be assessed by experts in the field, including MCC mission staff and any relevant embassy staff, with possible input from other international donor organizations that have expertise in the field. This is important as an on-the-ground reality check and serves to provide an informal ranking among proposals from each country (or region, depending on the extent of field staff).

Proposals should also be assessed on their technical feasibility, budgetary cost, and environmental impact, which might result in a variety of proposed modifications to the proposal before it is recommended for final approval.

Responsibility for final approval of contracts would reside with the board. For most projects board approval would be pro forma. But board approval would be decisive for contracts that are more complicated, such as those that received mixed reviews in the central competition, those that are exceptionally promising but are not squarely in the core competence of the MCA, and those that are controversial in the recipient country itself. The board should also be required to give special attention to projects that are exceptionally large by some standard metric, either relative to the total annual budget of the MCA (such as grants over $200 million) or relative to the recipient's budget (such as grants in excess of 5 percent of government expenditures). As explained in chapter 8, such an automatic board review requirement would be an important mechanism for congressional oversight.

Once proposals are approved, they should be made publicly available and posted on the Internet. This step will increase transparency in the selection process, provide a means by which citizens of recipient countries can read the proposals and learn what they can expect, and allow other proposal writers to see the kinds of activities approved by the MCC.

Building Capacity to Design Good Proposals

Regardless of whether NGOs are allowed to write proposals independently of the government, giving the responsibility for project and program design to recipient countries undoubtedly will increase the burden on organizations in those countries. There is simply no way to increase country ownership of development strategies and participation in the delivery of aid without placing greater demands on staff and other resources in the recipient country. There is a clear tension between, on the one hand, the desire to give recipient governments more voice in designing aid-financed projects and, on the other hand, the desire not to make more demands on overly burdened governments with limited numbers of trained staff. It is true that many MCA countries will initially lack the capacity to develop strong proposals and programs. However, the only way they will develop this capacity is if they are given the responsibility that requires it. Over time, requiring recipients to develop their own strategies will lead to more investment in developing these skills and ultimately more effective projects and programs with better results.

In the initial years some recipient countries may require technical assistance (local or international) in developing proposals and designing projects. If used appropriately, technical assistance could help improve the quality of the proposed activities and help achieve stronger results. One possibility would be to set aside a small amount of funds to be used for proposal development in MCA-eligible countries. Potential recipients initially could submit a very short concept paper. If the paper looked promising, a small amount of seed money ($5,000 to $50,000, or so) could be provided to enable the potential recipients to hire technical assistance and to cover proposal development costs. It is possible, of course, that governments or NGOs will simply hire outside expertise to write proposals on their behalf without investing their own time and effort. MCC staff on the ground in each country will have to work closely with potential recipients to ensure that technical assistance is used appropriately.

This approach, in which governments and NGOs in recipient countries are given the responsibility and flexibility to submit proposals for funding, is possible only if it is coupled with strong monitoring and evaluation that ensures that benchmarks are met during the program, lessons learned from one activity inform the design of others, and funds are allocated to programs with the strongest results.

Funding Modalities

Flexibility in financing modalities is of central importance to the success of the MCA. The MCA can have the greatest impact if its authorities extend to directly supporting recipient governments for sectorwide reforms and are not artificially confined to one-time expenses, such as the purchase of textbooks or construction of buildings, but can as easily cover ongoing training or maintenance. Although this approach would be a sharp departure from current U.S. development assistance, the greater flexibility is warranted by the MCA's focus on strong performers and could make a big difference in its impact.

The vast majority of U.S. foreign aid is used to fund specific projects. Only a limited amount is directed toward broader government programs (funded as budget support), mainly from the economic support fund (ESF) controlled by the State Department. Congress generally strongly favors project loans, for two reasons.

First, at least on the surface, project funds can be controlled and monitored more effectively than program funding, because the dollars going in can be traced to a specific activity. The purpose of the funds is clear, and funds can be traced more easily to see if they achieved their specified goal. Second, since the project is a discernible activity or structure, it can be identified as being funded with U.S. support. All donors, and the United States is no exception, like to plant a flag with their aid programs, and project aid allows them to do that.

However, project funding has limitations. First, the supposed control over spending is largely illusory. Money is fungible, and donor funding for one project can free up the recipient's budget for use in unrelated areas. For example, donor support to build a school that the government would have otherwise built with domestic resources could simply free government funds to buy a new airplane for the president. In this case the marginal impact of the donor funds is not to build a new school, however carefully monitored the school project may be, but to buy a plane. Second, individually funded projects are costly to the recipient because they are so heavily monitored and require a large commitment of time and money to address all donor concerns.

Third, donor-financed projects tend to hollow out the core administrative capacity of recipient governments rather than build it up. Donor projects usually are financed outside the budget, and the donors want to put in place strict financial controls. To do so, they hire away the strongest accountants, auditors, and technicians to work on their projects, leaving behind a weaker capacity to administer the government's projects and programs. Because they focus on their own projects, few donors pay much attention to building capacity in central budget administration, although this is arguably one of the most important institutions in the development process. Fourth, project funding provides much less flexibility for the recipient country than does program funding (by design), which inhibits recipient governments from allocating funds to their highest priorities. This lack of flexibility may be desirable in countries with untrustworthy, nonrepresentative, or incompetent governments, but it is counterproductive in countries where the government is accountable and committed to social investments.

The heavy reliance on project financing contributes to a related issue, known as the recurrent cost problem. Most project funding is used for capital and other start-up costs, with little allowed for financing ongoing (or recurrent) project costs, such as operations and maintenance or personnel costs. Donors see recurrent expenditures as harder to monitor and evaluate than capital or once-off expenditures, and they are wary about getting involved in long, open-ended commitments that financing recurrent costs might imply. In addition donors want recipients to contribute a share of project costs in order to demonstrate commitment and ownership, and the split between capital and recurrent costs provides a convenient rule for cost sharing.

However, a donor's reluctance to finance recurrent costs can cause major problems. Developing countries are littered with donor-funded roads and wells that quickly fell into disrepair for want of adequate maintenance funding. Once the original construction is completed, many development projects are chronically underfunded because recipient countries either cannot or will not devote sufficient funds to keep donor-initiated projects going.

Underwriting programs rather than individual projects can reduce (although not fully eliminate) many of these problems. With program funding going through the budget, the focus of attention shifts to strengthening local government institutions rather than hollowing them out. Donor monitoring can examine the entire budget, thus reducing the opportunities for governments to divert money to questionable items. When donors finance education projects, such as individual school buildings, they have much less leverage to question aircraft purchases than they do if they partially finance the budget. Also, requiring that grant submissions be presented in the context of the national budget will, over time, strengthen the role of the national budget as an institution and as a document for defining national priorities and making possible an informed public debate about trade-offs.

Monitoring and evaluating programs rather than projects is in some ways more complicated and in some ways easier. It is more complicated because the entire budget must be monitored (at least at a broad level), and it is harder to trace the impact of donor funds on specific outcomes. On the other hand, by monitoring the entire budget, donors have a much more accurate picture of the true impact of their funds. In addition the recurrent cost problem is generally less of an issue with program funding. With program funds, recipients can allocate money to activities that truly are high priority and can distribute funds as appropriate among capital and recurrent costs—a distinction that is often blurry and even arbitrary. Program funding is also administratively less costly than project funding.

The key to reconciling the project-program debate is to recognize that different approaches are appropriate in different circumstances. Since MCA-eligible countries, by definition, have a demonstrated track record of setting appropriate budget priorities and delivering effective results, the MCA can and should rely more on program funding. Proposals for program funds should set specific goals, including goals for improving budget and financial capacity, and articulate the activities the funds would help support. Careful tracking of baseline (preprogram) budget spending can clarify the marginal impact of program funds. This approach would significantly reduce the bureaucratic costs associated with myriad donor-funded projects and would allow governments in MCA-eligible countries to set their own priorities and build their budget capacity. But, in return for this flexibility, the United States should maintain strict standards in its program funds: If a recipient government's budget performance begins to falter with poor allocation of funds, mismanagement, or weakening audit and oversight systems, its funding should be cut. Recipients also could be required to contribute some funding, without making the somewhat arbitrary division that the donor should cover capital costs and the recipient recurrent costs.

For example, a government could propose that the MCA help fund its education program, specifying that it would like to build a certain number of schools, buy a certain number of textbooks, train some teachers, buy school supplies, establish curriculums and testing procedures, and so forth. It should also specify goals for strengthening its related budget and financial systems. It would estimate the total cost of the program, set specific goals, and request that the MCA fund a certain share of the program. A distinction would need to be drawn between funding for capital and recurrent costs. The important issue would be monitoring and evaluating progress toward the specified goals as the yardstick for continued funding.

Monitoring and Evaluation

The natural corollary to country ownership is country accountability for results. Strong monitoring and evaluation are essential to the MCA's success. Without a much stronger monitoring and evaluation (M&E) capacity than in past programs, the MCA will be doomed to fail. A broad thrust of the U.S. government's approach to the MCA should be a reallocation of administrative effort away from country strategy and project design and toward monitoring and evaluation. Much more effective M&E must be at the very core of the approach pioneered by the MCA, for three reasons.

First and most obvious is the emphasis in the MCA on achieving results. A core motivation for the MCA is that limited aid resources be directed to those activities that deliver the greatest results in terms of poverty reduction and development. In his speech proposing the MCA, President Bush strongly emphasized that the program would be driven by results. This change cannot occur without a solid M&E system built into the MCA process from inception to completion. It is essential that relevant baseline data are gathered at the outset of every project and program, and that progress is monitored continuously throughout the project. M&E cannot be added as an afterthought halfway through a program. In too many aid projects M&E begins only two years into the project (for a midterm review) and involves consultants who have not been involved in the project and who parachute in for a short review. These evaluations rarely achieve much good. Projects can be kept on track and more can be learned if M&E is an integral and ongoing aspect of projects and programs. Moreover, benchmarks can be modified and adjusted as appropriate. The main intent of the M&E process is not punitive. Rather it is to keep the program on track to achieve its concrete results. An effective M&E program is necessary to detect problems at an early stage and to make the necessary midcourse corrections.

The second reason is that strong M&E allows the incorporation of past results into new programs. Contracts funding new activities must include lessons learned from previous activities in order to continuously improve the effectiveness of the MCA. This process is easier said than done, however, and will require a focused strategy. For starters, the same review teams that approve projects should review monitoring reports. Evaluations of every MCA activity should be made publicly available to researchers and analysts, who can help decipher best practices in a wide variety of development activities.

The third reason for strong M&E is absorptive capacity; $5 billion is a large amount of money for approximately twenty low-income countries to absorb effectively.[11] The best way to monitor potential problems with absorptive capacity and to make the necessary adjustments in both the level and the direction of funding is with a serious M&E process.

Four separate aspects of monitoring and evaluation are critical: financial audit, concrete substantive outcomes targeted directly by the grant, institutional strengthening, and potential for replication or scaling up.

Financial audit should ensure that funds are spent where they are supposed to be spent, the project remains within budget, regulations on procurement and payment are followed, and funds are not stolen. This is a straightforward function that is already present in U.S. assistance programs. Clear violations, such as misappropriation of funds, could be grounds for prematurely terminating a grant.

The second goal of M&E is to measure progress on concrete outcomes that are the central target of the grant, such as primary school completion rates by girls. A core feature of the MCA approach is that, from the start, contracts should specify clear benchmarks and targets to meet during the course of the project. Some of these should be intermediate targets (such as building a certain number of schools, purchasing so many textbooks), and some should be longer-term goals (such as increasing the primary school completion rate or the immunization rate by a certain amount). The evaluation of concrete outcomes provides an invaluable mechanism for midcourse correction in program design, which can be agreed on by the recipient and the MCC. The total quality management approach in business provides a useful although incomplete analogy.

How should the U.S. government react when countries consistently miss specified performance benchmarks over a sustained period? The response should depend on the precise events and the extent of the problem. If a country regularly misses benchmarks on its education program, for example, but continues to do well on its health program, full funding for the health activity clearly should continue. On the education program, a graduated approach could be taken, depending on the extent of the problem. Some missed benchmarks could lead to a partial reduction in funding, with further reductions if problems persist. This kind of graduated approach is rarely used by donors, which typically either make full disbursements or none at all. Given this choice, when a relatively small number of benchmarks are missed, most donors opt to continue full funding. One result is that recipients learn that there is no penalty for missing a few benchmarks. A partial reduction in funding for missing some targets would help minimize this problem.

One reason that judgments on reducing funding need to be taken with care and discretion is that some projects and programs funded by the MCA may fail, even with governments that are fully committed and making their best efforts toward success. Strong and well-integrated M&E programs can take this into account and can make appropriate adjustments to benchmarks, as appropriate. Also, the MCA provides the opportunity for the U.S. government to allow well-intentioned governments to experiment (to some extent) with promising new ideas and approaches. Of course, if these new approaches fail, funds should be directed to other activities. But countries should not be deterred from trying promising new approaches because of overly harsh penalties for poor results.

Institutional strengthening should focus on improving internal systems (such as reducing the time it takes to close books at the end of the month and removing ineffective bureaucratic procedures), bolstering legal frameworks, and enhancing personnel capacity (through training, reorganization, and recruiting new staff, where necessary). Grant proposals should specify precise goals in these areas, just as they do in substantive areas. These kinds of institutional goals historically have been underemphasized by donors, although that has changed to some extent in recent years.

If the MCA is to effect a transformation in America's approach to aid over time, it should use the M&E process to generate learning on what works and what does not and what kinds of grants have the potential to be replicated in different environments or scaled up over time. All grants should require a final evaluation in order to advance this broader institutional goal, apart from evaluating the grantee's performance. For this purpose in particular, analyzing failures is as valuable as racking up successes.

Evaluating results is a tricky business, especially for these purposes. If a health project ends with the village showing a 10 percent decline in infant mortality after five years, how much of this is due to the project and how much is due to other factors? In many cases evaluators can learn a great deal by examining and comparing trends in adjacent villages, in the province, or in the nation as a whole. But this is only possible if comparable baseline data are available for these other groups. Even under the best of circumstances, these kinds of comparisons yield ambiguous conclusions.

The MCA provides the opportunity for introducing, for at least a small number of projects, a rigorous evaluation process involving randomized trials or comparisons with control and treatment groups, as is done with most medical trials and experiments.[12] A small amount of MCA funds—say, 3 to 5 percent of project funds—could be designated for projects that incorporate evaluations using these groups. Project design would specify a control group and systems for monitoring that group in tandem with the treatment group, throughout the life of the project. For example, if an NGO wanted to offer breakfast to schoolchildren to improve attendance and learning capacity, the proposal could designate a control village that did not introduce the program. Project monitors would track attendance, body weight, school achievement, and a range of other indicators in both villages throughout the life of the project.[13] Introducing control and treatment groups is time consuming and somewhat expensive, and this approach is not needed in all projects. It also raises ethical issues in some situations, especially for health care interventions, although the technique is both common and essential for testing medications throughout the world. Ultimately it is the surest way to evaluate what works and what does not, and the results would be invaluable for designing subsequent projects and making aid more effective.

How should monitoring and evaluation be carried out? As the administration has proposed, it should be the responsibility of both the recipient and the MCC. This is consistent with the need for both internal and external

M&E, as suggested by Radelet. On the internal side, each grantee should include in its proposal an M&E procedure designating who would perform it, how they would do it, and how the results would be measured and publicized. This internal process is central to the recipient understanding at an early stage whether activities are on track or not and provides opportunities for corrections, where necessary. On its own, however, internal M&E is not sufficient, because the recipient has obvious incentives to overlook problems and inflate results. To be effective, the internal review should be complemented by an independent external review, the mechanics of which are discussed in the next chapter.

Contract Length and Program Sustainability

Contract lengths should vary, depending on the circumstances in each country. In most cases contracts would be on the order of three to four years. The administration has proposed that contracts would contain incentive clauses to stimulate better performance. Presumably these clauses would be designed to reward countries that pass benchmarks early or by a wide margin with additional funding. This is an intriguing innovation, consistent with the idea of rewarding results. However, it would need to be carefully designed to avoid creating perverse incentives to lowball targets.

Perhaps the trickiest issue is to establish appropriate expectations for what happens at the end of each contract. On the one hand, donor-dependency is a real problem in many low-income countries, with recipients expecting that donors will continue funding for many years. This dependence can undermine the incentives to establish sound public finance institutions, including building a robust revenue base and an appropriate long-run level of expenditures. In the extreme, this concern would suggest that MCA funding be for short periods of time, perhaps for only one or two contracts, and then be terminated. On the other hand, development is a long process, even under the best of circumstances, and some programs require a modicum of certainty in their long-term financing to be successful. No country can build its health system in a sustainable way in three or four years. This concern would suggest providing recipients with certainty about continued funding, so long as the specified results are achieved.

It is clearly unrealistic to assume that activities initiated under the MCA will be self-sustaining once the initial contract terms ends. There is no way that the MCA can provide new financing of $250 million for three to four years and expect that activities will be completed or that the private sector will then step in to fill the gap. Indeed even holding out the threat of eliminating funding after one contract cycle could be counterproductive. Recipients would respond by writing proposals for only short-term, quick-start projects that can be completed quickly, even if these are not the most cost-effective and relevant from a development perspective. Key programs that require a longer commitment would not be proposed, as recipients would fear being stuck with large costs that they could not realistically cover in the short run.

However, it would be unwise to imply that MCA funding will continue forever. The right balance is to create the expectations that successful programs will receive continued funding at decreasing levels.

Clemens and Radelet show that, for the most successful low-income countries (the twenty-two countries that graduated from the World Bank's concessional lending facility), the half-life of aid was about twelve years. That is, aid (measured in constant dollars) declined by 50 percent over twelve years and by about 75 percent over twenty-four years.[14] Many MCA recipients will continue to be low-income countries with limited access to private sector financing for many years, even if all goes well. Consider Ghana, a prime candidate for the MCA, with current per capita income of $350. If it does everything absolutely right and achieves per capita growth of 7 percent per year (equivalent to about 9 percent overall growth, a rate achieved by only Korea, Botswana, and a few other countries), it will take Ghana twenty-one years to reach per capita income of $1,435.

New programs may require an initial scaling-up period to establish their effectiveness. But where scaled-up programs successfully achieve results, the expectation should be that over time new contracts with smaller amounts of money would follow. As a general rule, the second three-year contract should be about 85 to 90 percent of the first, and so on, so that after twelve years MCA funding would be between 40 and 60 percent of its original level. This kind of ramp-down should be a rule of thumb, not an absolute rule. Some activities can be ramped down faster, while others will take more time. The monitoring and evaluation process will be critical in establishing appropriate levels of subsequent funding.

Summary of Recommendations

The MCA should pioneer a sharply different approach to aid, one that places responsibility and accountability squarely in the hands of eligible countries—even as it seeks to build local capacity—from the design of the proposal through implementation and achievement of results. Our analysis strongly endorses the spirit of working in partnership with developing countries to achieve their own development strategies. While the concept of a contract between the MCA and grant recipients is useful in defining responsibilities and authorities on both sides, and should include both concrete sectoral goals and institution-strengthening goals, this approach should be tempered by realism about the inherent complexity of the development process.

The MCA should take a hybrid approach on the question of what kinds of organizations should be eligible to submit grant proposals, less restrictive than the government-only focus of the administration's proposal. The MCA should strike a balance, appropriate to the circumstances of each country, between strengthening the capability of the government (which has met the MCA tests on good governance, performance, and commitment to development), while also ensuring active space for civil society. This can be accomplished by encouraging but not requiring national governments to submit proposals that coordinate the activities of a range of actors—national and subnational, nongovernmental, for-profit, and official—while also leaving room for NGOs to submit proposals independently, where they do not win the support of the government.

Once the eligible pool of countries is established, the MCA should hold an open competition on a regular schedule, possibly twice a year, in order to select the best proposals from each pool. Central review of proposals should include both country and sector expertise, drawing on relevant agencies in the U.S. government, and must include outside expertise. Board review would be required for grant proposals that are controversial or exceed specified thresholds, relative either to the MCA budget or the budget of the grant recipient.

Finally, strong monitoring and evaluation are critical to the MCA's success and a natural corollary to the emphasis on country ownership. Monitoring and evaluation include four elements: financial audit, measuring progress on concrete outcomes targeted by grants, strengthening the internal capacity of the recipients for self-evaluation, and assessing the potential for scaling up or replication elsewhere.

6

Institutional and Operational Guidelines

The effectiveness of the Millennium Challenge Account will depend not only on good proposals but also on the institutional model and operational approaches guiding its implementation. This chapter reviews the advantages and disadvantages of various institutional models for the MCA and examines the board structure, staffing arrangements, and operational procedures that would best serve the MCA's implementation. It is recommended that there be a clearer relationship between the MCC and USAID, that the MCC's board be expanded, that staff detailed to the MCC be funded by MCA operational costs and not by outside agencies or companies, that new contracting methods be developed, and that mechanisms be put in place to expand the role of MCA countries in undertaking program implementation.

Institutional Models

Given its pioneering nature, the delivery mechanism for MCA assistance is of central importance. There are difficult trade-offs for consideration in the choice of the most promising institutional model. On the one hand, the delivery of MCA funds should be freed from bureaucratic inertia, should be sufficiently independent from political interference that funds are invested in meritorious recipients and not on the basis of foreign policy considerations, and should be allowed sufficient flexibility by Congress to operate expeditiously. These features provide a rationale for an independent agency governed by its own board. On the other hand, MCA operations should also draw upon existing expertise, avoid wasteful redundancies in overseas and headquarters staff,[1] and strengthen U.S. development policy by fostering greater coherence and better design. From this standpoint, the existence of two U.S. government agencies devoted to providing development assistance would appear to violate all the tenets of efficient, effective government (and common sense). These qualifications argue for the integration of the MCA with USAID.

Independent Corporation within USAID

Is it possible to integrate the MCA with USAID and also ensure independence, flexibility, and a demand-based competitive grant-making approach? There are two possible ways to accomplish these goals, although neither is flawless. In the most straightforward approach, the MCA could be housed in a new independent bureau within USAID. The MCA could be protected from bureaucratic contagion and distinguished from other USAID programs by appointing the head of the bureau to serve as both deputy (or assistant) administrator and the chief executive officer. Building on the precedent established by SEED (Support for Eastern European Democracy), FSA (Freedom Support Act), and other enterprise funds, the MCA could operate under the authority of an external board with USAID and State Department oversight. This, along with interagency staff rotations, would allow additional oversight by agencies other than USAID and also would inhibit political interference. Operational flexibility could be achieved with separate authorizing legislation (similar to SEED and FSA) including the congressional provision of the "notwithstanding authority" already provided to USAID's Office of Transition Initiatives, as described in chapter 2, and to some other agency programs. (Notwithstanding authority exempts aid from numerous prohibitions and requirements in the Foreign Assistance Act and thus expedites the delivery of funds.) Evaluation of results separate from other USAID accounts would permit the MCA to demonstrate its potential effectiveness (the hoped-for demonstration effect).

This arrangement would enhance coordination between USAID's development assistance and the MCA's programs. In particular it would streamline joint efforts to provide targeted assistance to "near miss" countries that, with modest improvements, could achieve future MCA eligibility. Further, it would eliminate the cost and time of establishing a new bureaucracy and leverage USAID's in-house expertise and overseas missions, while still affording the MCA a high degree of independence from more bureaucratic USAID operations. Finally, and given the largely experimental nature of the MCA, close proximity between the two would increase the likelihood that lessons learned from the implementation of the MCA could be translated into constructive modifications to USAID operations.

Opponents of this proposal could rightly argue that USAID is hindered by a complex and unwieldy bureaucracy, and few would defend the agency's efficiency (with important exceptions, such as disaster assistance). But many of the same mechanisms for ensuring operational flexibility and shielding the MCA could be available whether integrated with USAID or as an independent agency. Significantly, the administration's draft legislation provides for an independent board, "no-year" funding, and notwithstanding authority, and it has otherwise made clear that the MCA will be administered differently, and more efficiently, than conventional aid programs. No-year funding allows for aid to be allocated on an as-needed basis, as opposed to the more conventional one- or two-year funding requirements imposed on USAID's development assistance. One- or two-year funding requirements obligate funds to be committed to projects during the course of one or two fiscal years. If the funds are not committed (in other words, legally obligated through, for example, conclusion of a contract or agreement), the funds revert to the treasury and are essentially lost to the agency. The end of the fiscal year acts as a deadline that is unrelated to the merit or schedule of the project.

Absent these three provisions and the high-level commitment to avoiding the creation of layers of crippling bureaucracy, the MCA could ultimately prove as cumbersome as USAID's bilateral development assistance, regardless of its institutional home. Conversely, with these advantages, the MCA could be sufficiently shielded from cumbersome requirements that it could operate effectively even if it were placed within USAID.[2]

Merger

A more ambitious alternative would call for the merger of USAID and the MCA, in order to take advantage of synergies created by housing all economic development assistance programs under one roof. A merger implies the integration of two entities of equal stature, rather than the subordination of MCA to USAID. From the point of view of government efficiency and development policy, this is the most attractive alternative, because it would ensure the transfer to USAID of those elements of the MCA approach that are applicable in weaker policy environments (country ownership, select areas of core competence, and program support, albeit on a limited and heavily monitored basis). It would allow for an assistance continuum, whereby countries performing well with USAID's traditional development assistance programs could smoothly graduate to the MCA. This approach would significantly reduce costs and increase effectiveness, because both would rely on the same infrastructure, share professional expertise, rely on single overseas missions, and speak with one voice to development partners. The primary disadvantage would be that it would require a considerable investment of time and money to streamline USAID's excessive requirements, overhaul its outdated and inefficient financial systems, and reinvent its programming policies. Judging from the frequent reorganizations undertaken by successive administrations, this process would likely impede efforts to get the MCA up and running as soon as possible.

Independent Bureau within State Department

In considering its decision, the administration explored housing the MCA within the Department of State. Granting State Department authority over MCA development funds would have been consistent with other moves by the administration to increase the State Department's role in overseeing U.S. foreign assistance. The new $100 million in draw-down funds for complex political emergencies included in the administration's fiscal year 2004 budget proposal is designated for the State Department, and funds for the president's Emergency Plan for AIDS Relief are slated to fall under the authority of a State Department coordinator. The primary arguments against the MCA being placed solely under the authority of the State Department, however, are those that were made in the 1990s, when pressure from North Carolina Senator Jesse Helms led to consideration of merging USAID into the State Department. First, despite its considerable foreign policy expertise, the department has limited development experience, little operational (as opposed to policy) experience in the regional bureaus, and no capacity to administer a program budget as large as that of the MCA. Second, given that MCA funds are to be provided on the basis of performance and without reference to political considerations, housing the MCA within the Department of State could risk the appearance—if not the reality—of influence by foreign policy imperatives (although this problem may nonetheless exist with the designation of the secretary of state as chairman of the board).

Independent Agency

Following considerable internal debate, the administration concluded that the MCA should be managed by an independent entity, the Millennium Challenge Corporation (MCC). The administration's legislative proposal states that the MCC will be governed by a board of directors chaired by the secretary of state, and including the secretary of the treasury and director of the Office of Management and Budget. The CEO of the MCC will be a Senate-confirmed presidential appointee. The administration's proposal authorizes the MCC to establish overseas offices as it sees fit and to transfer money to other federal agencies and use the facilities of any U.S. government agency under agreed-upon terms.

Consideration was also given to placing the MCA within USAID, the agency mandated to oversee U.S. development assistance by the Foreign Assistance Act since 1961. Here the administration judged the advantages of USAID's in-house operational and development expertise, missions in most MCA-eligible countries, and its existing mandate to be less compelling than the disadvantages of excessive regulations, burdensome financial systems, and time-consuming programming requirements.[3] Effectively, in making its proposal for the MCC, the administration chose to design around USAID rather than confront the daunting task of reorganizing it.

Some administration officials argue that a new entity is needed because of the innovative and nontraditional approach of the MCA.[4] But this begs the question of why USAID should not also adopt this new approach, if indeed research and recent experience suggest that it is superior (at least those elements that are relevant to countries with weaker governance and policy environments). In this sense the creation of a new government entity defies policy and budgetary sense.

With the establishment of the MCC, the U.S. government will have two almost equally funded federal entities mandated to promote international development. One will be constrained by bureaucratic inertia and political interference, burdened by multiple, overlapping objectives, and charged with working all over the world employing a top-down, donor-driven approach that has been widely discredited. The other would be granted maximal flexibility to pursue a narrow mandate in a handful of countries based on a superior country ownership model. Even with the small staff that the administration proposes for the MCC, the cost of maintaining two federal agencies to administer development assistance is significant, particularly at a time when the international affairs budget faces increasing demands. The existence of two government development agencies, meanwhile, could sow confusion among implementing agencies and aid recipients, particularly if USAID operates on the basis of one set of operational guidelines and the MCC on another.

Governance

Whether the MCA operates as an independent agency or an independent entity within USAID, a strong and well-structured board is critical if the MCA is to achieve the requisite independence to undertake sound policies unencumbered by agency turf battles, political dictates, and excessive legislative burdens. The ideal structure would be one that strikes a balance between government and external interests, is small enough to be efficient yet broad enough to reflect a diversity of views, and allows for coordination with other U.S. policies affecting developing nations and bipartisan congressional engagement.

The administration has proposed that the board would be chaired by the secretary of state and include the secretary of the treasury and the Office of Management and Budget (OMB), and that a separate CEO would be appointed by the president with the advice and consent of the Senate. This structure bears some resemblance to other independent agencies examined by the administration, but it also has important differences that are instructive. Below we compare various possible models for the MCC on a host of dimensions, including governance structure.[5]

The Overseas Private Investment Corporation (OPIC) is an independent government agency with a four-year renewable charter, subject to reauthorization. It sells political risk insurance and loan guarantees to help U.S. businesses invest and compete in emerging markets and developing nations worldwide. It has 200 civil service employees,[6] with administrative expenses of $40 million, funds that are generated from operating revenue. OPIC has a board of fifteen members: seven from government and eight from outside government, two that represent small business, one from organized labor, and one representing cooperatives. The public sector directors serve ex officio; the private sector directors are appointed by the U.S. president, with the advice and consent of the Senate. All serve three-year terms, with staggered expiration dates. The president and CEO of OPIC are appointed by the U.S. president, with advice and consent from the Senate, and serve at the pleasure of the president. The OPIC president also serves as chairman of the board.

The Export-Import Bank (Ex-Im) is an independent government agency with a four-year renewable charter, subject to reauthorization. It provides guarantees of working capital loans for U.S. exporters, guarantees the repayment of loans or makes loans to foreign purchasers of U.S. goods and services, and provides credit insurance against nonpayment by foreign buyers for political or commercial risk. It has 400 civil service employees,[7] with administrative expenses of $68 million, funds generated from operating revenue. The U.S. trade representative and the secretary of commerce serve ex officio as nonvoting members of the Ex-Im board. Five board members are from the private sector; at least one represents small business, and no more than three can be of one political party. The board is appointed for four-year staggered terms by the U.S. president, with the advice and consent of the Senate, and serves at the pleasure of the president. The chairman of the board is the president and CEO of the bank; the vice chairman is vice president. Both are appointed by the U.S. president, with the advice and consent of the Senate, and serve simultaneous coequal terms.

The Trade and Development Agency (TDA) is an independent government agency that funds technical assistance, feasibility studies, and training, to support the development of modern infrastructure and a fair and open trading environment, for the advancement of economic development and U.S. commercial interests in developing and middle-income countries. It has fifty civil service employees,[8] with unspecified administrative expenses. It has no oversight board. The director is appointed by the U.S. president, with the advice and consent of the Senate, and serves at the pleasure of the president.

The Commodity Credit Corporation (CCC) is a wholly owned government corporation with a permanent charter. Its activities include stabilizing farm income and prices to increase exports of agricultural commodities, to compete against foreign agricultural exports, and to assist countries in meeting their food and fiber needs. Export guarantees are prohibited from use for foreign aid, foreign policy, or debt rescheduling. Its thirty employees (including the board and officers) are employees of the Department of Agriculture.[9] It shares staff with the Farm Services Agency, which has administrative expenses of $977 million. The CCC's eight board members serve ex officio and are appointed by the U.S. president, with the advice and consent of the Senate. A five-member advisory board (separate from the oversight board) consists of officers with experience in business and agriculture, no more than three of whom are of one political party. The secretary of agriculture serves as ex officio chairman of the board. The undersecretary for farm and foreign agricultural services serves as ex officio president.

The Ford Foundation is a private foundation that provides grants to developing countries. It has 600 employees worldwide, some serving under three-year contracts, others longer. Its administrative expenses are $53 million. Ford's oversight board consists of seventeen trustees experienced in government, private, and nonprofit sectors, as well as international interests.[10] New members are appointed by the sitting trustees and serve at their pleasure. The president is selected by the board from its membership and serves at the pleasure of the board.

The Global Fund to Fight AIDS, Tuberculosis, and Malaria (Global Fund) is a multilateral public-private partnership that manages resources to make a sustainable and significant contribution to the reduction of infections, illness, and death, thereby mitigating the impact of the three diseases and contributing to poverty reduction. It has sixty employees on loan from governments and multilateral agencies. Figures on its administrative expenses are not available. Its board has eighteen members: seven from developed countries, two from nongovernmental organizations, and two from the private sector. Five nonvoting members represent UNAIDS, the World Health Organization, the World Bank, and one member who lives with one of the three diseases. Board members are selected by constituents for two-year terms.[11] The chairman is elected by the board.

Within the U.S. government, the administration's preferred board structure is most similar to that of OPIC. Though its governance structure is similar to the MCC, OPIC is governed by a much more inclusive board, composed of a majority of representatives from outside government as well as the heads of relevant federal agencies (the secretaries of treasury, labor, commerce, and state, the U.S. trade representative, and the administrator of USAID).

Executive branch members of the MCC board should logically be drawn from among agencies with the expertise and mandates most relevant to the MCA. At a minimum this would include the State and Treasury Departments, as the administration has proposed, but also USAID. It is stunning that the OPIC board includes USAID but the MCC might not. USAID's board presence is critical, given the enormous potential overlap between the two organizations. It would ensure greater governmentwide consistency in board decisions, including final determinations of country eligibility, oversight of proposal reviews and programs, and insight into the suitability of contracting agencies with which USAID has direct and long experience.

In contrast the administration's proposed inclusion of the director of the White House Office of Management and Budget (OMB) presents a host of problems and offers little obvious value to the board, as OMB provides neither sectoral nor development expertise. OMB's ability to expedite MCC operations could easily be brought to bear at the direction of the president, rather than through assuming a seat on the board. More important, OMB's role in government is to arbitrate budgetary allocations between and among federal agencies. MCC oversight authority would give the OMB a vested interest in a single budgetary allocation and potentially compromise its neutrality, particularly as regards allocations of foreign aid among government agencies.

In addition to the secretaries of state and treasury and the administrator of USAID, the board might also include one other federal agency with relevant sectoral and international expertise from among the Departments of Health and Human Services, Agriculture, Commerce, and Education, and the U.S. trade representative. Inclusion of additional members from among this pool of candidates, however, should be determined with a view to the MCA's proposed program priorities. Also, as former USAID deputy administrator Carol Lancaster has pointed out, there is a danger of pressures to redirect MCA funds through other agencies (as is currently the practice with USAID) when heads of these agencies have seats on the board, especially in connection with the administration's proposal that the MCC be given authority to transfer funds to other federal agencies.[12] To minimize the dangers of an internal competition for funds within the executive branch, transfer authority should remain in the hands of Congress.

The second major difference between the proposed MCC board structure and the boards of OPIC, CCC, and Ex-Im (as well as the Enterprise Funds) is the absence of any outside representative on the board. A strong case can be made in favor of including outside representatives from both the development community and the private sector. This is the usual practice of independent corporations operated by the U.S. government, and it allows critical outside perspective and expertise to be brought to bear on board deliberations. The long-term interest of the MCA would be enhanced, as well, by granting foreign aid constituencies some degree of ownership.

As argued in detail in chapter 8, input from the legislative branch would serve that same long-term interest, which could be accommodated by having Congress make recommendations on outside board members. Bipartisan engagement, meanwhile, would lessen partisan political influence and foster operational consistency throughout successive administrations. This could be achieved by having Congress provide input on the appointment of four board members, one each appointed by the ranking majority and minority members of the Senate and House of Representatives.

Broad representation and consistency with the MCA's nonpolitical mandate could be ensured by providing a fixed six-year term for outside board members. This would provide some independence from the presidency, while also ensuring continuity from one administration to the next through the continued service of some board members. In sharp contrast to USAID and most government departments, but consistent with the practice of most independent institutions within the U.S. government, senior management of the MCC below the level of CEO should be hired on the basis of merit and not political appointment. Also consistent with independent corporations, such as Ex-Im and OPIC, the MCC should provide a high degree of transparency, including by subjecting its decisions to public notice. And finally, following the Ex-Im and OPIC models, the CEO should be appointed to the ninth board seat, as argued in greater detail in chapter 8.

Staffing

The streamlined approach proposed for the MCA dictates that its operations be lean and efficient. Staff should be kept to a reasonable minimum, maintain high morale, and benefit from rotating talent. It is also critical that good management principles be applied to MCC operations, and in particular that staff authority, responsibility, and results are well aligned. In the event of a heavy reliance on USAID mission staff or detailees from other agencies, the MCC's operations must reflect its true costs in order to prevent other agencies from carrying the burden of operating expenses and to permit a meaningful evaluation of performance.

The administration's proposed operational arrangements reflect some of these imperatives, but U.S. foreign assistance will be rendered less rather than more coherent unless clear lines of authority and responsibility are demarcated between the MCC and USAID. The lines between MCC and other U.S. government staff and institutions are blurred, while provisions proposed by the administration that would allow the private sector to detail paid staff to the MCC will at best risk the appearance of conflict of interest and at worst undermine fair competition. Meanwhile the administration's proposal lacks any reference to streamlining contracting and procurement practices and makes no provision for ensuring that program implementation gradually shifts away from reliance on the U.S. government and American contractors and toward recipient governments and their counterpart institutions.

Statements from the administration suggest that the MCC will have a staff of 100, in marked contrast to USAID, which has approximately 2,000 direct hire employees, 1,000 civil service employees, 1,000 foreign service officers, and 6,000 contract employees. The notion of a 100-member staff also contrasts in the extreme with comparable institutions. The MCC proposal suggests a ratio of one staff member for each $50 million in funds disbursed. No other bilateral or multilateral aid agency, independent government corporation, private foundation, or international financial institution comes close to approximating this ratio, as is shown in table 6-1. With a program rather than project focus and considerable reliance on outsourcing, the MCA should be able to achieve a greater disbursement ratio than existing bilateral aid agencies, but not by an order of magnitude. Looking at foundations, the National Science Foundation, which disburses roughly the same annual budget as that proposed for the MCA, has 1,300 staff, while the Bill and Melinda Gates Foundation employs a staff of over 200 to manage annual disbursements totaling only one-fifth of the MCA budget.[13] Even the Global Fund, which is the most analogous model and has a relatively high disbursement ratio, does not come close to the MCA (although the Global Fund numbers reflect only the first few years of operation).

The administration's proposal provides no detail on overseas staff, other than to propose that the MCC be authorized to establish overseas offices "as it sees fit." USAID administrator Andrew Natsios notes that he has been told that USAID will be expected to implement some MCA programs.[14] Perhaps more than any other element, the expectation that USAID missions will support implementation of MCA programs, along with the proposed reliance on USAID staff detailed to the MCA in Washington, underscores the illogic of the implied relationship between the MCC and USAID. On one hand the administration is proposing that a new, independent entity is required to administer the MCA rather than integrating it with USAID. On the other hand, that new entity is designed to rely heavily on USAID staff and USAID missions overseas.

The administration's proposal allows other U.S. government employees to be detailed to the MCC on a reimbursable or nonreimbursable basis. The implication that the MCC will operate with a remarkably lean staff structure is thus greatly overstated. While the intention may be that the MCC would cover the personnel costs of only 100 staff, it is authorized and likely to rely heavily on the staff of other agencies, and it is fair to assume that a majority of detailed staff would come from USAID. If detailed on a nonreimbursable basis, these and other government employees cost the MCC nothing and can be excluded from total staff counts. Home agencies, however,

Table 6-1. *Annual Assistance Flows Relative to Staff, for Various Donors*

Donor	*Number of employees*	*Disbursements, millions of dollars*[a]	*Disbursements per staff member, millions of dollars*
Bilateral aid agencies and countries			
MCA (proposed)	100	5,000.0	50.0
U.S. Agency for International Development	7,920	10,172.0	1.3[b]
Belgium	360	644.0	1.8
Canada	1,286	2,032.0	1.6
Denmark	338	1,434.0	4.2
European Community	3,219	4,460.0	1.4
Finland	185	321.0	1.7
Luxembourg	14	83.0	5.9
United Kingdom	1,077	3,315.0	3.1
U.S. independent agencies[c]			
U.S. Trade and Development Authority	75	51.8	0.7
Private foundations			
Bill & Melinda Gates Foundation	238	1,012.0	4.3
David and Lucille Packard Foundation	160	230.0	1.4
Ford Foundation	600	931.0	1.6
Kellogg Foundation	205	223.0	1.1
MacArthur Foundation	192	180.0	0.9
National Science Foundation	1,300	4,500.0	3.5
Open Society Institute (Soros Foundation)	500	261.0	0.5
Pew Charitable Trusts	140	230.0	1.6
Turner Foundation	16	70.0	4.4
International financial institutions			
Asian Development Bank	2,163	5,300.0	2.5
Inter-American Development Bank	1,770	7,900.0	4.5
International Financial Corporation	2,000	3,100.0	1.6

Table 6-1. (*continued*)

Donor	*Number of employees*	*Disbursements, millions of dollars*[a]	*Disbursements per staff member, millions of dollars*
International Fund for Agricultural Development	315	450.0	1.4
World Bank	10,000	19,500.0	2.0
Global trust funds			
Global Fund to Fight AIDS, Tuberculosis, and Malaria[a]	65	750.0[d]	11.5

Source: Lael Brainard, "Compassionate Conservatism Confronts Global Poverty?" *Washington Quarterly,* vol. 26, no. 2 (spring 2003), pp. 149–169; Steven Radelet, *Challenging Foreign Aid: A Policymaker's Guide to the Millennium Challenge Account* (Washington: Center for Global Development, 2003).

a. Figures in 2001 dollars. International Monetary Fund figure represents average 1998–2002.

b. This figure overstates the ratio of disbursements to staff. In a 2002 Development Cooperation report, the Organization for Economic Cooperation and Development found that AID administers only about half of U.S. net disbursements.

c. Excludes OPIC and Ex-Im. Disbursement figures for these agencies are not comparable, since their financing leverages private sector investment and trade contracts that are many times larger than the official subsidy.

d. Figure based on first and second rounds of Global Fund grants and represents half of two-year commitments for 2003 and 2004. This may be an overestimate; the Global Fund has said that "grant recipients are eligible for up to" this amount.

lose staff capacity while still incurring the costs. This arrangement discriminates against the contributing agency while allowing the MCC the pretense of operating with a smaller and thus more efficient staff. Further, the MCC would accrue the credit for efficient aid delivery despite USAID's having contributed much of the requisite staff and expertise. There would be no mechanism for measuring USAID's contribution or for giving it credit, thus further damaging morale and recruitment.

The administration also recommends that private sector companies and organizations be allowed to detail staff to the MCC on the condition that they cover salary costs. This risks at least the appearance of conflicts of interest and could possibly unfairly influence competition for MCC contracts. Many of the private sector companies with the human resource base and staff experience appropriate for the MCC will also be eligible for MCC contracts. Even if contracts with any company detailing staff to the MCC were prohibited during the tenure of that staff at the MCC, a "revolving door" provision for the private sector would allow a select group of providers to gain unfair advantage.

To make the MCA truly effective, the MCC should avail itself of the talent and perspective provided by staff rotations from other U.S. government agencies, the private sector, and nongovernmental organizations. But good management principles dictate a full accounting of personnel and other operating expenses to allow costs and results to be evaluated fairly. In order to accurately reflect the real costs of the MCA, core staff at headquarters and in the field should be designated as dedicated MCC staff, independent of any other agency or private entity, with personnel costs funded out of the MCC's own operational budget. Staff detailed from other U.S. government agencies should be provided only on a reimbursable basis, so that the MCC's real costs are captured, and home agencies are not required to incur personnel costs for staff working on behalf of another agency. Cost effectiveness would also dictate that USAID missions would cease operations in countries that qualify for the MCC, although this might prove problematic if countries move in and out of eligibility.

It is vital that the MCC be able to draw upon the insights and expertise of the private and nongovernmental sectors, but it is also critical that there be no appearance or fact of conflict of interest. Private companies and organizations should be encouraged to release staff to work for the MCC, but they should be prohibited from detailing paid staff to the MCC. Conflict of interest concerns could be further alleviated if private sector employees granted a leave of absence to work for the MCC were prohibited from working on any MCC-related contract for a designated period following their return to private employment.

Less important than claiming an arbitrary and unrealistically low staff ratio is ensuring that the MCC has the quality and number of staff required to fulfill core functions. In particular the MCC will need sufficient in-house experience to make swift decisions and will require central decision points allowing all actors—recipient governments, implementing agencies, contractors, and field counterparts—to make program modifications on an as-needed basis. At its core the MCC will have to manage multiple functions, including selection of eligible countries; assessment of potential nongovernmental and private sector partners; solicitation, review, and selection of grant proposals; management of relations with officials, local communities, NGOs, and the private sector in eligible countries; donor coordination; program oversight; board management; coordination within the U.S. government; reporting to the legislative branch; and public diplomacy. Even for functions that can be outsourced wholly or in part, such as the delivery of grant and technical assistance, procurement, and monitoring and evaluation, the MCC will require staff to manage the contracts.

Outsourcing

Even with a staff larger than the 100 originally envisaged by the administration, the MCC will necessarily have to rely on outsourcing critical management functions, delivery of goods and services, and monitoring and evaluation, in order to avoid creating an enormous bureaucracy. For the MCC to break new ground and pioneer a more flexible and efficient approach, it will need to break free of the approaches to contracting and procurement practiced by USAID. In addition the emphasis on selecting strong performers and graduating them implies that the MCC should gradually extend to grant recipients increasing responsibility for developing grant proposals, managing program implementation, and evaluating results.

Outsourcing will require compliance with a host of regulations, and the complexity of the process is best understood by examining the experience of USAID. That agency recently developed a new automated directives system (ADS), which sets forth rules and regulations governing programming, financial management, contracting and procurement, and other functions. Considered more user-friendly than the handbook system that preceded it, the ADS contains over 250 chapters in addition to the old handbooks that still remain in force. Thirty-one "most important" changes were appended in January 2003 alone. Contracting with external agencies is especially bureaucratic and slow. Following a 1994 dialogue with development partners, for example, USAID agreed to improve the quality of procedures, implement new timelines, and provide greater access and transparency. Specifically this meant reducing the number of documents required from new nongovernmental registrants from eighteen to eight and making decisions on noncompetitive awards within ninety days and competitive awards in less than six months.[15]

U.S. government procurement is overseen by the Office of Federal Procurement Policy in the White House Office of Management and Budget (OMB) and follows federal acquisition regulations. These are heavily influenced by the Department of Defense, the General Services Administration, and the National Aeronautics and Space Administration, who together are the highest-value procurers in the federal government. USAID procurement relies heavily on DoD and NASA personnel, in part because these two agencies have extensive procurement experience, but also because limited opportunities for promotion make it difficult for USAID to retain procurement staff. Career USAID officials point out, however, that DoD and NASA have experience in procuring goods and equipment but not the services that USAID more commonly requires.[16]

Procurement is also shaped by "buy America" provisions of the Foreign Assistance Act, which require that a majority of goods and services be acquired from American companies. While this "tied aid" successfully generates business for U.S. firms and most often results in the delivery of quality products, it can indirectly undermine development efforts. United States–funded projects in Africa, for example, must rely on American-made all-terrain vehicles. The private market in most of Africa, however, is dominated by Toyota. The result is that American-made trucks fall idle in a fairly short time, because local markets have neither sufficient spare parts nor enough mechanics required to maintain them. Similarly the Small Business Act requires federal agencies to allocate a percentage of contracts to specific types of small businesses in the United States. Efforts to address this domestic imperative, however, often mean that contracts are awarded less on the basis of quality and merit and more on the basis of fulfilling specific legislative requirements. Finally, as described in detail in chapter 8, earmarks can further complicate contracting and procurement by dictating that funds be awarded to specific implementing agencies or suppliers.

By exempting MCA funds from multiple provisions of the Foreign Assistance Act, notwithstanding authority will ease many of these constraints. The MCC's efficiency could be even further enhanced by the design of innovative contracting instruments. Typically contracting requires that a separate request for proposals, or RFP, be circulated for each project or component of a project. Once bids are received, they are evaluated, and contracts are negotiated with and awarded to the most competitive bidder. Because this is a time-consuming process requiring multiple contracts for each program, USAID also uses indefinite quantity contracts, or IQCs, which are considered much more flexible. Rather than being designed to fulfill the requirement of a specific project, an IQC is designed to bundle the requirements of several projects. An IQC might, for example, be awarded to an organization with training, implementation, and advisory skills in the health care sector. Once signed, an IQC is funded and available to fulfill the requirements of multiple similar projects in different countries. IQCs cut down on the time required to circulate and bid individual contracts for each project.

As an example, management of monitoring and evaluation functions would be well-served by IQCs. The MCC could contract an external agency with expertise in the health sector, for example, and by using an IQC allow that agency to monitor and evaluate health sector grants provided to multiple MCA countries. IQCs would be more efficient than circulating individual RFPs for each country and would also allow the contractor and the MCC to benefit from comparisons between and among different countries' experience in undertaking MCA health sector grants.

Many experienced USAID officials argue that task order contracts could prove even more effective than IQCs. In this case, funding is preapproved rather than being made available only after arduous contract negotiations are completed. A task order contract could also allow new funding to be added to an existing contract, thus extending its utility without its being interrupted, as in the case of IQCs or individual contracts, by renegotiation when the original contract sum is expended. Finally these former officials suggest that task order contracts include funds to cover mobilization costs and standby staffing.

In most cases contracts include specific allocations for travel and personnel; once expended, additional funds for these items must be renegotiated. If, for example, the MCC had a conventional contract with an outside firm to provide services in support of a major health sector development program in one MCA country, it could not request that firm to evaluate a new health care proposal from a second MCA country unless it renegotiated the original contract and added more funds to it. With the kind of task order contract proposed, the MCC could request the firm to go to the second country to conduct an evaluation, without either additional contract negotiations or the transfer of additional funds. Mobilization costs would cover travel requirements; standby staffing arrangements would allow the firm to compensate additional staff so that this sort of mission could be undertaken quickly. While mobilization and standby arrangements would increase overall contract costs, these and other provisions of task order contracts would considerably reduce the amount of time required to implement MCA programs.

Evaluation of the MCC

Finally, ensuring that MCC operations reflect the mandate of the MCA and are efficient and transparent requires that overall operations be evaluated on a regular basis. Here the General Accounting Office (GAO) could play a central role by assessing the efficacy of MCC operations and the implementation of MCA grants. MCC in turn could make midcourse corrections to ensure that the implementation of a new foreign aid instrument and the operations of a new government agency combine to meet the goals of the MCA.

Capacity Building

Another critical consideration is transferring expertise to MCA recipient governments by delegating the authority and responsibility for program implementation and evaluation to recipient governments and private institutions. The administration has proposed that the MCC provide technical assistance toward the development of MCA grant proposals. Maximizing the MCA's impact will require that ownership extend beyond program design and the preparation of proposals to also include program implementation, monitoring, and evaluation. At the outset it is reasonable to assume that the capacity of MCA recipients is likely to be limited. Building that capacity is critical to reduce the dependency of MCA grantees on the MCC, increase their capacity to manage other large-scale financial transactions and programs, and ultimately graduate.

An effort to gradually shift the responsibility and resources for implementation from MCC-funded American contractors to in-country institutions may meet with domestic political resistance. Some may argue that the risk of corruption is too high to warrant the delegation of critical operational functions to MCA governments and private institutions. A practical concern may be that local capacity constraints could undermine the swift implementation of MCA programs.

As a first step, technical assistance provided to support proposal preparation should move beyond the provision of outside experts to also include training local counterparts. Similarly the provision of financial management and the monitoring and evaluation of MCA programs should include a training component aimed at increasing the capacity of recipient government institutions. The MCC should allow for fair competition for procurement and other contracts among American and host country firms and establish a straightforward process for registration by private organizations and companies in MCA-eligible countries. The capacity of recipient governments could be further enhanced by ensuring that contractors implementing the monitoring and evaluation components of an MCA program are engaged in the entire process, beginning with the initial design of the proposal and selection of benchmarks. This would allow independent external monitors to evaluate all aspects of MCA implementation and thus to provide assessments to both MCA recipients and the MCC.

Summary of Recommendations

The administration should reconsider housing the MCA within USAID. It could constitute a new MCA bureau headed by an assistant or deputy USAID administrator and governed by an independent board with USAID and State Department oversight.

If the administration remains committed to the creation of the MCC, the MCC's board should not include OMB and should be expanded to include, in addition to the CEO and secretaries of state and treasury, the administrator of USAID, the secretaries of no more than one other relevant U.S. federal agency, and four representatives from outside the executive branch, one each designated by the ranking majority and minority members of the House and Senate. External members should be appointed to six-year terms, and Congress, rather than the MCC, should govern the transfer of MCA funds to other federal agencies by the MCC.

Core headquarters and overseas staff of the MCC should be detailed on a reimbursable basis only, and private sector companies should be prohibited from detailing paid staff.

The MCC should develop new contracting arrangements, including task order contracts that would allow for preapproved funding, would include a facility for adding new funds, and would cover mobilization and standby staff costs.

The MCC should enhance the ability of MCA countries to implement grant programs by including training and capacity-building components in all technical assistance, financial management, and other relevant assistance programs; by allowing competition for procurement and other service contracts by MCA country institutions; and by expediting the registration process for these entities.

Finally, MCC operations and MCA grant allocations and implementation should be periodically evaluated by the GAO.

7

U.S. Foreign Assistance and Development Programs

Even a smart design and a lot of money will not be enough to make a difference to U.S. foreign assistance, unless the Millennium Challenge Account reflects the lessons from past foreign aid failures and successes and complements other U.S. programs for developing countries. While the Bush administration seems intent on starting from a blank slate in order to avoid the problems of past foreign assistance programs, there has been scant reference to the precise nature of those problems and no discussion about the impact on U.S. Agency for International Development (USAID), which will maintain responsibility for the large majority of U.S. foreign economic assistance. Failure to identify the limitations of U.S. foreign assistance and to adapt the lessons learned to the MCA risks replicating many of those same problems and will undercut the potential for the MCA to transform U.S. development policy or strengthen U.S. foreign assistance. Meanwhile the president's decision to design around USAID rather than reform it has been interpreted as a clear vote of no-confidence, contributing to low morale among the staff at a time when they are being asked to take on additional difficult challenges.

This chapter describes the U.S. foreign assistance context, examines the key failings of U.S. foreign aid, and draws lessons from each to apply to the MCA. It concludes that the MCA will not achieve its own goals, and indeed runs a high risk of contributing to the proliferation of underperforming aid programs for the developing world, unless the U.S. government establishes a sharp distinction in its aid programs between foreign policy objectives and development priorities, establishes a process for driving coherence among multiple U.S. programs affecting developing nations, articulates a clear division of labor between the MCA and USAID, and rationalizes the multiple and often contradictory demands placed on USAID.

In a worst-case scenario the MCA will emerge as just one more account among a morass of overlapping U.S. aid programs and conditions. At one extreme, by maintaining too high a degree of selectivity, the MCA could remain beyond the reach of most poor nations. It then would be relevant only for the few stellar performers with deep local capacity to formulate and implement proposals, while USAID would remain the main source of U.S. funding for the far more numerous yet less capable countries. An elite minority of developing countries would benefit from program assistance invested in national development strategies, while a majority would rely on project aid and lifesaving welfare support.

There is also a danger that the MCA becomes the only game in town—the preferred fund not only for the best performers but also for weaker states and geopolitically significant countries. This outcome could emerge if the increased demand for national security–based assistance and the rapidly deteriorating budgetary environment conspire to undermine the integrity of the MCA. Indeed the administration's decision in November 2002 to expand the MCA pool of eligible countries to include not just the poorest but also lower-middle-income countries moved precisely in this direction, taking development advocates completely by surprise. With this change the eligibility pool encompasses nations who are among the largest beneficiaries of politically directed U.S. assistance but who no longer qualify for concessional lending from the World Bank, such as Russia, Jordan, Egypt, Colombia, Peru, and South Africa. In fiscal year 2002 these six countries received $1.25 billion in U.S. aid—one-fifth of all foreign economic (nondisaster) assistance.[1]

If protected from political interference and bureaucratic constraints, the MCA could demonstrate the potential for foreign aid to make a difference. Even if the MCA succeeds in its own right, however, the impact on global poverty will necessarily be limited because of the MCA's narrow coverage. The impact of U.S. aid on global poverty could be increased, however, if the

MCA is part of a broader strategy to transform U.S. policy toward the poorest countries over time—driving greater coherence among U.S. trade, aid, and investment policies, clarifying missions, and helping to rationalize existing aid programs.

An Inventory of U.S. Foreign Assistance Programs

The MCA will be the newest addition to a large group of separate U.S. foreign assistance accounts with varying degrees of flexibility and administered by a variety of agencies. Foreign assistance is often seen as synonymous with development aid, but the vast majority of U.S. foreign assistance has not historically had economic development as its primary purpose.

Within the foreign operations account of the U.S. budget, development and investment and export expansion programs represent nearly one-third of the fiscal 2003 total, or $6.0 billion. This category includes bilateral assistance, together with Title III food aid administered by USAID and the Department of Agriculture, support through the multilateral development banks and agencies, overseen by the Department of the Treasury, and funding for several independent entities, including the Peace Corps, the Inter-American and African Development Foundations, the Export-Import Bank (Ex-Im), the Overseas Private Investment Corporation (OPIC), and the Trade and Development Agency (TDA). Bilateral development programs account for roughly half of this category, comprising the development assistance (DA) and congressionally mandated child survival and health (CSH) funds, both administered by USAID. Heavily earmarked by Congress, appropriated on a single-year basis, and further constrained by USAID's cumbersome programming practices, DA is among the least flexible of U.S. foreign assistance instruments. Though DA is programmed to address development needs, decisions guiding country allocations are often based on foreign policy priorities.

Bilateral economic assistance allocated on the basis of political and security goals at 26 percent of the fiscal 2003 budget, or $4.84 billion, is much greater than bilateral development assistance. The economic support funds (ESF) account absorbs nearly half of these funds. ESF is allocated by the State Department, is administered by either State or USAID, and is the most flexible economic nonemergency assistance provided by the United States. In recent years more than half of ESF assistance has been provided in the form of cash transfers for budgetary or balance of payments support, with the rest programmed for development projects or to finance commodity purchases from the United States. ESF is also provided on a two-year basis, meaning that unexpended funds can be carried over to the following year. In designing the MCA, lawmakers and administration officials have looked at ESF as a possible model for providing financing through more flexible modalities (and therefore a larger average grant size) than is permitted under the DA account. A large share of ESF is earmarked for Egypt and Israel, who received more than half of total funds in the fiscal year 2003 budget request. Other funds provided on the basis of political and security interests include assistance for the former Soviet republics, Eastern Europe and the Baltic States, the Andean counterdrug initiative, and initiatives for counternarcotics, law enforcement, nonproliferation, counterterrorism, and demining.

Security assistance, which includes financing for foreign military purposes, accounts for $5.0 billion, or 27 percent of the fiscal 2003 budget. The majority of this category is for international military education and training and peacekeeping.

Humanitarian relief composes 9 percent of the fiscal 2003 foreign operations account, but it is often supplemented with the approval of Congress in the event of a major famine or other crisis. It includes disaster and emergency food aid programs administered by USAID and Migration and Refugee Assistance (MRA) programmed by the Department of State. (The Department of Defense, through Foreign Assistance Act draw-down authority, also provides humanitarian assistance, most often in the form of logistical support for U.S. operations, but these expenses are not reflected in this category.) Humanitarian assistance is quite flexible to enable swift delivery in times of crisis.

The United States also provides support to international organizations and programs, such as the World Trade Organization, and voluntary contributions to the United Nations and affiliated organizations. Once allocated, the United States exercises limited authority over these funds, which represent 1 percent of the fiscal 2003 foreign operations account.[2]

As U.S. international engagement has increased, so too has new assistance administered through U.S. agencies not traditionally responsible for foreign aid, such as the Health and Human Services Department. There is a clear trend toward USAID controlling a shrinking share of overall foreign assistance. In a 2002 Development Cooperation report, the Organization for Economic Cooperation and Development found that USAID administers only about half of U.S. net overseas development assistance.[3] The State Department, the Agriculture Department, the Treasury Department, and the Defense Department are important players on foreign aid, in addition to USAID.

Not included in the above programs but of increasing desirability to both U.S. policymakers and recipients are debt relief, market access through trade preferences, and support for trade and investment. In fiscal years 2001 and 2002, Congress appropriated $676 million to cover the U.S. contribution to the highly indebted poor country (HIPC) trust fund and the writing down of bilateral debt. Trade preference programs for developing nations are provided primarily through the African Growth and Opportunity Act (AGOA), the Caribbean Basin Initiative (CBI), the Andean Trade Preference Act (ATPA), and the umbrella generalized system of preferences (GSP), which are administered by the Department of Commerce and the U.S. trade representative. Trade and investment support is provided by Ex-Im, OPIC, and TDA. The Treasury Department has the lead authority for U.S. involvement in multilateral development programs and in negotiating bilateral investment treaties.

The Record of Foreign Assistance: What We Can Learn

According to the Bush administration's 2002 national security strategy, "Decades of massive development assistance have failed to spur economic growth in the poorest countries. Worse, development aid has often served to prop up failed policies, relieving the pressure for reform and perpetuating misery. Results of aid are typically measured in dollars spent by donors, not in the rates of growth and poverty reduction achieved by recipients. These are indicators of a failed strategy."[4] The administration has thus proposed investing MCA dollars in so-called "good performers," building on the assumption that the greatest gains can be achieved in countries governed by rule of law, engaged in economic reform, and committed to health and education.

That international foreign assistance has failed to spur the sustained development of the world's poorest countries is not seriously in dispute.[5] But U.S. aid has failed for much more complicated reasons than suggested above, and the MCA risks falling into the same traps unless they are explicitly addressed in the MCA's design.

Moreover, it is important to understand that development efforts have had some notable successes in the past half century. Incomes are rising throughout much of the world, the number of democracies has dramatically increased,[6] and the poorest countries have made important progress in narrowing the gap with the richest countries on child survival, life expectancy, declines in infant mortality, and literacy. The countries accounting for the poorest fifth of the world population have seen life expectancy rise from thirty-seven to sixty-six in just three decades, although the AIDS pandemic now threatens this remarkable achievement.[7] By most accounts, foreign assistance has made important contributions through immunization campaigns, child survival strategies, and improvements to agricultural productivity. Improved sanitation combined with inexpensive oral rehydration therapy has led to a two-thirds drop in deaths from diarrheal disease between 1980 and 1999.[8] In one of the biggest triumphs of science and political will, smallpox has been completely eradicated (although bioterrorism could threaten this achievement), and polio is well on its way to eradication. But too many of the world's poorest countries have failed to close the income gap, despite high levels of foreign assistance.

Many foreign assistance programs fail because they are overcome by events beyond their scope of influence or by external factors. In the late 1980s, for example, many bilateral aid donors considered Rwanda a development success. Just before it erupted into chaos and killing in 2000 and again last year, Côte d'Ivoire was considered a "good performer" and would have qualified for the MCA. Donors did not anticipate instability in either of these countries, nor were they aware that considerable aid investments would be lost to unforeseen crises.

International policies outside the scope of aid programs, including those shaping the international terms of trade, also pose important constraints. Despite the market access provided to Africa by the African Growth and Opportunity Act, for example, U.S. and EU agricultural subsidies continue to constrain the development of African agricultural production. Trade preferences under AGOA are conditional on African governments liberalizing agricultural markets, but do not address the more important obstacles facing would-be African agricultural exporters of subsidies in the richest markets. OECD countries pay their farmers more than $300 billion a year in subsidies, more than five times total spending on overseas development assistance and greater than the national income of all sub-Saharan African nations combined.[9] The average cow in European Union nations receives $2.20 a day in government support,[10] while three billion people in the world live on less than $2 a day.[11]

In and of itself the MCA will not transcend either unforeseen crises or international policy constraints. Its effectiveness can be increased, however, if it complements the foreign assistance apparatus of which it will become a part. Further it must avoid the unique problems characterizing U.S. foreign assistance, which are described in some detail below.

A Servant to Two Masters: Development and Foreign Policy

Development policy and foreign policy frequently pull U.S. foreign assistance programs in different directions. Too often, U.S. economic assistance is equated with development assistance, contributing greatly to aid's discredit. It makes little sense, however, to measure the return of investment in economic terms, when aid dollars were allocated according to geopolitical criteria in the first place.[12] In some cases the aid has yielded the desired geopolitical outcomes while failing to yield economic gains, and in other cases it has failed on both fronts. Most examples of aid lost to corruption, waste, or diversion—as was the case in Zaire, Liberia, Sudan, and Somalia—were allocated according to cold-war logic. The billions of aid dollars poured into Egypt since the Camp David Peace Accords may have yielded foreign policy gains, even though they have failed to produce durable economic or political modernization. On the other hand, even politically motivated assistance can yield impressive economic dividends where recipients are committed to reform and have sound economic policies, as happened in Taiwan and South Korea.

It is important to distinguish between the principles that guide the allocation of U.S. aid among countries and the purposes for which aid is spent in those countries. Strictly speaking, for assistance to have the greatest impact on a nation's development, the funds not only must be spent on economic development but also must be allocated on the basis of development worthiness. As described above, the bulk of U.S. foreign assistance is allocated according to political and security criteria over and above development goals. Indeed, the MCA represents the first and only package of assistance allocated solely on the basis of development criteria. ESF is overtly political; though it is disbursed in support of development programs, most DA country allocations are made on the basis of foreign policy interests. But even though the proposed allocation to the MCA represents an enormous increase in bilateral development assistance, it pales by comparison to an expanding budget for politically directed assistance.[13]

"Political" foreign aid is arrayed against a number of traditional interests. The United States has for decades used foreign assistance as a political reward, in the case of Egypt and Israel in the wake of the Camp David Accords. Similarly foreign assistance is often provided to support the capacity of a recipient country to implement policies supportive of U.S. interests, as in the case of Plan Colombia, which provided $1.3 billion in 2000, mainly to stem the flow of illegal drugs to the United States.[14] In other cases foreign aid is provided for relative virtue. Jordan, for example, is slated to receive $250 million this year because it is among the most moderate and pro-American states in the turbulent Middle East. Most of these overtly political needs are addressed with ESF funds, but DA resources are also tapped to address political imperatives. Table 7-1 provides an overview of the various foreign policy purposes of foreign aid.

Because the war against terrorism and the war in Iraq have defined a new breed of post-cold-war allies, the majority of total U.S. aid dollars will continue to go to countries selected on the basis of political over and above development criteria, even if allocations under the MCA are factored in. Following the September 11, 2001, attacks, for example, Congress approved a $600 million cash grant to the government of Pakistan. Unlike the aid proposed in the MCA, aid to Pakistan is not conditioned upon good development performance; indeed, Pakistan has some of the worst health and education indicators in the world. The top ten recipients of U.S. foreign assistance in the fiscal year 2003 budget request are neither the world's poorest countries nor the best development partners. All, however, are key foreign policy allies. Politically directed assistance strengthens the ability of the United States to carry out its foreign policy but does not necessarily bring about sustainable development gains. Despite receiving over $55 billion in international aid in the past twenty-five years, Egypt's government spending on education fell 10 percent during the 1990s, and the availability of safe water has actually declined during the past several years.[15]

The development assistance administered by USAID is used to support local development efforts, but even for these programs recipient country designations often reflect foreign policy over and above need or performance criteria. The top DA recipients in the fiscal year 2004 budget request, for example, are Afghanistan, Pakistan, Sudan, and Indonesia. Development assistance is also used to support high-risk windows of opportunity, including postconflict transitions, which may or may not yield significant development gains. The Federal Republic of Yugoslavia is a leading recipient of DA, for example, and it is anticipated that the administration will make a supplemental budget request to Congress including both ESF and DA for postintervention Iraq.

If the MCA is to demonstrate the potential effectiveness of aid allocated to the best development investments, its mandate must be defined narrowly so that foreign policy and political pressures can be avoided. Basing country eligibility on stringent criteria will help ensure that only meritorious countries benefit from MCA assistance. Pressure to use the MCA as a means of providing political rewards may also be limited by the fact that few of the world's lowest-income countries are of geopolitical interest to the United

Table 7-1. *Foreign Policy Goals of U.S. Assistance Programs*

Type of beneficiary	*Foreign policy goal*	*Example*	*Assistance programs*[a]
Strategic partner	To maintain goodwill or provide a political reward deemed vital to U.S. interests.	Egypt	ESF, FSA, SEED
Quid pro quo	To secure cooperation on a particular activity (for example, counternarcotics, nonproliferation). Mainly targeted at cooperative activity but may encompass development assistance.	Colombia	INCLE, IMET, FMF, NADR
Regional linchpin	To help maintain stability of country that serves as a critical anchor and whose instability could have ripple effects throughout region. Targeted at development.	South Africa	DA, CSH
Failing or postconflict	To avoid vortex of instability that poses risks in region or more generally; or to reconstruct former adversary.	Afghanistan	Transition assistance
Modest salience, stable	To maintain the support and goodwill in multilateral arenas and elsewhere of stable countries where the United States has moderate to negligible direct interests in their economic development.	Senegal	DA, CSH
Humanitarian crises	To address humanitarian emergencies regardless of the strategic or development worthiness of the affected countries.	Hurricane Mitch	OFDA, MRA, emergency food aid

a. Economic support fund (ESF); Freedom Support Act (FSA); support for Eastern European democracy (SEED); international narcotics control and law enforcement (INCLE); international military education and training (IMET); foreign military financing (FMF); nonproliferation, antiterrorism, demining, and related programs (NADR); development assistance (DA); child survival and health (CSH); Office of Foreign Disaster Assistance (OFDA); migration and refugee assistance (MRA).

States. However, the administration's proposed increase in income eligibility from an initial $1,435 per capita to $2,975 in fiscal year 2006 could render the MCA vulnerable to political influence. Egypt and Jordan, for example, could become eligible if the per capita income level is increased. With the Millennium Challenge Corporation board allowed discretion in ruling on MCA country designations, eligibility could be stretched to address the growing demands of national security. Maintaining the ceiling for per capita incomes at the $1,435 level would greatly reduce this risk.

Fewer Goals, Greater Flexibility

Many observers view the administration's decision to establish the MCC as an indictment of USAID. They see it as part of a broader trend toward marginalization of USAID, with erosion of its role and budget ultimately leading to its demise. By way of illustration, it is worth noting that of the $2.5 billion in new foreign assistance money requested in the Bush administration's fiscal year 2004 budget request, less than 1 percent goes to USAID.[16] The administration's decision to create a new aid agency rather than to reform USAID suggests, at the very least, a lack of confidence in the agency's ability to implement the MCA. But while critics are right to point to the limitations and ineffectiveness of USAID, they are wrong to assume that the agency's flaws are driven solely by intent. The primary limitations to USAID's effectiveness include a shifting and often troubled relationship with the Department of State, the overlay of domestic politics, its lack of focus, and the dominance of an unwieldy bureaucracy. Misdiagnosing USAID's weaknesses could leave the MCA similarly vulnerable.

Since its creation in 1961, USAID has functioned both as an independent agency and, since the mid-1990s, as an autonomous agency operating under the authority of the secretary of state. The shift did nothing to solve USAID's internal problems and little to lessen tensions between USAID staff, who believe that DA should be protected from politics, and State Department officials, who view DA as a tool for promoting the foreign policy agenda of the United States. Instead USAID is now tugged in two different and often contradictory directions, pushed by the State Department and other agencies to fashion programs that can buttress U.S. foreign policy, and pulled from within toward programs that focus more squarely on economic development.

The strong institutional and programmatic influence of domestic politics poses an additional constraint. Each incoming administration nominates political appointees to serve as USAID administrators and top management. Because each new administration brings with it a unique approach to development and new priorities, USAID undergoes massive reorganization every four or eight years. Changing priorities every few years is inconsistent with economic development, which is, by its very nature, a long-term process. It disrupts ongoing programs, generates high costs, and demands the reorientation of a huge bureaucracy. Political debates about the role and future of USAID, meanwhile, have often crippled the agency, most dramatically in the case of the Atwood-Helms battle over whether USAID should remain an independent agency or fall under the authority of the Department of State. Domestic politics can also distort agency programs, both through earmarks imposed by Congress and by the imposition of program requirements favored by domestic political constituencies. The most striking example of this phenomenon is what is sometimes called the Mexico City provision on family planning, or the "global gag rule," which dictates that nongovernmental organizations that receive family planning assistance from USAID cannot provide abortion services, even with funds from sources other than USAID. Nor can they provide information about abortion or refer women to other services, even where abortion is legal, though they can advocate against abortion. On his first day in office President Bush reinstated this policy, first put in place by President Reagan in 1987 and subsequently rescinded by the Clinton administration. While positions pro or con may satisfy or dismay Republican and Democratic constituencies, the impact on development programming is disruptive and confusing to recipients as they are funded, defunded, and refunded in response to changes in U.S. administrations.[17]

Congress places further demands on USAID by frequently earmarking aid, requiring that it be directed to specific countries, programs, or American implementing agencies and contractors. Speaking of the fiscal year 2002 Foreign Appropriations Bill, Senator John McCain observed the often troublesome nature of earmarks when he noted that "Fragile allies suffering from civil unrest and economic decay will not be helped by this bill's provision of $2.3 million in core support for the International Fertilizer Development Center, or the report language's recommendation of $4 million for its work. Peanuts, orangutans, gorillas, neotropical raptors, tropical fish, and exotic plants also receive the committee's attention, though it's unclear why any individual making a list of critical international security, economic, and humanitarian concerns worth addressing would target these otherwise meritorious flora and fauna. . . . The committee has [also] disturbingly singled out for funding a laundry list of American universities—some with multibillion-dollar endowments—in contravention of the usual merit-based process of allocating scarce foreign assistance dollars to the most worthy causes."[18]

USAID also suffers from a lack of focus. More often than not, country programs are composed of individual projects designed to meet multiple objectives. Regional and functional funds are heavily stovepiped, and there is little coordination among separate interventions by USAID's relief, food aid, technical, functional, and regional bureaus. While USAID was more focused on single objectives in decades past, the agency's more recent tendency has been to engage in all sectors and thus spread limited assistance too thin to have measurable impact.

Finally, bureaucratic constraints reduce USAID's programmatic and operational efficiencies. While some USAID accounts are provided bureaucratic flexibility, internal requirements and congressional earmarks tightly prescribe the bulk of the DA budget. A rocky relationship with Congress has caused staff to overinterpret legislative requirements and thus avoid risk. At the same time, while new administrations regularly overhaul the management of the agency, they often fail to rescind past regulations. As a result agency staffing has shifted toward bureaucratic managers and away from field professionals. This trend was exacerbated by budget cuts in the 1980s and 1990s that were taken primarily in the field and from among professional development staff, leaving a disproportionate layer of midlevel management in Washington. Former deputy USAID administrator Carol Lancaster observes that AID is further impaired by cumbersome programming procedures that are inconsistent with the type of activities being supported and by the fact that most USAID officers—and contractors—serve only three years in recipient countries, thus reducing staff's ability to negotiate foreign cultures and practices.[19]

The MCA legislation drafted by the White House suggests a commitment to freeing the MCC from some of the bureaucratic constraints faced by USAID. The administration wisely proposes the provision of MCA assistance to countries notwithstanding any other provision of law with the exception of prohibiting MCA assistance to countries that are ineligible to receive assistance under part one of the Foreign Assistance Act of 1961.[20] Notwithstanding authority will exempt the MCA from a broad range of prohibitions and requirements and thus expedite programming. The provision that MCA funds will be no-year means that funds will remain available until they are expended; in contrast USAID funds must be obligated within a single year. But, as described in the next chapter, this critical operational flexibility will not be sustained over time in the absence of a new relationship with Congress.

Even with a high degree of bureaucratic freedom, however, the MCA could prove vulnerable to other constraints facing USAID, including the influence of domestic politics. The establishment of a bipartisan board, as outlined in chapter 5, is critical to ensuring that MCA programming is not unduly influenced by either major political party and that the MCC is not subjected to crippling reorganizations each time a new administration takes office. And attempts to stretch the MCA's mandate to incorporate other than pure developmental objectives could also dilute its effectiveness. Protecting the MCA's mandate, therefore, will also require that both the administration and Congress avoid the temptation to use the MCA to address international political aims or to appease domestic constituencies.

The MCA must also avoid the kind of program overreach that undermines USAID. The administration has already made reference to multiple program areas, including budget support for various community, sector, or national initiatives; infrastructure development; commodity financing; training and technical assistance; capitalization of enterprise funds or foundations; agricultural development; education; enterprise and private sector development; governance; health; and trade and investment capacity building.[21] Instead the MCC should seek to develop specific sectoral expertise and fund programs in the six areas outlined in chapter 4 that reflect recipient country priorities but also play to the MCC's comparative advantage.

Ensuring Policy Coherence

U.S. foreign assistance fails to achieve maximum impact in part because aid is administered through a multiplicity of overlapping but uncoordinated programs and agencies. U.S. agencies involved in foreign assistance programs include not only the most likely suspects—USAID, the Departments of State, Agriculture, and Treasury, and the Peace Corps—but also the Departments of Defense, Education, Health and Human Services, Commerce, and Transportation; the U.S. trade representative; the IRS and INS; the Export-Import Bank, OPIC, and TDA; the Small Business Administration; and the Federal Aeronautics Administration. Even within USAID there are multiple funding streams. A country might initially qualify for humanitarian assistance from the Office of Foreign Disaster Assistance but then, as the crisis eases, qualify for assistance from the Office of Transition Initiatives. It might graduate to DA but even then receive separate funding from accounts created in support of special initiatives. Lest the MCA contribute to further institutional incoherence, it is necessary to define a clear relationship between the MCC and USAID, ensure consistency and complementarities between and among U.S. government agencies engaged in development, and identify an interagency coordination mechanism having the full support of senior policymakers.

In addition to those proposed for the MCA, for example, there are a number of other criteria by which the United States determines a country's economic worthiness, including both highly indebted poor country (HIPC) standards and those required for benefits under AGOA, CBI, and ATPA. Overlap between these is, currently, strikingly low. HIPC, for example, targets those countries where debt burdens are deemed to be an obstacle to poverty reduction and growth and includes fairly stringent selection criteria on income and the degree of indebtedness and openness.[22] It further requires that a significant portion of the proceeds be devoted to the same types of social investments included in the MCA selection criteria. Yet, remarkably, only seven of the twenty-seven countries that have been approved for HIPC are likely to be eligible for the MCA, while the remaining sixteen countries likely to qualify for the MCA are not HIPC-eligible. On the trade side, thirty-six countries have been approved for AGOA, but of these only five are likely to qualify for the MCA initially, along with only three of twenty-four CBI-eligible countries and two of those eligible for ATPA.

The creation of another independent agency to support international development with its own idiosyncratic conditions threatens to add to an already confusing proliferation of U.S. programs and agencies. U.S. development assistance will not achieve maximal efficiency and impact unless it is part of a coherent strategy that also includes trade and investment programs, debt relief, and multilateral programs. Especially for the most reform-oriented countries singled out by the MCA, the prospects for graduating rest centrally on improved trade and investment prospects. This is also particularly important if, as proposed by the administration, the MCC operates in lower-middle-income countries, where trade and investment opportunities tend to be more important to growth and poverty reduction than are aid flows. It makes little sense to grade a country on its trade openness and provide foreign aid to improve its trade regime but then provide less favorable market access than is available to other countries (who might be politically more important but less committed to market reform). This argues for an approach in which the most reform-oriented poor nations would also qualify for the most flexible terms on trade access, debt treatment, development assistance, and export and investment programs. Unfortunately the obstacles to this approach are high, including jurisdiction problems across agencies within the executive branch and across committees in the legislative branch.

Past efforts to integrate U.S. assistance programs have not met with success. In the mid-1990s, then USAID administrator Brian Atwood signed a directive ordering that programs in a ten-country pilot region be coordinated through integrated strategic programs that would harmonize funding from multiple USAID accounts and integrate USAID programs with those funded by other U.S. government agencies. The effort failed, in part because of bureaucratic resistance but also because there was insufficient demand from senior decisionmakers to comply with the directive.

Rather than create a new mechanism, the administration would be well advised to mandate a policy coordination process led from the White House, using existing mechanisms of the National Security Council (NSC) and National Economic Council (NEC). It should ensure deployment of all the development tools in the U.S. arsenal in a mutually reinforcing way to assist poor countries to make the transition to sustained growth. This should include foreign aid, technical assistance, debt relief, trade preferences or trade agreements, export credits, investment support, and bilateral investment treaties. Already charged with interagency coordination, the NSC and NEC have the benefit of broad governmental rather than agency-specific perspectives. Together the two have expertise in the foreign policy and development dimensions of foreign assistance, while their placement in the executive office of the president provides them with sufficient stature to drive the coordination that is currently lacking and may be resisted.

Defining Complementary Missions for MCA and USAID

Since the inception of the Marshall Plan in 1948, six separate agencies have been created to address international development—only one of which exists today, as shown in box 7-1. Unlike past efforts, the MCC would create a new development agency without either replacing or triggering the reorganization of already existing foreign assistance programs. This has the potential to lead to bureaucratic duplication and misalignment of staff responsibilities and performance evaluation, especially in countries that become eligible for the MCA, most of which will already have AID missions.

A clear division of labor between USAID and the MCC (whether as a new agency or as part of a merged entity) is critical to the programmatic and operational effectiveness of both agencies. For the MCA this means a strict focus on development worthiness and a narrow program scope. But it also means that the MCA should not rely on implicit cross subsidization and support from USAID through nonreimbursed detailees or support from USAID mission staff on the ground, as is currently envisaged in the administration's proposal. To do so would create wasteful duplication and needless turf fights, would muddy program evaluation, and would further diffuse USAID's mission and undermine morale.

No comment has been offered on whether MCA countries will remain eligible for DA funds. With the MCA available to only a handful of eligible countries, the administration should logically reserve DA resources for the remaining majority of low-income countries. Eligible to compete for heavily funded development assistance packages of their own design, MCA countries would lose existing DA funds. These, in turn, would revert to USAID for allocation to other priorities. This is particularly important in light of the fact that DA resources are decreasing and may be stretched by demands associated with the war in Iraq.[23]

Coordination in the field is much more difficult to address and, perhaps more than any other feature of the administration's proposal, points to the flaws in the MCC's institutional design. The administration's legislative proposal authorizes the MCC to establish overseas offices "as it sees fit." USAID administrator Andrew Natsios has suggested, meanwhile, that the agency will assume some role in implementing MCA programs.[24] And indeed, it appears that the proposed lean staffing structure of the MCC relies on cross subsidization from USAID in the field. This approach defies basic business management practices, as it would require USAID to dedicate staff and expertise to support the MCA but without receiving any of the institutional benefits of the MCA's success. Instead USAID would continue to be judged on the effectiveness of bureaucratically constrained DA programs in countries that are, by definition, not among the developing world's best performers and are thus unlikely to generate stellar results.

Short of crafting a new institutional model for the MCA, no fully satisfactory means exist to resolve how two separate agencies with a single development purpose might coexist on the ground. More generally, however, logic would dictate that the MCC open and finance its own offices in MCA countries, and USAID maintain missions in other countries with DA and other programs. But this arrangement is not without its vulnerabilities. Had the MCA been established two years ago, Côte d'Ivoire would have been found eligible. (In fact, because the data used to determine eligibility are dated, Côte d'Ivoire could qualify today.) The USAID mission would therefore have closed, and an MCC office would have opened. But then, quite unexpectedly, Côte d'Ivoire suddenly fell victim to widespread civil strife, a

(*text continues on page 164*)

Box 7-1. *U.S. Foreign Aid Agencies, 1948–95*

1948–51	**Economic Cooperation Agency (ECA)**
	1951 Congress replaces the ECA with the Mutual Security Agency.
1951–53	**Mutual Security Agency (MSA)**
	1953 Congress replaces the MSA with the Foreign Operations Administration.
1953–54	**Foreign Operations Administration (FOA)**
	1954 The Mutual Security Act revises and consolidates all previous foreign assistance legislation, creating the International Cooperation Agency in 1954. Placed under the authority of the State Department, the ICA has less authority than its predecessors.
1954–61	**International Cooperation Agency (ICA)**
	1959 The Draper Committee report recommends a unified economic and technical assistance agency outside the Department of State, long-range planning on a country-by-country basis, and the decentralization of authority to the field.
	1960 The Senate Foreign Relations Committee sponsors a Brookings Institution report recommending the creation of a foreign aid department with cabinet-level status. The report proposes consolidating the Development Loan Fund, the Export-Import Bank, the ICA, and authority over the Food for Peace program. The Ford Foundation, however, calls for the consolidation of foreign assistance within the Department of State.
1961–present	**U.S. Agency for International Development (USAID)**
	1961 President Kennedy calls for a new program with flexibility for short-term emergencies; commitment to long-term development; commitment to education at all levels; emphasis on recipient nation's roles through

public administration, taxes and social justice; and orderly planning for national and regional development. Secretary of State George Ball creates a task force on the reorganization of foreign assistance. Senator William Fulbright secures passage of the Act for International Development, authorizing the creation of the U.S. Agency for International Development.

1973 The Foreign Assistance Act (FAA) decrees that foreign assistance should focus on food and nutrition, population planning and health, and education and human resource development.

1978 Senator Hubert Humphrey attempts to overhaul foreign assistance through the International Development Cooperation Act.

1979–95 **International Development Cooperation Agency (IDCA)**

1979 President Carter establishes the International Development Cooperation Agency to oversee USAID.

1981 IDCA loses funding under the Reagan administration

1985 The International Security and Development Cooperation Act is the last general foreign assistance authorization enacted.

1995 The Foreign Affairs Reform and Restructuring Act abolishes IDCA, and USAID becomes a statutory agency, with the administrator reporting to and under the direct authority and foreign policy guidance of the secretary of state. The act also abolishes the Arms Control and Disarmament Agency and the U.S. Information Agency, consolidating their functions into the Department of State.

Source: Adapted from USAID, "Brief Chronology and Highlights of the History of U.S. Foreign Assistance Activities," October 2002 (www.usaid.gov/about/chronology.html [April 2003]).

military coup, a flawed election, and, finally, open conflict. In circumstances such as this, should the MCC office shut down and, conditions allowing, USAID return—all at considerable cost to the taxpayer?

The one sensible area of overlap between the MCC and USAID would be in those countries that fail to qualify for the MCA by virtue of one or two indicators or that are just below the median on several indicators. It is precisely in such near-miss countries that the promise of vastly increased foreign assistance could be catalytic in encouraging policy reforms, in contrast to poorly performing states, where the government is unlikely to possess the capacity to close the gap. Moreover this category is likely to include some developmentally important countries, such as Uganda, which has pioneered an effective development strategy while retaining severe deficiencies in governance. In these cases, limited MCA funding should be provided as challenge grants to address those areas that are weak, but under USAID's supervision. In cases where the goal is to graduate a near-miss country from a USAID program to MCA eligibility, the MCC might house a representative in the resident USAID mission.

A Sharper Mission for USAID

Finally greater clarity must be given to USAID's core mission. U.S. foreign assistance is driven by a multiplicity of competing goals and objectives and not by a strategic framework. The manifold demands on USAID result in unfocused aid programs, arrayed against a plethora of programmatic objectives. Worse, the multiplicity of foreign assistance goals adds up to an incomplete whole, leaving important gaps. Filling these gaps will require broadening the impact of the MCA on the world's poor, a dedicated effort to expand the pool of eligible recipients, and sharpening the mission of USAID to reflect new global realities.

As amended, the Foreign Assistance Act of 1961 includes thirty-two discrete objectives for foreign aid. USAID's goals include economic growth, agriculture and trade, global health, including HIV/AIDS and other infectious diseases, democratization, conflict prevention, and humanitarian assistance. The administration's fiscal year 2003 budget request outlines yet another set of goals and objectives for international assistance: maintaining and strengthening the international coalition against terror and the core alliance with NATO member countries (Japan, Australia, and South Korea); integrating Russia and China into cooperative frameworks; preventing conflict and promoting reconciliation in Africa, the Balkans, the Middle East, and northeast and south Asia; combating the proliferation of weapons of mass destruction; enlisting new support from Pakistan and other countries in the region; helping to open markets, encourage investment, promote environmentally sound development, and expand economic opportunities around the world; and promoting human rights, democracy, and other American values, including freedom of religion.[25] The foreign assistance goals outlined in the 2002 national security strategy include meeting commitments to "expand the circle of development by opening societies and building the infrastructure of democracy; promote freedom and support those who struggle nonviolently for it; disrupt and destroy terrorist organizations by . . . diminishing the underlying conditions that spawn terrorism; making investments in health and education; promote the connection between trade and development; and provide resources to aid countries that have met the challenge of national reform."[26] Finally the MCA adds the goal of reducing poverty through promoting sustained economic growth in developing countries committed to implementing good policies.[27]

The net result is that U.S. foreign assistance is not guided by a concise strategic framework but is instead allocated haphazardly to meet individual agency and congressional imperatives. The increased effectiveness of U.S. foreign assistance demands, however, a coherent strategy in which assistance instruments are arrayed against policy requirements. Absent the more deliberate allocation of foreign assistance, key priorities will go unmet.

Even with over fifty stated objectives, for example, there are costly gaps in the U.S. foreign assistance program on failed and poorly performing states. Despite the growing recognition given to the threat posed to U.S. national security by weak states, for example, the foreign assistance program lacks the strategies and resources to address this vulnerability. In the 2002 national security strategy, the administration points out that "The events of September 11, 2001, taught the U.S. that weak states like Afghanistan can pose as great a danger to the national interest as strong states. Poverty does not make poor people into terrorists and murderers. Yet poverty, weak institutions, and corruption can make weak states vulnerable to terrorist networks and drug cartels within their borders."[28] However, as foreign policy analysts have pointed out, "Current development strategies leave little place for significant, nonhumanitarian expenditures in failing states, much less those that have already gone into the abyss. There are occasional exceptions in high-profile cases where the U.S. military is deployed, as in Afghanistan and Bosnia, but these are rare."[29] Early statements by President Bush suggested that the MCA would be an effective tool for addressing weak states: "We will challenge the poverty and hopelessness and lack of education and failed governments that too often allow conditions that terrorists can seize and try to turn to their advantage." However, by focusing solely on good performers, the MCA will not, by definition, assist either weak states or failed institutions.

Even with the addition of the MCA, efforts to combat global poverty will remain incomplete because the strong eligibility conditions are likely to exclude many of the world's poorest countries. Sub-Saharan Africa is the only region of the world to experience negative growth rates over the past twenty years; during the 1990s the number of people in extreme poverty rose from 242 million to 300 million. Twenty countries, with more than half of sub-Saharan Africa's people, are poorer now than in 1990, and twenty-three are poorer than in 1975.[30] Based on current criteria, however, the MCA will impact only a handful of African countries, composing only 12 percent of the continent's population. Further, none of the likely first-year recipients is a real or potential regional economic power, and none of the countries identified as "strategic" in the national security strategy qualifies.[31] As presently funded, the ESF account cannot effectively fill this gap.

The administration's fiscal year 2004 request for ESF for Africa reflects a reduction of almost 40 percent from the fiscal year 2002 actual budget while, by contrast, the request for Europe (primarily Turkey) shows a fivefold increase. Similarly the DA account is already sufficiently overstretched to prevent it from having any additional impact. InterAction, a coalition of 160 American NGOs, has expressed concern that "the president's budget includes virtually no increases for core development and humanitarian accounts from last year's request. Furthermore, the funding requested for development assistance, child survival, disaster assistance, and refugees is actually below the level approved by Congress for this year."[32] In the fiscal year 2004 budget proposal, just over half of all DA for Africa goes to child survival and health programs, which are often effective in promoting immunization and meeting other basic health care needs but which do little to impact governments' institutional capacity, invest in the productive sectors of national economies, or promote science and technology tailored to the particular challenges of poor nations, especially those in tropical regions. In the fiscal year 2004 budget request, the balance of DA for sub-Saharan Africa is divided among twenty-six countries, three regional programs, and seven sector-based initiatives, with per-country allocations averaging at just under $10 million.

As recommended in chapter 3, the coverage of the MCA in Africa and poor countries more generally could be increased by maintaining income eligibility levels at $1,435 per capita, evaluating eligibility for countries in two separate groups based on per capita incomes, and setting the hurdles at rather than above the medians in each group. Most importantly the number of potentially eligible countries could be expanded over time by setting aside a portion of MCA funding to assist the near-miss countries to achieve eligibility. But other modalities complementary to the MCA are required if the administration seriously hopes to employ a coherent foreign assistance program to tackle the challenges posed by failed and poorly performing states. USAID's mission must be sharpened and other development resources applied more deliberately.

Successive administrations have failed to reorient USAID to new global realities. This, combined with the reduction in professional staff and problematical relationships with Congress and the State Department, has caused the agency to lose its creative edge and to concentrate on relatively safe development projects rather than on strategic interventions.[33] Meanwhile USAID's internal analyses and external programming tend to focus more on functional than regional approaches to development. As a result there is no apparent development rationale for country allocations, and programs are instead based on multiple functional priorities. What is needed is a two-pronged strategy based on a new approach to country allocations and the prioritization of functional interventions.

USAID's increased effectiveness requires greater clarity in its core mission, which could be summarized in five goals (focused primarily on types of countries rather than broad functional goals):

—providing humanitarian assistance;

—supporting sustainable development, democracy, and governance, where considerations of foreign policy, regional stability, and transnational cooperation are vital;

—countering the threat posed by weak and failing states;

—helping postconflict countries through transitions; and

—addressing poverty, sustainable development, and governance challenges in moderate-to-poorly-performing poor countries.

With the MCA taking on responsibility for the world's best-performing poor countries, USAID should logically focus DA on other kinds of states, including weak and postconflict states. The articulation of a USAID strategy complementary to and consistent with the MCA would combine DA and MCA resources in a logical continuum in which countries that achieve a strong policy environment would graduate from USAID to the MCA. Further, some degree of coverage of the gaps in the current foreign assistance program would be ensured.

USAID funding can also be utilized more effectively in moderately-to-poorly-performing poor countries and failed states. Gene Sperling and Tom Hart have argued that countries that may not qualify as good performers nonetheless could succeed in selected priority areas, such as AIDS prevention, education, the provision of clean water, or agriculture.[34] In these cases, large sector-based investments would be far more effective than the customary packages of project assistance. Susan Rice advocates a wide range of targeted interventions that could prove effective in countries with poor policy environments. These include help in establishing zones of relative security and economic opportunity in failed states, seed monies for a range of high-impact investments in countries undergoing transitions, and small-scale development investments in zones of ongoing conflict.[35]

Summary of Recommendations

Even if the MCA succeeds on its own terms, it may fail in making the United States a more effective development partner, unless there is a greater effort to ensure complementarity and coherence among the many U.S. programs and agencies oriented toward development. Moreover the MCA's success will be measured not only in terms of its impact on reducing global poverty but also on the extent to which it restores congressional and public confidence in U.S. foreign assistance. For these reasons, our recommendations are aimed not only at the MCA but also at its place in the broader range of foreign assistance policies and institutions.

Further, deliberate steps should be taken to sharpen USAID's mission to complement the MCC (whether through a new agency or as part of a merged entity). Recent statements by the administrator of USAID committing the agency to support the MCC would compound USAID's diffuse mission, exacerbate morale and recruitment problems, and muddy the evaluation of individual program performance against costs. Instead AID should give greater attention to five core missions: to meet humanitarian needs; to support sustainable development, democracy, and governance where considerations of foreign policy, regional stability, and transnational cooperation are vital; to address poverty, sustainable development, and governance challenges in weaker-performing poor nations; to help reconstruction in post-conflict situations; and to counter the threat posed by weak and vulnerable states, a mission that has suffered neglect at great cost in recent years.

The division of labor would also be immensely more compelling if MCA income eligibility were maintained at the $1,435 level, in order to reduce the risk of potential political influence posed by the inclusion of middle-income countries and to maximize resource availability for low-income countries. Instead of expanding coverage at higher income levels, MCA coverage could expand among low-income countries by modifying eligibility criteria to allow countries meeting rather than exceeding median levels and by setting aside MCA funding to assist near-miss countries to move toward future eligibility. For these near-miss countries, it is recommended that MCA funds be used in partnership with AID to address those areas that are weak.

The administration must designate clear responsibility for coordination between and among the MCA and other development programs, ideally to the NSC and NEC. Further it must define a clear and mutually beneficial relationship between the MCA and MCC and USAID.

The failures of foreign aid also offer clear lessons for the design of the MCA itself, which are incorporated into the recommendations above on the design, operations, and structure of the MCA.

While the priorities of recipient countries should drive the MCC's program priorities, the administration should refrain from opening up the MCC to all sectors, as USAID has done. Instead the MCC should seek to develop specific sectoral expertise and fund programs that reflect recipient country priorities but also play to the MCC's comparative advantage.

The integrity of the MCA should be further protected from political influence by bipartisan representation on the board of the MCC and a commitment by both the administration and Congress to avoid using the MCA to meet international political requirements or appease domestic constituencies.

8

A New Partnership between Congress and the Administration

In this chapter, we turn our attention to the role of Congress. The preceding chapters have highlighted those elements of program design and implementation by the executive branch that will be critical to the success of the Millennium Challenge Account (MCA) and U.S. programs to combat global poverty more broadly. But none of this will be possible without strong support from Congress. The purpose of this chapter is to highlight key aspects of program design that would lay the groundwork for a partnership between Congress and the executive branch in support of a successful MCA.

Historian Edward S. Corwin once noted that the U.S. Constitution presents the president and Congress with an "invitation to struggle" for control over foreign policy.[1] It divides responsibility for foreign affairs between the political branches of government. As Louis Henkin observes, the Constitution provides a "starkly incomplete, indeed skimpy . . . blueprint for the governance of our foreign affairs."[2] The Constitution confers on the president certain explicit powers over foreign affairs, including the authority to make treaties, as well as to appoint and receive ambassadors.[3] As these functions (negotiation and representation) are the heart of diplomacy, the president, his secretary of state, and other executive branch staff are responsible for carrying out U.S. foreign policy. In addition, the Constitution vests in the president full authority to implement laws and government programs, including by extension those relating to foreign aid.[4]

Yet presidential foreign affairs powers are far from absolute; the Constitution also envisions a significant role for the legislative branch. Congress has, for example, the sole power to raise and support armies as well as to declare war.[5] The Senate, in addition, provides necessary advice and consent to U.S. treaty ratification and confirms senior foreign diplomatic appointments. Most important for this discussion, only Congress can authorize and appropriate federal monies, including those for foreign aid.[6] Collectively these powers afford Congress ample opportunity to influence U.S. foreign policy and development assistance programs. Although it is difficult to divine which branch has the greater say on foreign aid,[7] it is clear that a "substantial role for the Congress in U.S. international diplomacy is a given. It is that point from which all serious discussion about how to make the process work better should begin."[8]

Congress already shapes current foreign aid programs enormously, particularly through the congressional budget process. Congress has employed a variety of statutory restrictions on foreign aid (box 8-1) and informal constraints on foreign aid (box 8-2). Congressional activism, generally not welcomed by presidents, has made foreign aid programs more accountable but also at times more cumbersome. The administration's proposal to create a new agency, the Millennium Challenge Corporation (MCC), to implement the MCA should be understood as a reaction in part to the perceived failure of Congress and the president to work together effectively in the past on many foreign aid programs.

As the preceding chapters make clear, the MCA and the MCC are intended to pioneer an entirely new approach to foreign aid. Almost every aspect of the design and operation will necessarily differ from how U.S. foreign aid programs have operated in recent years. Yet in one respect the role of Congress vis-à-vis the MCC is fixed. Congress's basic functions on the MCC—enacting authorization legislation and appropriations acts, as well as overseeing executive branch implementation of those laws—will be similar to the role Congress currently plays in foreign aid. At another level, however, the relationship between the MCC and Congress is a blank slate. Congress and the president have an enormous opportunity to initiate a new partnership in designing the agency and its mandate. Currently pending design decisions will shape the

(*text continues on page 174*)

Box 8-1. *Statutory Restrictions on Foreign Aid*

Congress uses a variety of practices to shape not only the level of foreign aid spending but also where, how, and for what international aid funds are spent:

Prohibitions. These are outright bars on the president providing foreign assistance to individual countries, such as Burma, or to governments that engage in certain types of behavior, such as human rights violations or coups against democratic governments, or for particular types of aid activities, such as abortions or police training.[1] The Foreign Assistance Act and annual Foreign Operations Appropriations Acts contain several dozen of these blanket prohibitions.[2]

Earmarks. Sometimes called spending floors, earmarks are appropriations directed by law toward particular activities, such as child survival, or toward individual countries, such as Egypt and Israel, or toward specific institutions, such as international nongovernmental organizations.[3] The fiscal year 2003 Omnibus Appropriations Act included nearly forty earmarks, accounting for 52 percent of bilateral economic assistance (see table 7-1).

Tied aid. Foreign assistance must be spent in ways that meet certain general conditions (such as obligations to buy American-made products whenever possible) or for particular projects. The Congressional Research Service reports that 70 percent of AID program funding went to U.S. contractors between October 1999 and September 2000, and 90 percent of foreign food aid expenditures was directed to U.S. suppliers.[4]

Spending caps. These are provisions that set maximum spending limits on an activity, such as funding for unpopular international organizations.[5] Spending caps, if they are low, can undercut executive branch initiatives and force policy changes.

Organizational mandates. Congress may require the executive branch to create an office dedicated to an issue of particular concern to Congress.[6] Seemingly bureaucratic dictates often have significant policy ramifications, as was the case in requiring the U.S. embassy to Israel to be located in Jerusalem.

Policy statements. Congress may seek to change U.S. policy explicitly through foreign affairs legislation. These laws can state that "it shall be the policy of the United States to" do one thing or another.[7] Some of these provisions are limited, in that they purport only to be the "sense of the Congress."[8]

Reporting requirements. Reporting requirements can be permanent (such as the yearly obligation of AID to justify its programs) or ad hoc (such as a report on antiterrorism assistance to Pakistan).[9] Reporting requirements expose executive branch decisions to political scrutiny and, if made burdensome, can also undermine unpopular programs by diverting funds and staff.

1. Foreign Assistance Act of 1961, as amended (FAA), 22 U.S.C. 32.1.1.

2. See, for example, P.L. 107-115, H.R. 2506, Foreign Operations Appropriations Act, sections on Burma, Debt Restructuring (human rights), and Child Survival and Health Programs Fund (family planning).

3. David Weiner, "New Perspectives on Foreign Aid," working paper, Center for Global Development (2002).

4. Curt Tarnoff and Larry Nowels, "Foreign Aid: An Introductory Overview of U.S. Programs and Policy," Congressional Research Service Report for Congress, April 6, 2001.

5. See, for example, P.L. 107-115, H.R. 2506, Foreign Operations Appropriations Act (limitation on expenses).

6. House Appropriations Committee, Report 107-663, Foreign Operations, Export Financing, and Related Programs, Appropriations Bill 2003, includes a requirement to change the office of Women in Development in the Bureau for Economic Growth and Trade to the office of Women and Effective Development in the Bureau for Policy and Program Coordination. See Title II-Bilateral Economic Assistance, Development Assistance, subsection "Global Issues: The Role of Girls and Women in Development," page 24.

7. See, for example, P.L. 107-115 (H.R. 2506), Foreign Operations Appropriations Act (policy on terminating the Arab League boycott of Israel and normalizing relations with Israel).

8. See, for example, ibid., section 2376 (nuclear proliferation policy in South Asia).

9. See, for example, ibid., Other Bilateral Economic Assistance, Economic Support Fund, subsection "Assistance for Eastern Europe and the Baltic States," page 9; also see P.L. 107-38, Emergency Supplemental Appropriations Act for Recovery from and Response to Terrorist Attacks on the United States (H.R. 2888), Office of Management and the Budget News Release 2001-57, "President Bush Announces $9.3 billion in Emergency Funds," November 9, 2001.

Box 8-2. *Informal Restrictions on Foreign Aid*

Congress employs a variety of informal or nonbinding mechanisms for influencing foreign aid policy.

Notifications. Notification requirements prohibit the executive branch from taking action until some period (usually fifteen days) after it has notified Congress of its intention to act.[1] The procedural delay provides Congress a window to raise objections. Notifications are sometimes called wait-and-see clauses because of the uncertainties they create. Upon receipt of an aid notification, a lone member of Congress may choose to inform the aid agency, often through the oversight committee chairman, that he or she objects to the proposed action and requests a hold on executive branch action pending further consultation. The executive branch can legally ignore the hold request (once the required notification period has expired) or try to accommodate the concerns raised. In the interest of maintaining allies in Congress, presidents often honor the wishes of individual members, particularly powerful members of key committees.

Soft earmarks. Earmarks come in nonbinding forms, too. Congress frequently seeks to direct foreign aid expenditures by placing requests in committee reports. The executive branch goes to great lengths to honor these congressional spending directives. The conference report for fiscal year 2002 Foreign Affairs Appropriations Act contained nearly a hundred specific soft earmarks.[2]

Procedural delay. Congress may demand some change in administration behavior or policy before taking other, sometimes unrelated, action that the president desires. The Senate Foreign Relations Com-

very character of the MCC and its relation to Congress. In enacting the MCA authorizing legislation, the goal should be to create an agency that is at once accountable to Congress, defers to congressional policy views, carries out the coherent, achievable mission created by legislation, and yet has the operational flexibility needed to respond to evolving international circumstances. The MCC, in short, will need much of the flexibility President Bush has requested but much more congressional policy input than the White House has acknowledged.[9] This chapter analyzes precisely how to reach these elu-

mittee has frequently delayed consideration of political nominees and treaties in objection to administration policy. In 1995 former senator Jesse Helms (R-N.C.), then chairman of the Senate Foreign Relations Committee, declared that he was "taking hostages again" until President Clinton agreed that AID should be subject to the policy direction of the State Department.[3]

Public statements. Members of Congress use public hearings, committee reports, and floor speeches to signal their desires regarding foreign aid. The executive branch gives these views significant weight in implementing foreign aid laws.

Informal reporting. Members of Congress submit to the executive branch voluminous informal requests for information, frequently generated by inquiries from their constituents or political supporters. AID responded to over a thousand such letters from Congress in fiscal year 2002.[4] Like statutory reporting requirements, congressional interest has a significant effect on the behavior of foreign aid agencies and occupies agency staff time.

1. See, for example, P.L. 107-115, H.R. 2506, Foreign Operations Appropriations Act, Department of State International Narcotics Control and Enforcement, or Transfers between Accounts.

2. Senator John McCain lists many of these nonbinding spending directives in his press release of October 24, 2001. A count of earmarks was conducted manually in February 2003.

3. Al Kamen, "In the Loop," *Washington Post,* June 26, 1995, quoted in William Bacchus, *The Price of American Foreign Policy* (1997), Pennsylvania State University Press.

4. Personal communication from AID Legislative Correspondence Unit, February 2003.

sive goals—accountability, policy deference, a coherent achievable mission, and operational flexibility.

Accountability

The accountability of a foreign affairs agency depends on a variety of considerations, including the integrity of its leaders, its bureaucratic personality, and the stresses of immediate political circumstances.[10] Perhaps the greatest factors, however, are those over which Congress has some control, including the agency's governance structure, transparency in decisionmaking, and openness to public participation.[11] Let us consider how each of these factors should play out in the MCC.

Governance

A poorly governed agency will not be accountable. At best a poorly managed agency will be inefficient and unresponsive to congressional concerns, at worst it will misuse public funds and adopt harmful policies. Congress should give the MCC four management characteristics to help ensure that the agency is governed well. They are: clear lines of management authority, an adequate professional staff, some degree of political independence, and strong grant monitoring and evaluation procedures.

MANAGEMENT. Congress works best with agencies that have clear lines of management authority. In exercising its oversight function, Congress needs to know whom to hold accountable. Ordinarily it is the agency head and senior officers confirmed by the Senate. Under the administration's plan, unfortunately, determining who will be in charge of MCC policy may prove difficult. President Bush has proposed giving the MCC a board of directors, chaired by the secretary of state and composed of other cabinet-level officers, and also a chief executive officer responsible for general management. To whom would Congress turn when it has questions? The CEO would be responsible for implementing policy but would take policy direction from the board. The secretary of state would lead the board but would have little time to devote to its oversight. The president would be responsible ultimately but would not ordinarily be available to appear before Congress to facilitate congressional oversight.

The administration closely examined the Overseas Private Investment Corporation (OPIC) as a possible model for the MCC. OPIC's experience, however, suggests two lessons that are not reflected in the current design. First, the participation of cabinet officials in policy oversight is largely illusory. Cabinet secretaries rarely if ever attend OPIC board meetings, but rather they delegate representation to lower-level officials. Second, a board composed heavily of representatives of other federal agencies is a mixed blessing. Although it brings some useful breadth of perspective, it may also subject the agency to political pressure to help further outside agendas. In contrast, consolidating authority under the chief executive would enhance accountability and help keep the focus of the agency on its own mission.

In this sense the Export-Import Bank (Ex-Im) and OPIC model of combining the role of director and chairman of the board may be better. This structure would make sense regardless of whether Congress chooses to make the MCC an independent agency or merge it with another entity, such as USAID. In either event the head of the MCC should have sufficient authority to make policy and be held accountable.

Congress, in addition, should adjust the composition of the board to ensure balance among valuable diverse perspectives of government agencies, the private sector, nongovernmental organizations, and others. Here OPIC's diverse board provides a useful model. Its representation is split between government appointees serving ex officio and outside directors. Following a similar model, as argued in chapter 6, the MCC board should include executive branch and outside directors in equal numbers with the MCC chairman occupying the final slot. The outside director slots are also important vehicles for ensuring political balance and congressional input. The balance between internal and external representation and the need for bipartisan oversight could be achieved if the majority and ranking minority members of the House and Senate appointed the four external members of the board, as recommended in chapter 6.

STAFF. Congress would be well advised to make sure that the MCC has a sufficiently large and nonpartisan work force to respond to Congress's requests for both general information and rigorous analyses of program performance. The administration has proposed the creation of a lean, short-term work force. The MCC is to have no more than 100 employees, and the staff is expected to stay on for no more than five years without a waiver from the MCC chief executive. The administration contends that this approach will promote efficiency and prevent the creation of an entrenched bureaucracy. Chapter 5 explains why the size of the staff and the implicit cross subsidy from USAID and others on staff support is not optimal from the point of view of the organization itself, in particular with regard to management incentives and evaluating results. On top of this, such a plan would not serve Congress. A thin staff with a high turnover rate is ill suited to respond to Congress's legitimate requests for information on program operations and will have difficulty tracking program performance and maintaining financial accountability.

The president's proposal, furthermore, may raise questions regarding the status of temporary employees. Would these outside staff members receive civil service protections? Would not employing individuals on the payroll of private sector organizations raise questions of conflict of interest? How would these decisions affect which grants receive approval? While there may be merit to the president's proposals on other grounds, the interests of Congress would be served better by a professional staff of a size appropriate to the demands, with a sufficient number employed on a long-term basis to create institutional memory. For some fraction of the staff, civil service protection (or some other form of appointment that makes employment independent of the president or outside organizations with interests other than the MCA) would reduce political pressure on the staff and enhance their accountability to Congress. Indeed all the models considered by the administration as relatively lean and efficient independent agencies (OPIC, Ex-Im, Trade and Development Agency) have civil service staff. (See chapter 6.)

INDEPENDENCE. As President Bush has said, raising living standards in the developing world is key to our long-run security. The MCA should be dedicated to that foreign policy purpose solely and have the independence needed to pursue the mission without political pressure from other executive branch agencies. If the theory of the MCA is to invest only in countries that have adopted sound development policies, then Congress should by statute reserve MCA appropriations for those countries. Without some degree of independence from the State Department and other foreign affairs agencies, the MCC would likely face pressure to make grants relating to the immediate political needs of the executive branch, such as the latest international security crisis or an upcoming presidential visit to a foreign land. MCA grants directed to countries with poor development policies, even if they are key allies in the war on terror or any other major political objective, would only turn the MCA into exactly the type of old-style politically directed economic aid everyone claims they wish to avoid in this context.

This does not mean that the United States should not support key allies regardless of their development policies. One can make a compelling case for high levels of foreign aid allocated according to geostrategic objectives—helping to stabilize economies in transition, regional powers, and failing states, as well as shoring up allies in the wars against terror, drug trafficking, and other ills. Aid of this type is vital to protecting U.S. interests. Now that USAID is under the direction of the secretary of state, moreover, that office has the tools necessary to ensure that non-MCA aid advances our broad foreign policy interests apart from international development. Congress should appropriate sufficient geostrategic foreign aid to meet our foreign policy objectives. The MCA, however, should be reserved for its stated purpose—supporting growth, poverty reduction, and sustainable development in poor nations with sound policy and good governance.

Congress can enhance the independence of the MCA in a variety of specific ways. First, it could designate the MCA a true independent agency, thus ensuring that current ethics prohibitions on White House personnel lobbying independent agencies would apply to the MCA. Second, Congress could define the agency's mandate narrowly to leave the MCC and the president little opportunity to divert MCA funds for strategic foreign policy purposes. Third, Congress could make sure the MCA focuses on the poorest nations with sound policy environments rather than middle-income countries, which tend to be of greater strategic importance to the United States. (See chapter 3 for a full discussion of income-related eligibility criteria and chapter 9 for a discussion of the current aid status of lower-middle-income countries likely to be eligible for the MCA under the administration's plan.)

MONITORING AND EVALUATION. Congress has a strong interest in ensuring that MCA appropriations are used wisely. Because the MCA will make grants (rather than manage projects), monitoring program expenditures to ensure financial accountability and evaluating program performance to improve future grant making will prove vital. To make the MCC accountable on these points, Congress should give considerable attention to the agency's capacity to monitor and evaluate grants. Congress should mandate that the MCC adopt the very best practices learned in the private sector, as outlined more fully in chapter 5. Moreover Congress could mandate that the General Accounting Office also play a role in monitoring and evaluation, including by regularly assessing MCC operations and auditing grants above a specific dollar amount.

Transparency

"Sunshine is the best disinfectant," as Justice Louis Brandeis's frequently quoted maxim maintains.[12] Transparency in decisionmaking leads to accountability. Making the MCC highly transparent is perhaps the single best way for Congress to enhance its accountability and strengthen congressional oversight. Congress, more than any other institution or private party, has standing to question executive branch actions, can compel disclosure of pertinent facts, and is a forum for public debate about U.S. policy. But Congress's effectiveness in serving as a check-and-balance to the executive branch on the MCA will depend on the quality of the information it receives. To know whether the MCC is doing its job well, Congress should require the MCC to prepare the following:

—A periodic strategy paper timed to coincide with the debate on the multiyear reauthorization of the MCA, which is recommended in the next section. The paper would spell out the administration's funding priorities for future years. The report would signal publicly substantive areas where the MCC has a strong interest in providing funding (health or education, for example). Congress would then take these priorities into account as it formulates the MCA's new authorizing legislation. Developing countries, in turn, would be able to submit grants with advanced understanding of U.S. funding priorities. The strategy paper would also provide a comprehensive retrospective analysis of the effectiveness of past MCA funding in achieving the development goals for which funding was provided.

—An annual report that provides the following: an explanation of how the most recent country eligibility decisions were made; an accounting of all MCA obligations and expenditures during the prior fiscal year; country-by-country analysis of results, with in-depth examination of the largest MCA grants and recipients; and analysis of effects on global issues, including democracy promotion, rule of law, respect for human rights, education, health, and the environment.

In addition to these regular reports, Congress should require notification in advance when the MCC intends to take certain types of actions. For the reasons described in box 8-2, above, executive branch obligations to notify Congress in advance of agency action empower members of Congress to request that the administration "hold" pending consultation with Congress. The executive branch almost always honors these hold requests, even when they create indefinite delay. Because of the uncertainty created by the ever-present risk of congressional holds and the ability of a lone member of Congress to trump the president's foreign aid policies, advance notification provisions should be used only sparingly. Congress would have a compelling interest when the administration intends to do any of the following:

—Approve a particularly large-scale funding proposal (either on an absolute basis or as a share of a recipient's budget).

—Approve a proposal for a project that falls into a statutorily defined category of highly sensitive areas. This category should be adopted as part of the MCA's authorizing legislation. It could include projects that are in particular countries of concern (as determined by statute) or that could have significant adverse effects on certain disadvantaged populations (such as ethnic or religious minorities) or the environment.

—Deviate significantly from its previously reported funding priorities (as reflected in the above-referenced strategy paper).

Public Participation

Congress should also require the MCC to seek public participation in its decisionmaking. The executive branch is sometimes required by statute to seek public participation through cumbersome procedures that include *Federal Register* notices and official advisory committees subject to open hearing requirements in the Federal Advisory Committee Act. The Bush administration's commitment to post all MCA grant proposals on the web for public comment, in contrast, would help disseminate information broadly through efficient information technologies. Imposing additional public disclosure obligations may not prove necessary.

Public disclosure alone, however, would not be enough to ensure effective public participation. Web-based disclosure should occur during MCA consideration of grant proposals (at least sixty days) to ensure that the public has time to submit relevant information for the consideration of decisionmakers. At the conclusion of this period, in addition, the MCC should be required to disclose the general tenor and weight of public sentiment. Doing so would help guide Congress in future policy consultations with the MCC. Codifying these public participation provisions in the MCA authorizing act would not only enhance the public accountability of the MCC but also Congress's ability to hear from outside groups when the MCC may be going astray. Giving the public a stake in the MCC would have the added benefit of enhancing public support for the MCA.

Policy Deference

For an effective partnership, Congress must have assurance that the MCC will follow its policy lead. Congress has traditionally employed many tools to promote policy deference on foreign aid (as described in the boxes above) which sometimes have had the mostly unintended consequences of making foreign assistance programs cumbersome and often unresponsive to local needs or conditions. It is noteworthy that Congress has not deployed one of its most powerful mechanisms for exerting policy control—authorizing legislation—for nearly two decades. One of the central recommendations of this chapter is that Congress should authorize the MCC for a limited term and then exercise its powers through regular reauthorizations to provide up-to-date policy guidance and limit the executive branch's discretion to use the MCA to achieve short-term political objectives.

Here again, as for the governance structure and staffing recommendations above, Ex-Im and OPIC are useful analogies, although not perfect, because their missions are somewhat simpler than the MCA. Both operate under renewable mandates that are subject to a regular four-year authorization cycle. Most observers would agree that the appropriations process for these agencies has typically been less encumbered than it has been for USAID, at least in part because there is regular policy oversight through the authorization process.

Congress should authorize the MCC for a limited term. The length of the term should balance the need for congressional review to make adjustments to the MCC, especially in its early years, with the need to provide stable incentives for countries that are working to achieve eligibility. These considerations argue for a six-year reauthorization cycle initially. (Congress recently extended the reauthorization cycle for OPIC and Ex-Im from three years to four years.) To ensure policy deference, the authorization process should do the following:

—Define a narrow mission for the agency that would bar it from taking immediate foreign policy considerations into account, just as Ex-Im is required to make funding decisions based solely on commercial criteria.[13]

—Spell out in general terms political factors (such as respect for human rights) that must be met for a government to receive funding. One approach would be to incorporate the basic conditions on assistance from the Foreign Assistance Act, as the administration has proposed.

—Set out broad principles for the country selection criteria and require the president both to adopt regulations for implementing them and to follow predetermined procedures for subsequently adjusting implementation in order to create stable incentives and discourage political manipulation.

—Require the president to apply eligibility criteria universally.

—Require the president to adopt regulations laying out standard procedures for the review of grant proposals.

A Coherent Mission

What the MCA needs from Congress most of all is a clear mission statement. Existing aid agencies are handicapped by a multitude of often competing objectives. One never knows whether to judge USAID, for example, by whether its programs support key political allies, respond to humanitarian disasters, foster democracy, promote U.S. grain exports, or alleviate poverty. Because most USAID programs are meant to achieve a number of these objectives simultaneously, it is not surprising that they sometimes fail to achieve much in any one area. Given the enormous importance of political factors (terrorism, counternarcotics, nonproliferation) in allocating funds managed by USAID, the agency itself hardly knows how to judge its performance.

The MCA needs to be different. The executive branch needs a clear, coherent, and achievable mission. That mission should be to support growth, poverty reduction, and sustainable development in poor nations with a demonstrated record of sound policy, social investment, and good governance by underwriting meritorious strategies designed and implemented by recipients. It will be up to Congress, initially, to define that mission in the MCA authorizing bill. The mission of the MCA must be narrow enough for Congress to have confidence that the MCC will follow its policy lead. In addition Congress should renew the MCA's mandate through regular, limited authorization acts, as recommended above.

Congress can enhance the deference of the MCC by limiting the agency's authority to depart from a well-defined statutory scheme. But before focusing on the perils of excessive agency discretion, it is worth acknowledging that some discretion is necessary and desirable. Explicitly granting the president unlimited authority to reject grant proposals would enhance aid effectiveness. No country has a right to U.S. assistance. The executive branch should have the authority to deny U.S. funding to any nation for any project, unless explicitly directed by statute. Binding the president's hands would undercut our ability to respond to changed international circumstances (such as armed conflict) or matters of concern to the United States (such as terrorism).

Extensive agency discretion to approve funding for otherwise ineligible countries or projects, however, would risk making the MCC unaccountable to the policy preferences of Congress. Without appropriate checks, the executive branch could seek to use the MCA as a tool to achieve short-term political objectives in violation of the MCA's objective of investing only in countries with sound policy environments and well-designed proposals. To guard against this risk, Congress should define the agency's mandate as narrowly as possible. Just as Ex-Im is required to make funding decisions based solely on commercial criteria, the MCA should be required to approve projects only if they would contribute to growth, poverty reduction, and sustainable development.[14] If additional funds are required for humanitarian, security, and other politically driven assistance, they should be appropriated separately. Adding these objectives to the MCA would condemn the initiative to policy incoherence and failure. It would be merely the latest version of the old economic aid paradigm.

To flesh out the MCA's mission and give it substance, Congress should enact a durable set of statutory requirements to guide grant making. These requirements should be reviewed and renewed as part of the multiyear authorization process. Congress should legislate in broad terms. For instance it should define the basic conditions for MCA eligibility (for example, whether or not democracy should be considered in determining eligibility) but then should leave it to the MCC to select the indicators that determine whether a country satisfies the conditions. Congress should require that these indicators be adopted by the MCC as formal regulations, so as to ensure consistency and clear, objective application. Congress, for example, could prohibit assistance to corrupt governments but leave to the MCC the discretion to determine how Transparency International's rankings should be taken into account when applying the corruption condition. This approach would mirror how Congress treats domestic regulatory agencies and, because regulations can be altered more easily than statutes, allow the MCC to fine-tune the eligibility indicators with experience. Congress would be able to judge whether MCA regulations were consistent with statutory guidance through regular reporting requirements and could, when necessary, override agency decisions in authorizing legislation.

Operational Flexibility

Congressional interests would be well served by giving the MCC the operational flexibility necessary to achieve the MCA's statutory objectives. The central logic of the MCA—a demand-driven, grant-making entity protected from political interests and committed to support the best proposals—necessitates an entirely new approach to foreign aid appropriations, in some respects more akin to OPIC and Ex-Im than to USAID.[15] Moreover if Congress allows itself to be drawn into overseeing the minutiae of funding decisions, the MCC will lack the authority to run an efficient and coherent program. Differences on operational detail will crowd out any serious discussions of policy between Congress and the president.

The MCA simply will not work as envisioned unless Congress avoids the temptation to earmark funds, tie aid, create extraneous political litmus tests, micromanage expenditures, elaborate funding directives, and impose inflexible procedural requirements.[16] We fully recognize that it is much easier to recommend this forbearance in principle than to achieve it in practice, as demonstrated by the past two decades of foreign aid reform efforts—many initiated by Congress—and many of which have failed, as described in box 8-3. As shown in table 8-1, bilateral development assistance and politically allocated economic assistance are heavily earmarked, affecting over half the funds, whereas disaster and transition assistance is much less encumbered. How these practices have worked in the past and why they would undercut the MCA are described, respectively, in the boxes above and in chapter 6. Here we explain why Congress itself might find these practices counterproductive in overseeing the MCA.

Earmarking and Tied Aid

The MCA is supposed to fund the best proposals from qualifying donor countries on a competitive, demand-driven basis. It should be self-evident that the MCC cannot make grants on the basis of a legitimate, genuine competition among recipient-designated proposals if Congress decides ahead of time which types of proposals or countries shall receive U.S. support or what types of entities (small businesses, American companies) will carry out the proposed grants. Earmarks and tied aid are inconsistent with allocating grants on the basis of demand and competition. Moreover they would undercut the beneficial effects of MCA grants in poor countries. Countries with earmarks would have little incentive to submit high-quality proposals. Countries without earmarks and countries that did not qualify for the MCA would have reduced incentives to make needed policy reforms because they would know that few MCA funds were genuinely open for competition. As described in chapters 4 and 5, an integral part of the MCA's design is that recipient governments over time should build capacity for developing grant proposals and bidding out for implementation and delivery, which would be impossible under strict interpretations of existing contracting and procurement regulations. Specific considerations regarding directing aid through contracting and procurement rules are discussed below.

Extraneous Political Litmus Tests

The MCA will be much less effective as a means of encouraging development reforms if Congress chooses to use MCA monies to leverage unrelated policy changes that have little to do with development and poverty

Box 8-3. *Foreign Aid Reform Efforts over the Past Two Decades*

The Hamilton-Gilman report. In 1989 the breakup of the Soviet Union spurred calls on Capitol Hill to reform aid policy. Representatives Lee Hamilton (D-Indiana) and Ben Gilman (R-New York), who chair a House Foreign Affairs Committee task force, declared the Foreign Assistance Act obsolete. Their report recommends fewer objectives and congressional restrictions (earmarks, tied aid, conditions, prohibitions).[1] Although the Hamilton-Gilman report was written into legislation that passed the House twice, it was not taken up by the Senate. The first Bush administration proposed its own reforms, but a variety of groups argued for the status quo, and neither reforms nor an authorization act was passed that year.

The Ferris Commission. In 1992, the final year of the George Bush administration, congressional displeasure with USAID and critical reports on the agency from the General Accounting Office led Congress to establish a commission to look into foreign aid.[2] The commission, chaired by George M. Ferris Jr., called for reducing the number of objectives of foreign aid, scrapping the Foreign Assistance Act, integrating AID into the State Department, and reorganizing its programs by function (such as humanitarian assistance) rather than geographic area. The Bush administration countered with its own reforms, and by the spring of 1992 attention had shifted from foreign aid to the upcoming presidential elections.

Foreign aid summit. Before January 1993 two other reform studies were conducted, one by the Carnegie Endowment for International Peace (chaired by Ambassador Richard Holbrooke) and the other by the State Department itself.[3] The new administration launched three new studies of foreign aid, one by the State Department, one by the National Security Council, and one by the National Performance Review Task Force (Vice President Gore's "reinventing gov-

reduction. While U.S. taxpayer funds should not support governments that actively undermine U.S. national interests, we should not use MCA funds to press poor nations to adopt a U.S. approach to unrelated issues that are largely domestic in nature. Congress should outline certain minimum political conditions (such as those already in the Foreign Assistance Act)

ernment" task force). These studies suggest focusing aid more on global concerns, such as the environment and health, and less on particular countries. In September 1993 Lee Hamilton convened a "foreign aid summit" attended by most of the major players in the debate, including congressional leadership and Secretary of State Warren Christopher. Despite consensus in 1994 to push for aid reform, domestic issues held center stage, and the midterm election in November (the "Gingrich revolution") brought new leadership to Capitol Hill.

AID subordination to the State Department. In April 1997 President Clinton announced that he favored integrating AID into the State Department in order to secure support for the administration's foreign affairs agenda, in particular to prevail over Senate Foreign Relations Committee Chair Jesse Helms. The idea, but not the specific form of a merger, was enacted into law a year later.[4] In December 1998, however, under pressure from Senator Helms to abolish AID, the Clinton administration struck a bargain with Senator Helms. USAID survived and maintained its mission, substantive goals, basic authorities, and development programs, but the director of AID had to report to the secretary of state, starting on April 1, 1999.

1. Report of the Task Force on Foreign Assistance, to the Committee on Foreign Affairs, U.S. House of Representatives, February 1, 1989 (see pages 22–49).

2. Commission on the Management of the Agency for International Development Programs, Fiscal Year 1991 Foreign Operations Appropriations Act, P.L. 101-513, sec. 557, November 1990.

3. "Memorandum to the President-Elect: Harnessing Process to Purpose," Carnegie Endowment for International Peace, 1992. "State 2000: A New Model for Managing Foreign Affairs," Department of State, 1992.

4. Foreign Affairs Reform and Restructuring Act of 1998, P.L. 105-277, div. G.

and then leave it to the MCC, in consultation with Congress, to weigh, on a case-by-case basis, whether other political criteria should disqualify a particular country or proposal. Otherwise the appropriations and authorization acts for the MCA will become a constant fight among single-issue special interests seeking leverage over other governments.

Table 8-1. *Earmarks in Bilateral Assistance Administered by USAID, Fiscal Year 2003*

Categories of assistance	*Assistance (millions of dollars)*	*Earmarks (percent)*[a]	
		Hard	*Soft*
Bilateral development aid	$3,226	3.3	52.3
Child survival and health programs	1,837	0.3	71.4
Development assistance	1,389	7.2	27.1
Humanitarian assistance	280	0.0	21.4
International disaster assistance	230	0.0	26.1
Transition initiatives	50	0.0	0.0
Politically allocated economic assistance	3,605	41.2	9.7
Development credit authority	25	0.0	0.0
Economic support fund	2,270	59.5	11.7
International Fund for Ireland	25	100.0	0.0
Assistance for Eastern Europe and the Baltic States (SEED Act)	525	1.0	0.6
Assistance for the independent states of the former Soviet Union (Freedom Act)	760	14.3	10.7
Total or average	14,220	18.9	19.3

Source: Adapted from Omnibus Appropriations Act for fiscal year 2003, P.L.108-7, Div. E—Foreign Operations, Export Financing, and Related Programs Appropriations.

a. Soft earmarks use the language "should" or "not," while hard earmarks use "shall" or "must be."

Advance Notifications

The MCA will need the flexibility to approve and disburse grants quickly and efficiently. The Congress will be tempted to require the MCA to notify it in advance of every action that could potentially prove of interest to Congress and then wait before proceeding (see box 8-2). So-called wait-and-see notification provisions, which also apply to agency decisions to reprogram funds (shift them from one purpose to another), enable individual members of Congress to essentially veto agency actions through procedural delay. While regular reporting and timely notification are essential for Congress to oversee the MCA, Congress should not make routine MCA grant decisions subject to advance congressional notification. Doing so would put Congress in the business of reviewing specific routine grants rather than remaining engaged on high-level policy. This is the wrong approach and would turn the MCC into a slow, inefficient grant-making version of USAID. If the proposal to establish the MCC outside USAID was intended to enhance flexibility and efficiency, it hardly makes sense to recreate the MCA in USAID's image. The opportunity for genuine reform would be lost.

Procedural requirements that create delay and uncertainty, moreover, increase costs and drive away potential private sector partners. For the MCA to be a nimble entity that can build public-private coalitions, respond to changing international circumstances, and achieve progress on development, Congress should empower it to make routine grant decisions. Congress should then hold the MCA accountable for its decisions through the legislative process. Congress may wish to create a small exception to this rule by requiring advance notification of certain particularly large projects or projects in countries of particular political interest to Congress, as suggested above in the discussion of accountability.

Contracting and Procurement

The MCC will need Congress to design new rules for contracting and procuring goods and services. This is true for several reasons. First, by retaining too much operational authority in the hands of the MCC and American contractors, we would reinforce donor dependency and undercut a central mission of the MCA: building up the capacity of recipients so as to encourage graduation. Second, existing practices concerning contracting and procurement have made U.S. aid programs inflexible, slow, and bureaucratic, as discussed in chapter 6. Part of the problem has been that these rules, designed by Congress initially for domestic agencies, do not take into sufficient account the realities of international operations. USAID also has contributed to the problem by interpreting existing requirements in a cumbersome and overly broad manner, in part for fear of congressional criticism for not taking seriously enough obligations to contract fairly and buy American products. To succeed, the MCC requires a fresh start. If the MCA will be authorized within the confines of the Foreign Assistance Act, the MCC should have the authority to operate "notwithstanding" provisions of that act, as the Bush administration has proposed. Alternatively Congress could adopt new waiver procedures that would streamline agency contracting and procurement.

No-Year Money

The MCC will need the flexibility to say no to unmeritorious grant proposals without jeopardizing its appropriations. Congress's general practice in foreign aid requires agencies to return monies unused by the conclusion of the fiscal year to the U.S. Treasury. This would be fundamentally at odds with the demand-driven, competitively allocated logic of the MCA. As it currently operates, this practice creates a perverse incentive for aid agencies to spend cash on hand as the new fiscal year approaches. These late year expenditures are often not in furtherance of the agency's highest priorities but are in areas where the agency can rapidly spend monies appropriated to them. To break this cycle of poor decisionmaking, Congress should create positive incentives for the MCC to wait for worthy funding proposals. The best way to achieve this would be to allow appropriations for the MCC to remain valid for several years. If the MCC builds up an excessive unused reserve, Congress could reduce future year funding, as it currently does with Ex-Im. Appropriations of this type are generally referred to as no-year funds because they do not need to be spent within the given fiscal year. Congress has been reluctant in the past to appropriate no-year funds because of the desire to keep foreign aid agencies accountable. But the recommendations above regarding congressional input into the governing structure of the MCC board, limited term authorization acts, and the annual appropriations process should provide meaningful alternative oversight mechanisms. Further accountability could be achieved through broad strictures on the amount of excess reserves that could be transferred from one year to the next or by requiring all appropriated funds to be used within a several-year horizon (for example, four-year money).

The Political Compromise

The new partnership between the legislative and executive branches suggested above would maintain the political balance of power on foreign aid. The executive branch would give Congress a larger voice in setting aid policy by making itself fully accountable to Congress. In return the executive branch would receive a clear mandate and operational flexibility for the MCA. Congress, for its part, would pull back from day-to-day monitoring of aid spending and in return would set overarching development policy and oversee the effectiveness of U.S. aid. The new political compromise would maintain the standing of each political branch of government, while also enhancing the efficacy of U.S. aid programs.

Congress, with the agreement of the president, should enshrine the principles behind this new compromise into law. The authorizing act for the MCA should state explicitly not only the policy objectives of the MCC but also the envisioned relationship between the MCC and Congress. By codifying the roles and expectations of each branch of government, Congress and the president would lay down markers about how they will act. The principles would also strengthen the hand of MCA champions, who could seek to enforce the political bargain down the road.

How durable would this political compromise prove? As with most political arrangements between the president and Congress, its success would depend on goodwill and personal relationships. Congress cannot make a law that it cannot change with the very next law. At any time Congress could pass legislation that violates the spirit of the MCA. Short of the Constitution and judicial review, there is no formal restraint on Congress other than the president's veto power. Similarly any president who wishes to minimize the role of Congress can seek to do so by interpreting the laws with bias. Reporting can be minimized. Obligations to notify and consult with Congress can be made hollow by ignoring the wishes of the legislature. The durability of the political compromise suggested here, as with any political pact, will depend on people as well as process. The thesis of this chapter, however, is that fundamental design decisions could also make a difference.

Conclusion

By following the recommendations presented above, Congress and the president can help make the MCC accountable and effective and thereby create a dynamic new partnership on foreign aid policy. Congress will have an enormous role in designing, funding, overseeing, and altering the MCA. Congress has shown historically its desire and capacity to influence foreign aid policy, and it has employed with increasing frequency and effectiveness a variety of legislative mechanisms to consolidate its control. Similarly the executive branch has proven that it cannot implement foreign aid laws effectively without clear mandates and operational flexibility. Failures in past aid programs have demonstrated repeatedly the high cost of poor cooperation and mistrust between Congress and the president.

The MCA provides a historic opportunity to correct the errors of the past. Almost every aspect of how the MCA works will differ from how aid agencies do business under current laws. For this new approach to succeed, however, the president and Congress will need to develop a new aid relationship. In drafting the MCA authorization bill, Congress should give great attention to program design decisions that will affect the accountability of the MCC. Congress should focus on and maintain input into how the agency is governed (its management, staff, independence, and monitoring and evaluation of grants), as well as the transparency of and public participation in the agency's decisionmaking. It should command policy deference by giving the MCC a limited term and by requiring a regular reauthorization process that reviews the principles governing country selection and program coverage. And Congress should give the MCC a narrow and clear mandate without regard to other foreign policy goals, just as has been done with other independent foreign affairs agencies. Congress also should grant the president significant operational flexibility to ensure that the MCC is responsive, efficient, and effective. Certain of Congress's historic practices on foreign aid—including earmarking and tying aid, as well as inflexible procurement and contracting rules and extraneous political litmus tests—would be fundamentally incompatible with the demand-driven, competitive, grant-making logic of the MCA and its envisioned method of operation.

If Congress gives careful attention to the initial design of the MCA, it will have ample opportunity to influence MCA policy under this new approach. A new partnership built on accountability, policy deference, a narrow, coherent mission, and operational flexibility would maintain the balance of power between Congress and the executive branch. Forging this new political compromise, however, will be difficult, as few legislative guarantees exist. Success will depend on the good faith of both branches of government. The first step is for Congress and the president to enact and approve authorizing legislation that reflects the spirit of this new potential partnership.

To help Congress and the president define the terms of the new partnership that is needed for the MCA, the president should quickly designate a personal adviser who could represent the administration before Congress in crafting the MCA legislation. The president could consider announcing that this individual would be his likely nominee to be the CEO of the MCC, should Congress approve the creation of the agency.

Summary of Recommendations

To enhance accountability, Congress should give the MCC the following:

—a strong agency head fully accountable for policy, with a seat on and preferably[17] leadership of the board of directors;

—a board of directors balanced between administration representatives and outside members, who should be selected with input from Congress;

—an adequate, stable professional staff;

—independent agency status;

—the very best monitoring and evaluation procedures;

—obligations to report regularly on priorities, expenditures, and performance, timed to coincide with reauthorization;

—a duty to notify Congress in advance in extraordinary circumstances, such as grants of an unusually large size;

—obligations to solicit public participation through web postings and solicitation of comments.

To ensure policy deference, Congress should authorize the MCC for a limited term and exercise oversight thereafter through a regular and rigorous reauthorization process that would do the following:

—define a narrow mission, largely free from immediate foreign policy considerations, with the exception of limited political factors that would be disqualifying;

—set out principles for the country selection criteria and require the president to adopt regulations for implementing or modifying them;

—set out principles regarding program areas and entities eligible to compete for funds and require the president to adopt regulations laying out standard procedures for the review of grant proposals.

For a clear mission, Congress should give the MCC the following:

—a mandate to support growth, poverty reduction, and sustainable development in poor nations with sound policy and good governance;

—a limited and durable set of legislative prohibitions on certain kinds of assistance;

—clear statutory standards for judging country eligibility that are applied universally;

—uniform procedures for reviewing grants that are followed consistently;

To afford operational flexibility, Congress should do the following:

—appropriate funds free of earmarks or ties, to the extent practicable;

—appropriate no-year funds;

—exempt the MCC from contracting and procurement rules (or enact new waiver procedures);

—avoid advance notification requirements for routine grant decisions.

9

Funding the Millennium Challenge Account

Last but not least, we come to the issue of money. This chapter assesses the projected budget for the Millennium Challenge Account. It starts by placing the proposed MCA funding in context by considering broader trends in the U.S. budget for foreign assistance and the allocation between development assistance and other types of foreign aid. The MCA is sizable in relation to current levels of U.S. development assistance and the combined income of the select group of initially eligible countries, but, even with full funding of the MCA, U.S. official aid would be small compared to aid from other donors, as a share of income and relative to the overall cost of addressing global poverty. Even so, lawmakers will find it challenging to make room for MCA funding while also addressing the administration's new pledges for HIV/AIDS and the likelihood of vast new aid demands to reward allies and reconstruct war-torn countries in the current grim budget environment.[1]

As a presidential initiative, the MCA is likely to receive special treatment in the budget process. Even so, given budget pressures, the administration has already scaled back its initial MCA request to Congress, and it is extremely unlikely it will reach $5 billion in the promised three years—or perhaps ever. There is an even greater danger that the less prominent and less popular development aid programs administered by USAID will be progressively squeezed over time even though the need is as great as ever, due to a combination of budget pressures and deterioration in the beneficiary pool, as the best performers move to the MCA. A second danger is that the expanding geopolitical calls on aid, together with the expansion of the MCA to lower-middle-income countries, could conspire to make the MCA the lead fund not just for the best performers but also for politically important countries.

U.S. Foreign Assistance in Context

To assess the significance of the proposed size of the MCA, it is helpful to start with overall trends in U.S. foreign assistance, and in particular in foreign economic assistance, excluding security assistance. Looking back over the past four decades, it is clear that U.S. foreign assistance has been closely connected to national security priorities and especially the cold war and developments in the Middle East. The end of the anticommunist imperative associated with the cold war, deep disillusionment with aid's many failures, and the drive to balance the budget produced a slash-and-burn approach to U.S. economic aid during the 1990s. As a result U.S. foreign economic assistance fell in absolute terms and as a share of the budget, from $15 billion (in 2003 dollars), or over 3 percent of total outlays in 1962, at the time of the Cuban missile crisis, to $11 billion, or just over 0.5 percent, in the early 2000s (see table 9-1). During that time, the new democracies of Eastern Europe and the newly independent states of the former Soviet Union for the first time were allocated a large share of the shrinking pie.

The declining share of U.S. income devoted to aid has provoked a growing chorus of criticism from abroad and particularly from Europe. European officials have repeatedly attempted to negotiate binding minimum commitments on aid levels at the Organization for Economic Cooperation and Development (OECD) well in excess of current U.S. levels. The United States spends 0.1 percent of GDP on development aid, compared with 0.33 percent for the European Union. More broadly, although the United States is one of the top two donors in absolute terms (Japan is the other), it compares poorly with other industrial countries when assistance is measured as a share of national income, as shown in figure 9-1. Similarly, on a per capita basis, U.S. foreign aid spending of $34 per year is only about half the industrial country average of $67.[2]

Table 9-1. *Trends in U.S. Foreign Economic Assistance, 1962–2002*[a]

Years	*Economic aid (billions of 2003 dollars)*	*Economic aid as a share of GDP (percent)*	*Economic aid as a share of budget outlays (percent)*
1962–69	15.55	0.44	2.36
1970–79	10.87	0.21	1.07
1980–89	13.64	0.20	0.92
1990–99	12.33	0.14	0.68
2000–03	11.45	0.11	0.57

Source: Authors' calculations based on Isaac Shapiro and Nancy Birdsall, "How Does the Proposed Level of Foreign Economic Aid under the Bush Budget Compare with Historical Levels, and What Would Be the Effects of Bush's New 'Millennium Challenge Account'?" Center on Budget and Policy Priorities and Center for Global Development, March 20, 2002.

a. Figures represent the average over the given time period. Economic aid here corresponds to the categories development aid, politically allocated economic assistance, and humanitarian assistance, as used in table 9-2. For a detailed explanation of differences between pre-1992 data and recent data, see Isaac Shapiro, "As a Share of the Economy and the Budget, U.S. Development and Humanitarian Aid Would Drop to Post–WWII Lows in 2002," Center on Budget and Policy Priorities, June 18, 2001.

The OECD definition of official development assistance (ODA) includes all assistance that has a developmental impact, regardless of the intended purpose or eligibility criteria. By this definition, which requires a threshold grant element and is confined to lower- and middle-income countries, the United States disbursed roughly $9.5 billion in ODA in 2001, including strategically directed assistance to Egypt and humanitarian assistance.

Of course American officials defend the record on aid by noting the important contribution made to growth and poverty reduction by the U.S. private sector through imports, direct investment, remittances, and transfers from U.S. businesses and charitable organizations. They further note that the United States shoulders a much larger share of the burden on maintaining global peace and stability through defense expenditures.[3]

Public Support for Foreign Aid

The transatlantic divergence on official foreign aid reflects deep cultural differences that are also evident in transatlantic disparities on domestic social safety nets and the relative roles of the public and private sectors in the provision of social insurance. Polling finds consistently that Americans

Figure 9-1. *Foreign Assistance, United States and Other OECD Countries, 2000*

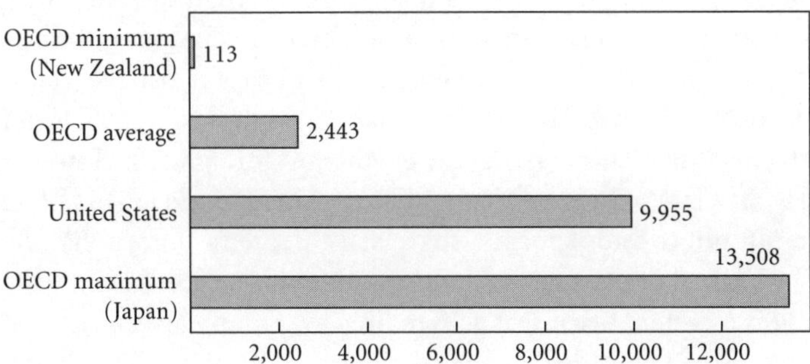

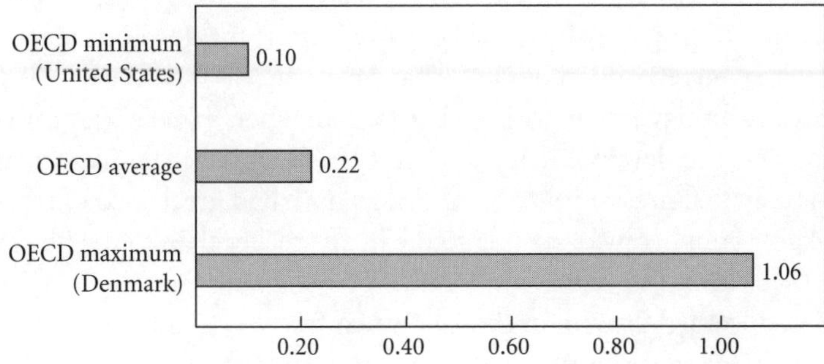

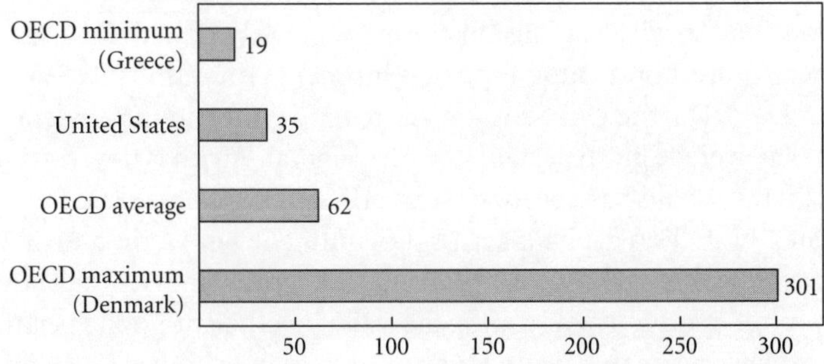

Source: Jean-Claude Faure, "Development Co-Operation, 2001 Report," *Organization for Economic Cooperation and Development DAC Journal,* vol. 3, no. 1 (2002), pp. 200, 201, 207. Data on official development assistance per capita converted into 2001 dollars using Organization for Economic Cooperation and Development, Development Assistance Committee deflators.

believe that too much money is spent on foreign aid. Yet the same polls reveal an interesting paradox that is also robust. Americans feel that the appropriate amount of foreign aid is far higher than the amount the U.S. actually spends. For instance, a 2001 poll by the Program on International Policy Attitudes found that 61 percent of Americans believe that the U.S. spends too much on foreign aid, and that the average American believes that 24 percent of the federal budget is devoted to foreign aid. However, when asked what share of the budget should be devoted to foreign aid, the average American put the appropriate share at 14 percent—more than fourteen times the actual current level.[4] Polling also finds that Americans believe foreign aid is misspent because it goes mainly to corrupt governments and that poor people benefit little. As shown below, it is true that a large share of U.S. economic aid is allocated to strategic allies for foreign policy reasons and is not based on economic performance.[5] Moreover Americans have other spending priorities. Poverty alleviation abroad takes a back seat to using available funds at home for education, health care, or tax cuts.

But the polling may be missing some important developments. When faced with concrete and immediate challenges, such as famine and HIV/AIDS, Americans display much greater charity than when asked about foreign aid and longer-term development and poverty in the abstract. Similarly it appears anecdotally that grass-roots organizations have had great success recently in mobilizing support by "speaking to the heart" rather than to the head, which is the focus of most polling.

Indeed toward the end of the 1990s two forces began to turn the tide on foreign aid for the poorest countries. First, the global scourge of HIV/AIDS, which claimed over three million lives in 2002 alone, has made the case for foreign assistance that much more urgent. The disease costs not only the lives of those infected but also undermines the effectiveness of all development efforts. The HIV/AIDS pandemic threatens to reverse the impressive gains on child survival and health, life expectancy, productivity, and literacy that heretofore stood among the development community's clearest successes.[6] UNAIDS, the United Nations agency devoted to the epidemic, estimates that average life expectancy in sub-Saharan Africa is now fifteen years lower than it would have been without HIV/AIDS.[7] The disease has already generated 11 million orphans across the continent, with estimates of 25 million by the end of the decade.[8] HIV/AIDS has also undermined advances in economic productivity, straining already insufficient public health budgets and leaving both private and public sector employers struggling to hire and train replacements for dying and debilitated workers. The disease has disproportionately afflicted the regions of the world least able to shoulder the enormous financial and institutional burden associated with preventing and treating the disease, with sub-Saharan Africa, the world's poorest region, showing the highest prevalence rates.[9]

Second, and related, aid activists have developed a powerful four-part recipe for mobilizing public support for assistance to poor countries:[10] the adoption of a simple and compelling goal, champions with tremendous name recognition, coalitions that transcend national borders and include opposite ends of the political spectrum, and a focus on high-profile international gatherings. The first big victory came in 1998, when the global rock star Bono of U2 made common cause with the pope in persuading leaders of the richest nations to adopt an unprecedented initiative to forgive the debt of the poorest nations. A similarly eclectic coalition, including Bill Gates and some of the economics profession's best and brightest, has helped rivet world attention on the HIV/AIDS pandemic and other infectious diseases. Efforts have also been launched to mobilize support for achieving universal primary education and for the millennium development goals more generally. The year 2000 marked a turning point: Even as U.S. budget authority for development aid fell overall, President Clinton received congressional authorization for nearly $1 billion for debt forgiveness and the global fight against HIV/AIDS. The numbers have been increasing ever since.[11]

Foreign Assistance: A Servant to Two Masters

To assess the relative size of the MCA, it is important to locate it within the U.S. budget for foreign assistance. Most analysis of U.S. economic aid trends, including the section above, remains at a high level of aggregation. Too often U.S. economic assistance is equated with development assistance, which has contributed greatly to the discrediting of aid. In reality, as explained in chapter 7, much of what is considered economic assistance in the U.S. budget, such as the economic support fund (ESF), is allocated according to the logic of national security, rewarding allies, helping to transform former adversaries, and shoring up cooperation on counternarcotics, antiterrorism, and nonproliferation.

It is important to distinguish between the principles guiding the allocation of aid among countries and the purposes on which aid is spent. Most development experts believe that for assistance to have the greatest development impact it must not only be spent on economic development but also be allocated to countries on the basis of their commitment to sound development policies. It turns out that the majority of what is considered economic assistance in the U.S. budget is directed to countries based on political considerations, even though the money itself is used for economic purposes. At most a third of U.S. bilateral economic assistance (and a smaller portion of overall aid) is allocated among countries based on development considerations. This bilateral development aid is divided between the development assistance (DA) and child survival and health (CSH) accounts (which are sometimes combined).

In principle, pure development assistance should be allocated to the investments with the highest marginal value, determined by the extent of need (or the marginal social value) and the policy environment. The multilateral development banks condition development assistance on per capita income levels, with the poorest countries receiving assistance on the easiest terms, conditioned on policy performance.

The MCA would attempt to isolate the highest potential investments by targeting only the best-performing poor countries. In contrast much of existing bilateral U.S. development assistance (DA and CSH) reflects U.S. political and economic objectives as well as assessed needs. And it is not typically conditioned on the policy and institutional environment.

Table 9-2 provides a breakdown of the U.S. budget for foreign aid, referred to as the foreign operations function, or function 150, of the U.S. budget. The OECD's cross-country comparisons of official assistance and most discussions of foreign economic assistance, such as the first section above, include not only the development assistance category but also the categories of politically allocated economic assistance (such as aid to Egypt) and humanitarian assistance shown in the table. (The OECD further subdivides the numbers into official assistance, which includes lower-middle-income countries, and official development assistance, which is confined to low-income countries.) Table 9-2 shows that less than one third of the roughly $18 billion U.S. foreign assistance budget is devoted to development assistance, in the strict sense that both the eligibility criteria and the programmatic impact focus on development, as well as trade and investment support.[12] Of this, slightly more than half, or $3.14 billion, is bilateral development assistance (including child survival and health programs). Another one quarter of aid is directed toward economic ends but is allocated according to political criteria. The remainder is humanitarian assistance and contributions to international organizations as well as noneconomic security assistance, such as financing of military sales.

From these facts, two striking comparisons emerge. First, the proposed $5 billion magnitude of the MCA is nearly double the size of existing U.S.

Table 9-2. *Foreign Assistance in the Foreign Operations Function, Fiscal Year 2003*

Type of assistance	*Appropriation (billions of dollars)*	*Percent of total*	*Lead agency*
Development aid and trade and investment programs	**5.97**	**32.4**	
Development assistance	3.14	17.0	AID
Food aid for development[a]	0.60		State and AID
Multilateral development programs	1.31		Treasury and State
U.S. export, investment programs, Peace Corps, and development foundations	0.92		Independent agencies
Politically allocated economic assistance	**4.77**	**25.9**	
Economic support funds (ESF)	2.27		State and AID
Assistance for Eastern Europe and the Baltic States (SEED)	0.53		State and AID
Assistance for the independent states of the former Soviet Union (FSA)	0.76		State and AID
International narcotics control and law enforcement (INCLE)[b]	0.90		State
Nonproliferation, antiterrorism, demining, and related programs (NADR)[b]	0.31		State
Humanitarian assistance	**1.68**	**9.1**	
Migration and refugee assistance (MRA)	0.79		State
Disaster assistance	0.29		AID
Emergency food aid[a]	0.60		AID
Security assistance	**4.94**	**26.8**	
Foreign military financing (FMF)	4.07		State lead, DoD implementation
International military education and training (IMET)	0.08		State lead, DoD implementation
Peacekeeping operations and international peacekeeping	0.79		State lead, DoD implementation
International organizations and programs	**1.06**	**5.8**	State

Source: P.L. 108-7.

a. Emergency food aid does not include P.L. 480, Title I, programs or section 416(b) surplus commodity programs administered by the Department of Agriculture. Food aid for development and emergency food aid are each estimated as one-half of total P.L. 480, Title II, appropriations.

b. International narcotics control and law enforcement includes funding for the Andean counterdrug initiative. In fact, less than half of the counternarcotics assistance is devoted to development. The remainder, which is devoted to interdiction, may fit better conceptually in the security assistance category, and similarly for the spending on nonproliferation, antiterrorism, demining, and related programs.

Table 9-3. *MCA Resource Transfer, as Share of Recipient Income*

Initially eligible MCA countries[a]	*2001 combined gross national income (billions of 2001 dollars)*	*MCA funding ($5 billion) as share of gross national income (percent)*
Years one and two	169.5	2.9
Year three	151.4	3.3
Total	320.9	1.6

Source: World Bank Country Data.

a. See chapter 3 for list of eligible countries. Totals also include those countries that have been deemed likely to qualify if the median score counts to pass a hurdle.

bilateral development assistance programs. But second, it is clear that the U.S. engages much more heavily in bilateral economic aid for political purposes—with funding nearly twice as high as for development.

The Size of the MCA Relative to the Need

Another way to assess the proposed size of the MCA is to compare likely aid flows against the size of the economies likely to qualify for MCA funding. Table 9-3 compares the size of the MCA with the combined incomes of a group of the most likely recipient countries. Under the boldest scenario, in which the full year-three $5 billion in funding is confined to countries with per capita incomes below $1,435, as recommended in earlier chapters, the MCA would represent a resource transfer of 2.9 percent of combined income. When year-three countries are included in the analysis, the ratio of MCA funds to combined recipient income falls to 1.6 percent.

For purposes of comparison, table 9-4 shows comparable ratios for past recipients of U.S. aid. Aid success stories such as South Korea and Costa Rica for decades received aid flows that were an order of magnitude greater as a share of income. In South Korea foreign aid ranged between 30 and 60 percent of the government budget during the 1950s and was still 8.6 percent of national income in the early 1970s, after strong growth had been achieved.[13] But many countries receiving large amounts of aid have shown mixed and even poor records, like Egypt, Kenya, and Zambia.

A $5 billion per year fund would represent an important but incomplete U.S. down payment on international efforts to promote growth and

Table 9-4. *Foreign Aid as a Percent of Gross National Product, Select U.S. Aid Recipients, 1970–1993*[a]

Country	*1970–74*	*1975–79*	*1980–84*	*1985–89*	*1990–93*
Botswana	36.6	18.2	13.0	11.8	4.3
Costa Rica	3.4	3.8	6.7	9.3	7.0
Egypt	5.6	21.1	12.0	10.9	16.0
Honduras	3.0	4.5	8.7	8.8	7.4
Philippines	4.2	3.9	3.5	5.1	6.9
South Korea[b]	8.6	3.8	1.8	0.6	0.2
Tunisia	7.7	7.3	7.6	7.9	7.2
Zambia	5.1	7.8	10.4	20.2	31.1

Source: Congressional Budget Office, based on data from AID, OECD, and the World Bank (www.cbo.gov/showdoc.cfm?index=8&sequence=5).

a. Data reflect averages for the period shown.

b. South Korea received a substantial amount of foreign aid in the 1950s and 1960s, amounts far in excess of that received since 1970.

sustainable development in poor nations. It would increase the share of U.S. income devoted to ODA from the current 0.10 percent to nearly 0.15 percent, a significant increase but nonetheless well below the OECD average of 0.33 percent and the international target of 0.70 percent. It is also incomplete relative to the assessed need for achieving the eight millennium development goals (MDGs) by 2015 (see chapter 2). This is a particularly pertinent benchmark for purposes of international credibility (if not for policy), because President Bush announced the MCA as the U.S. contribution to the global effort to achieve international goals on growth and poverty reduction with special reference to the MDGs at the UN Conference on Financing for Development in Monterrey, Mexico. The purpose of the summit was ostensibly to secure financing commitments for this global effort, which was estimated at $50 billion in additional aid a year, by an officially appointed group chaired by former Mexican President Ernesto Zedillo and including former U.S. Treasury Secretary Robert Rubin. This would roughly double current annual international aid flows of $53 billion, $30 billion of which goes to the world's poorest nations.[14] Using this figure as a baseline, the annual U.S. share would amount to between $8.5 billion (based on the U.S. share of International Monetary Fund and World Bank capital) and $20.7 billion per year (based on the U.S. share in OECD donor GDP of 41.3 percent).[15] According to the Zedillo group, the additional $50 billion would comprise $12 billion per year to meet the millennium education goals, $20 billion a year to halve poverty, and $10 billion per year to achieve the health targets. The World Health Organization Commission on Macroeconomics and Health puts the price tag on health at double that amount, estimating that it will cost the international community roughly $22 billion by 2007 (or an additional 1 percent of GDP) to reach two-thirds of the population affected by HIV/AIDS and target the major communicable diseases and maternal and perinatal conditions in low-income countries.

Budget Trade-offs

The tension between development and foreign policy is particularly salient because the MCA is being crafted at a time when national security has returned to the forefront of the nation's consciousness to an extent not seen since the cold war. With allocations based solely on economic performance and governance, the MCA would be the closest to a development purist's blueprint for aid that the United States has ever attempted. In many respects the MCA is precisely the sort of fund that development advocates had hoped would emerge as the cold war wound down. Yet paradoxically the MCA, which would be the largest single increase in pure development assistance, was announced in the context of the war against terrorism, a few months after the tragedy of September 11, 2001, with the words: "We fight against poverty because hope is an answer to terror."[16]

Security experts were puzzled by the proposal to sharply increase pure development assistance at a moment of greatly increased need for political funding to reward allies in the antiterrorism coalition, to shore up frontline states, and to stabilize failed states. President Bush made the case for the MCA in terms of the fight against terrorism: "We also work for prosperity and opportunity because they help defeat terror. . . . When governments fail to meet the most basic needs of their people, these failed states can become havens for terror."[17] However, few such countries could in fact meet economic performance and governance tests.

Indeed the administration's decision in November 2002 to expand the pool of eligible countries to include countries with per capita incomes between $1,435 and $2,975 rendered the MCA more suitable for geopolitical objectives, taking development advocates completely by surprise. Although the effects on poverty reduction and growth of including these richer countries can be debated, it is undeniable that this device is essential to bring strategically significant countries such as Jordan and Egypt into the tent. Table 9-5 shows the amount of foreign economic assistance that currently goes to the countries that are most likely to qualify for the MCA in

Table 9-5. *Fiscal Year 2003 Request, U.S. Economic Assistance for MCA-Eligible Countries*
Millions of dollars

	Program[b]				
Country income level[a]	*DA/CSH*	*ESF*	*SEED/FSA*	*INCLE development*	*Total*[c]
Years one and two (percent)	265 (10)	52 (2)	70 (6)	42 (14)	429 (7)
Year three (percent)	68 (2)	250 (11)	28 (2)	0 (0)	346 (5)
All MCA eligible (percent)	333 (12)	302 (13)	98 (8)	42 (14)	775 (12)
All countries, total	2,740	2,290	1,250	291	6,571

Source: State Department, fiscal year 2004, 150 account, budget request tables.

a. Percent indicates total assistance to all countries in each category.

b. Abbreviations are development assistance (DA); child survival and health (CSH); economic support fund (ESF); support for Eastern European Democracy (SEED); Freedom Support Act (FSA); and International Narcotics Control and Law Enforcement (INCLE).

c. Totals include those countries deemed likely to qualify if a median score counts to pass a hurdle.

the first three years. The inclusion of the richer group considerably expands the overlap with existing assistance programs allocated according to political considerations. Year-three countries that could qualify for the MCA account for 11 percent of the geopolitical economic support fund and for $0.35 billion in current aid overall. There is a danger that the MCA will succumb to budget pressures over time, increasingly taking the place of existing politically driven economic aid programs and thereby undermining the strict focus on performance and developmental merit.

With the inclusion of the year-three group, the MCA overlaps with one-eighth of current economic assistance. By themselves, likely MCA poorer countries account for 7 percent of existing assistance, or $0.4 billion, less than one-tenth of promised funding levels. Whether MCA funding would come on top of existing funding for these countries, free up this assistance to be allocated elsewhere, or eventually effectively substitute for this assistance is thus a central issue.

This raises the second danger: that the budgetary squeeze will gradually erode funding for the vast majority of poor countries that are unlikely soon to qualify for the MCA but where poverty remains acute. The deteriorating budget outlook raises the stakes. In the words of former Office of Management and the Budget director Mitch Daniels: “Unexpected new defense and homeland security spending is needed to protect America from new threats. Given these two developments, it is absolutely essential that we set aside business as usual and keep tight control over all other spending."[18] And external events are creating huge new demands on the already overtaxed foreign aid account. In fiscal 2002 terrorism-related demands led to an increase of $3.2 billion in two supplemental budgets. For fiscal 2004 the administration has requested increases in political and economic assistance by $1.77 billion over 2003, and this does not include supplemental funding to cover aid to allies such as Turkey and reconstruction after the war with Iraq, which have been estimated at up to $20 billion a year overall.[19]

Given strong bipartisan support for terrorism-related needs, the HIV/AIDS pandemic, and most likely the MCA, there is an important risk that lower-visibility accounts will get squeezed. Already the administration has proposed cuts for funding for child survival and maternal health programs unrelated to HIV/AIDS to make room for the new priorities.[20] This is consistent with a longer-standing tendency to squeeze foreign aid funding in areas that are key long-run determinants of poverty reduction and growth but have low public salience, such as science and technology, economic reform, agriculture, and primary education.[21] In this context the traditional development assistance account—the main source of U.S. bilateral support for most poor nations—appears particularly vulnerable.

This precise trend is evident in the administration's fiscal 2004 foreign aid request for the following five years. Table 9-6 decomposes the administration's fiscal year 2004 request for fiscal years 2004–2008 into the aid categories discussed above. The administration's request would cut both bilateral development programs, DA and CSH, in real terms by roughly 1 percent and 4 percent a year, respectively, relative to fiscal 2003 appropriations. The HIV/AIDS pandemic would receive vastly expanded funding, consistent with the breathtaking expansion of needs. Congress appropriated $1.4 billion for HIV/AIDS in 2003—a 40 percent increase over the previous year. President Bush has proposed continuing this pattern with a further 40 percent increase in his fiscal 2004 request and continued growth in the following years for a five-year cumulative $7.8 billion increase over the 2003 baseline (which is not explicitly broken out in table 9-6).[22]

Despite the high profile of the MCA, there is a risk that it will follow a pattern seen elsewhere, in which actual budgeted amounts fall far short of pledges. In this regard it is striking that the administration's actual fiscal 2004 request for the MCA falls short relative to the administration's previous statements.[23] In Monterrey the president committed to a 50 percent

Table 9-6. *Real Growth in Foreign Assistance Programs, Administration's Budget Request, Fiscal Year 2004*

Billions of 2003 dollars, unless otherwise noted

Type of assistance	*2003 appro-priation*	*Fiscal year request*					*Ave. ann. growth (%, 2003–08)*
		2004	*2005*	*2006*	*2007*	*2008*	
Development aid and trade and investment programs	5.42	6.46	7.27	8.19	8.77	8.99	10.64
Bilateral development assistance	1.39	1.32	1.30	1.31	1.31	1.32	–0.96
Child survival and health	1.84	1.46	1.47	1.48	1.48	1.50	–4.03
Global AIDS initiative	0.00	0.44	1.20	1.71	2.24	2.39	n.a.
Millennium Challenge Account	0.00	1.27	1.28[a]	1.28[a]	1.29[a]	1.30[a]	n.a.
Multilateral development programs	1.31	1.52	1.53	1.53	1.54	1.56	3.57
U.S. export, investment programs, Peace Corps, and development foundations	0.89	0.44	0.50	0.89	0.91	0.93	0.86
Politically allocated economic assistance	4.76	4.84	4.86	4.88	4.91	4.95	0.78
Humanitarian assistance	1.08	0.97	0.98	0.98	0.99	1.00	–1.55
Security assistance	4.94	5.04	5.05	5.08	5.11	5.15	0.84
International organizations and programs	1.06	1.30	1.30	1.31	1.31	1.32	4.54
Total	17.26	18.61	19.46	20.45	21.09	21.41	4.40

Source: Authors' calculations using data from Office of Management and Budget, Public Budget Database, Budget Authority table (www.whitehouse.gov/omb/budget/fy2004/db.html). Data converted to real 2003 dollars using the "All Other" Composite Outlay Deflator series, Fiscal Year 2004 Budget of the U.S. Government Historical Tables (Government Printing Office, 2003), p.183.

a. Food aid for development and emergency food aid are estimated to be one half of total (P.L. 480, Title II funding).

increase in assistance to developing countries, resulting in a $5 billion annual increase by fiscal 2006. Administration officials issued an important further clarification that the new assistance would total $10 billion cumulatively in the three years 2004 to 2006. Subsequently, in June 2002, the White House issued an update showing "illustrative funding levels" for the Millennium Challenge Account of $1.7 billion in fiscal year 2003, $3.3 billion in 2004, and $5 billion in 2006.[24]

By comparison the fiscal 2004 request of $1.3 billion is more than 20 percent below the illustrative funding level, which puts a greater burden on the following two years to achieve the remaining $8.7 billion cumulative increase. Further confusing matters, the administration published budget projections for fiscal years 2004 through 2008 that remain below $1.5 billion annually and cumulatively total only $4 billion.[25] OMB officials have indicated privately that these numbers will be corrected, but there is concern, given the pattern of overpledging and underfunding mentioned above.

Because the administration opted to create a new agency to administer the MCA rather than using the existing infrastructure of USAID, the actual ability to disburse funding may be well below the fiscal year 2004 request of $1.3 billion (indeed, outlays are projected to be only one-half the requested authorization). It is critical for U.S. credibility abroad that the administration follow through on its pledges to increase development aid by $10 billion cumulatively by fiscal 2006. But realism dictates that the money may move more slowly, given the determination to set up a new independent bureaucracy from scratch, as with the experience of the Global Fund to Fight AIDS, Tuberculosis, and Malaria. Given the many pressing calls on fiscal resources, Congress might use a combination of advance appropriations and no-year money (explained in box 9-1) to signal that the promised amount of money will be safeguarded for use when the MCA is able to spend it well, without tying up current funds that are badly needed elsewhere.

Summary of Recommendations

The administration's promised funding for the MCA represents an enormous increase in existing U.S. bilateral development assistance, but existing levels are low, relative both to other donors as a share of income and to U.S. politically allocated economic assistance. Relative to need, the MCA could make an important but manageable contribution to the resources available to potential recipients, and as such represent a sizable but still

Box 9-1. *Appropriations: The Basics*

The appropriation of funds is divided into three categories.

—Appropriations legislation provides a government agency with budget authority, which entitles the agency to commit the designated funds through employment agreements, purchase orders, and other contracts.

—These commitments are called obligations. Obligations may be short-term contracts, which must be paid in the fiscal year in which they are negotiated (such as employment agreements), or may be long-term contracts, to be paid in future years (such as large construction contracts).

—Payments of obligations are called outlays. Although the majority of outlays derive from obligations made in the current fiscal year, some outlays derive from long-term obligations made in previous fiscal years.

The time during which funds remain available is also critical. Depending on the type of appropriations granted, unspent budget authority, both obligated and unobligated balances, may be carried over into future years. There are three possibilities:

—One-year appropriations: Budget authority expires at the end of the fiscal year for which it is appropriated. While funds obligated to long-term contracts to be paid in future years carry over, unobligated funds are revoked at the end of the fiscal year.

—Multiyear appropriations: Budget authority remains valid until a specified date.

—No-year appropriations: Budget authority remains valid until all appropriated funds have been obligated.

Source: Allen Schick, *The Federal Budget: Politics, Policy, Process* (Brookings, 1995).

incomplete U.S. contribution to the overall bill for achieving a sustained improvement in living standards in the poorest countries.

In the years ahead it will be important to examine the foreign aid budget in fine detail to ward against the danger of cuts to assistance that has lower public salience but where the needs are nonetheless great, from a combination of budget pressures and deterioration in the beneficiary pool, as the best performers migrate to the MCA. Traditional DA is among the most vulnerable programs in the foreign assistance account because of its low public salience, but it is critically important as the key funding source for some of the world's neediest populations (it is also critical to make DA more effective, as recommended in the preceding chapter).

It is also important to guard against the MCA becoming the central source of economic assistance to geopolitically important countries that are part of the expanded income range eligibility pool. Not only could a disproportionate share of MCA resources be directed away from the poorest nations, but the strict standards of the MCA could be undermined, as political considerations creep in. As recommended in chapters 3 and 7, this could be prevented by excluding countries with incomes above $1,435. Another possible way to prevent this development without unfairly excluding otherwise meritorious year-three countries that have large poor populations (such as South Africa) would be to exclude only those countries in the richer group that receive significant funding from U.S. political foreign aid accounts, such as the economic support fund, and require some cooling off period, such as two years, after a country ceases receiving large amounts of aid from politically determined accounts, before the MCA approves its grants.

If it is necessary to create a new agency to implement the MCA, it is unlikely that the account will be able to disburse the promised amounts while maintaining high standards in its first year of operation and possibly longer. It is nonetheless critical that the United States deliver on the promised funding levels. Congress could use a combination of advance appropriations and no-year money to ensure that the promised funds will be available when there is the ability to use them well, without unnecessarily tying up resources that are badly needed for a variety of purposes.

10

Making a Difference to Global Poverty

The United States has a vital national interest in being a good development partner to the many countries around the world struggling with poverty. President Bush's proposal to create a $5 billion Millennium Challenge Account (MCA) creates a rare and important opportunity to pioneer a more effective partnership. But, welcome as they are, new money and a good idea are not enough. Critical design and implementation decisions require urgent attention for the new fund to succeed on its own terms, as well as to strengthen international cooperation and broader U.S. development policy. *The Other War: Global Poverty and the Millennium Challenge Account* identifies ten key drivers of success and provides recommendations for each.

Driver 1: Piggyback on and Learn from International Efforts

It would be a terrible irony if the laudable goals of the MCA were undercut by perceptions that it is one more instance of the United States going it alone. But the risk of adding to concerns about unilateralism is real, since both the MCA and the president's Emergency Plan for AIDS Relief bypass international efforts and existing aid agencies in favor of U.S. programs with idiosyncratic eligibility criteria and newly invented institutional arrangements. Although unveiled for a United Nations conference, the Bush administration's legislative proposal for the MCA appears curiously uninformed by efforts to coordinate and cooperate at the international level, and there has been little consultation with other donors. The past several years have seen intense debate and some important advances at the international level on improving development strategies. The MCA should be crafted to reinforce those elements of international cooperation that are succeeding and to integrate lessons from recent initiatives.

Recommendation: Don't Go It Alone

American taxpayer dollars could be greatly leveraged if they piggybacked on the efforts of the poverty-reduction strategy papers (PRSP) process to pioneer the country ownership model that animates the MCA—putting resources toward the development strategies and plans developed by governments, with input from civil society as a central element. As the PRSP process goes forward, it is providing valuable lessons about the promises and the pitfalls of requiring participation by local civil society and about institutional capacity in poor countries. These lessons are directly relevant to the operations of the MCA. There may be economies of scale for the MCA, meanwhile, in collaborating with the monitoring and evaluation mechanisms established by the PRSP process.

For the United States to present as its contribution to international efforts a Millennium Challenge Account that makes no reference to the millennium development goals will be seen as a bad case of unilateralism and, more importantly, bad policy. The millennium development goals (MDGs) have become the organizing principle for a host of mutually reinforcing international and bilateral poverty reduction efforts. The Millennium Challenge Corporation (MCC) should consider consistency with the MDGs in its grant making and include MDG targets in its assessments, where appropriate.

The Global Fund to Fight AIDS, Tuberculosis, and Malaria (Global Fund) provides the most relevant set of comparisons and contrasts on the demand-driven, results-oriented grant-making approach, based on competition among locally designed proposals. Lacking the strict selection criteria envisaged for the MCA, the Global Fund covers a vastly broader group of countries, which will provide valuable data for assessing whether the MCA's demand-driven approach could be compatible with broader coverage of poor countries over time.

On selection criteria, the highly indebted poor countries (HIPC) debt relief initiative may provide the most interesting parallel. HIPC differs from the MCA in that it has a narrow mandate, and the quantitative criteria select for unsustainable debt burdens, while judgments on policy performance are largely qualitative. Nonetheless HIPC is the first and best-known development program that uses a set of publicly available quantitative indicators to determine eligibility, making possible a transparent and open selection process. Three years into the life of the HIPC program, as the outcomes emerged, public pressure led to a significant modification of the eligibility criteria (and enhanced relief), and several adjustments have been made to the selection process for similar reasons. MCA criteria too should be reexamined as results emerge.

Driver 2: A Narrow Core Mission

In contrast to the sprawling mission and multiple objectives of USAID, the MCA should develop a core competence around a limited set of areas in order to achieve greatest effectiveness. The mission of the MCA should be to support growth, poverty reduction, and sustainable development in poor nations with a record of sound policy, social investment, and good governance, by underwriting meritorious strategies designed and implemented by recipients. Four key criteria should determine the sectors on which MCA should focus its grant making:

—evidence that the sector is an important determinant of growth and poverty reduction;

—inclusion of the sector in the MDGs, whose importance to poverty reduction is a matter of international consensus;

—evidence that public intervention is needed in the sector to address areas where private investment falls short of the socially desirable level; and

—an established track record of foreign aid delivering results in the sector and evidence the U.S. has particular expertise and experience there.

The compatibility between a program area and the demand-driven, recipient-led approach of the MCA should also be considered.

The core focus of the MCA should thus encompass five areas and reserve a final area for further study:

Core Competence 1: Basic Health

Basic health should be a priority focus of the MCA, as it is for three of the eight MDGs. Substantial research suggests that increases in child survival and life expectancy and reductions in morbidity have important development benefits, including improvements in productivity, savings and investment, and educational investments, and (with a lag) more sustainable population growth patterns. Official international efforts have an impressive record in health, in areas like vaccines and oral rehydration therapy, which have led to measurable and highly cost-effective improvements. A compelling case can be made that the market on its own would yield socially suboptimal health outcomes.

Core Competence 2: Primary Education

Targeting primary education for all girls and boys should be a core focus of the MCA, as it is for two of the eight MDGs. Primary education has obvious direct economic benefits but also important indirect benefits. Girls' literacy has been linked to better health outcomes for families and more sustainable fertility patterns. Foreign aid's record on education, while mixed, holds out hope for good outcomes from well-designed programs that focus on the quality and not just the quantity of educational attainment.

Core Competence 3: Environmental Sustainability and Clean Energy

Ensuring sustainable resources as well as safe water and clean air should be a core programmatic focus of the MCA, based on all of the criteria above. The absence of the environment from the administration's proposal is a startling omission, especially since it has been a high priority for the United States historically. Pressing immediate economic needs and poor environmental regulatory capacity in many poor countries result in unhealthy air and water, irreversible trade-offs between the interests of current and future generations, and harmful spillovers to people living outside the border. The case for foreign aid to rebalance the equation is strong. Developing countries are also eager to obtain the most modern clean energy technologies available. In addition, the MCA should follow all other U.S. aid, trade, and investment programs in requiring environmental impact analyses of relevant grants. The MCA provides an important opportunity for building up the capacity of recipient governments to undertake this type of review for their own purposes.

Core Competence 4: Agricultural Development

Agriculture should be a core focus because of its central role in employing the majority of the work force and as the initial driver of productivity and growth in many poor nations. However, it is important for foreign aid programs to avoid competing with private sector activities. The MCA should target collective goods that are underprovided by the market and where assistance can be put to good use, such as rural infrastructure, research applied to local conditions, and collective marketing arrangements.

Core Competence 5: Strengthening the Policy Environment for Private Sector Development

The MCA should strengthen the policy environment for private sector development. There is no compelling reason to single out (as the administration proposes) trade and foreign investment as more important to a dynamic and vibrant private sector than, for instance, financial market supervision, a viable bankruptcy regime, competition policy, and regulations conducive to small business creation. The MCA should not support enterprise funds or other direct financing to business—with the possible exception of microfinance. The MCA's grant-making approach is ill-suited to the role of financial intermediary, the record of U.S. government enterprise funds is mixed, and the MCA should not duplicate the work of existing U.S. and multilateral institutions dedicated to financing trade and foreign investment.

Reserve for Further Study: Governance

Although governance meets many of the above criteria, it differs from the program priorities recommended above in that there is uncertainty about the demand in potential recipient countries. To ascertain the extent of demand before building in-house expertise at the MCA, we recommend that the MCA encourage the submission of governance proposals but initially subcontract out (on a reimbursed basis) any such proposals to USAID for assessment, monitoring, and evaluation. On democracy, in contrast, we suggest that the small staff of the MCA is ill-suited to the intensive, hands-on nature of democracy programs, and USAID should retain responsibility.

Driver 3: Targeting Countries in the Right Income Range

In a move that took many development advocates by surprise, the administration proposed broadening the eligibility pool in year three to include countries with incomes between $1,435 and $2,975. This has raised concerns that resources will be diverted from countries with far greater needs. Although some of the countries in the richer group have many people living in poverty, they have access to a much wider array of financial resources to address these problems. In addition, the richer group encompasses nations already among the largest beneficiaries of politically directed U.S. assistance, raising the risk that the MCA could be used to replace current aid flows for those that qualify. For instance, this income group includes Russia, Jordan, Egypt, Colombia, and Peru, which together received $1.32 billion in U.S. economic assistance in fiscal 2002—one-fifth of foreign economic assistance for nonemergency programs.

Recommendation: Keep the Focus on the Poorest Countries

Countries in the $1,435-to-$2,975 income range should continue to have access to traditional forms of U.S. assistance, rather than being included in the MCA. If they are nonetheless included, we recommend excluding those countries that receive significant funding from U.S. political foreign aid accounts, such as economic support funds, and requiring a two-year cooling-off period between the time political aid ends and MCA funding begins. This will help guard against geopolitical creep, without unfairly excluding meritorious lower-middle-income countries with high poverty (such as South Africa). In addition a ceiling (up to a maximum of $1 billion a year) should be put on funds available to the lower-middle-income group.

Within the narrower income range, we recommend that MCA-eligible countries be split into two groups, the first with incomes of $875 or less, the World Bank's current operational cutoff for International Development Association (IDA) eligibility, and the second with incomes between $875 and $1,435, the World Bank's historical cutoff for IDA. The first group would include the sixty-eight poorest countries in the world, and the second group would be composed of another nineteen poor countries. Structuring the selection so that the two groups compete separately for funding is likely to broaden the group of the poorest countries that meet the selection criteria, by enabling them to compete only against nations at a similar level of poverty.

Driver 4: Getting the Selection Process Right

The administration has highlighted the selection criteria as the defining aspect of the MCA. Funding only the best performers not only intends to create good incentives for reform but also is the underlying rationale for giving the recipients greater ownership and the administering agency greater flexibility in the use of funds. Getting the selection criteria right is, therefore, absolutely critical. The data are unlikely to be fully up to the task, however, creating inevitable scope for discretion (which in turn puts greater onus on the board and the statutory mandate of the MCA, as discussed below).

On the surface, the proposed approach is as analytical and objective as one is likely to find in the policy realm. It is appealing insofar as it lays out a transparent methodology against which the results can be compared to check for fairness and objectivity. In principle the data should measure those variables that empirical research has shown to be the best predictors of poverty reduction and growth. Broadly speaking, the Bush administration's indicators—responsible fiscal and monetary management, investments in basic health and education, economic openness, efficient regulation, and accountable and efficient governance—conform to this approach. And the inclusion of political rights and civil liberties is important in its own right.

The list of countries generated by the dry run of the selection methodology in chapter 3 includes many countries that would seem appropriate for the MCA but also yields some surprises, such as Vietnam, which seem inconsistent with the MCA's general policy thrust. These problems suggest several modifications to the selection process:

Recommendation: Reduce Reliance on the Median as the Hurdle

The selection criteria will not provide effective incentives for reform if they are moving targets. The administration should move as quickly as it can to adopt absolute hurdles for as many indicators as possible—as is already the case for inflation—perhaps using the medians from the first year as a guide.

The analysis also would suggest setting the hurdles at the median rather than above it, a small modification that would achieve broader coverage among poor countries without any sacrifice of rigor.

The administration should refine some of the indicators that measure countries on a narrow scale, such that most countries are bunched together at or near the median. The Heritage Foundation/Wall Street Journal trade policy index is the weakest indicator in this area, but the Freedom House civil liberties and political rights indexes are also of concern. In these cases, a country whose performance is above the median but is measured poorly could be erroneously excluded, and the reverse. Until the data are refined, some method less vulnerable to error should be used (such as that proposed for corruption, below).

Recommendation: Change Treatment of Corruption

The proposal to eliminate all countries with corruption scores below the median should be reexamined. The data used for this indicator (along with most other indicators) are not robust and accurate enough to be the sole basis for eliminating countries regardless of their performance in other areas. As an alternative, the worst corruption offenders, where the data indicate a 75 percent chance or greater that the true score is below the median, could be eliminated immediately. Other countries would remain eligible and could qualify if they meet half the hurdles in each of the three categories, even if they miss on the corruption indicator.

Recommendation: Improve the Indicators

As discussed above, HIPC underwent a major revision to its selection indicators three years after its inception, as the operational implications became clear. The architects of the MCA would be wise to build in a process for refining the selection methodology early in the life of the program.

—The administration should commission other indicators that could be used in place of or to supplement the indicators with evident weaknesses. Most immediately, the set of four indicators for investing in people should be expanded to include the ratio of girls to boys in primary schools and primary school enrollment rates, plus one additional measure of health outcomes. On a somewhat longer schedule, the MCA should address the weakness of the trade index by working with the World Trade Organization and the United Nations to access data on actual barriers to trade.

—The selection process raises many complex technical issues that have important implications for MCA coverage. To thoroughly address these issues on a regular basis, the administration and Congress should establish an independent panel of outside experts to review the selection methodology on an annual basis.

—Procedurally a trade-off exists between establishing a stable set of incentives for applicant countries and improving the data and methodology over time. A similar trade-off exists between ensuring congressional policy direction on the indicators and permitting the administration discretion to change them in response to experience. Congress should provide policy guidance in the authorizing legislation on the key categories for the selection process and income groups and require the administration to undertake a regulatory process for implementing and revising the selection criteria, with the usual provisions for public comment and advance notification.

Driver 5: A New Approach to Aid

The MCA should pioneer a sharply different approach to aid, one that places responsibility and accountability squarely in the hands of eligible countries, even as it seeks to build local capacity from proposal design through implementation and assessment of results. Our analysis strongly endorses the spirit of working in partnership with developing countries to achieve their own development strategies.

Recommendation: Balance Contract Specificity and Flexibility for Innovation

The concept of a contract between the MCA and grant recipients is useful in defining responsibilities and authorities on both sides. But the contractual precision should be tempered by realism about the inherent long-term and risky nature of the development process. The MCA should expect disappointments and even outright failures; to do otherwise would discourage innovative proposals.

Recommendation: Select the Best Proposals

Once the eligible pool of countries is established, the MCA should hold an open competition for the best grant proposals on a regular schedule, twice a year, so that all proposals in each round can be compared against each other fairly. The core assessment of competing proposals should be undertaken by country-sector teams that incorporate the views of experts from inside the MCA and other relevant U.S. agencies as well as external experts on every proposal. This would also take into account input from the field and on technical feasibility.

Board review would be required for grant proposals that are controversial or exceed 5 percent of either the MCA annual budget or the budget of the grant recipient.

Recommendation: Facilitate Participation by NGOs and the Private Sector

The MCA should strike a balance, appropriate to the circumstances of each country, between strengthening the capability of the government and ensuring active space for civil society. This suggests a hybrid approach on the question of what kinds of organizations should be eligible to submit grant proposals, one less restrictive than the government-only focus of the administration's proposal. This can be accomplished by encouraging but not requiring national governments to submit proposals that coordinate the activities of a range of actors—national, subnational, nongovernmental, and for-profit—while also leaving room for NGOs and subnational governments to submit proposals independently. While encouraging the same kind of coordination and broad-based participation as the Global Fund, this approach would not necessarily require the establishment of a new country coordinating mechanism, while leaving room for direct funding of NGOs that meet certain standards of legitimacy and effectiveness. The difference is justified in part because of the MCA's narrower focus on governments that have met tests of good governance, effectiveness, and commitment, and by permitting direct funding of NGOs as a check.

Recommendation: Ensure Flexible Funding Modalities

The MCA should have substantial flexibility in tailoring the type of financing to the particular country and sectoral emphasis of each proposal. It must have the capacity to fund programs and not just projects, to provide support directly through the national budget, and to underwrite recurring expenses, such as operating costs, maintenance, and salaries, as well as capital or one-time costs.

Although funding programs through budget support has risks, there are also compelling advantages. With program funding going through the budget, the focus of attention shifts to strengthening government institutions rather than hollowing them out. Donor monitoring can examine the entire budget, thus reducing the opportunities for governments to divert money to questionable items. In addition, over time, requiring that grant submissions be presented in the context of the national budget will help strengthen the budget as a process for defining national priorities and facilitating an informed public debate about trade-offs.

Recommendation: Make Monitoring and Evaluation of Concrete Outcomes a Priority

Strong monitoring and evaluation are critical to the MCA's success and a natural corollary to the emphasis on country ownership. Monitoring and evaluation should include four elements: financial audit, measuring progress on the concrete outcomes targeted by the grants, strengthening the internal capacity of the recipients for self-evaluation, and assessing the potential for scaling up or replication elsewhere.

Driver 6: A New Bureaucracy?

Many elements of the Overseas Private Investment Corporation (OPIC), the Export-Import Bank (Ex-Im), and the enterprise funds are suggestive for the MCA—especially on governance, status, and staffing. USAID, with its wide range of programs and missions, provides a rich set of both positive and negative examples.

Perhaps the hardest-fought issue in the administration's internal deliberations on the MCA was where to house it. The State Department was ruled out, correctly in our judgment. The perception if not the reality of a foreign policy overlay to the selection process would have been unavoidable, and the lack of program experience was equally compelling.

Strong arguments can be made on both sides of the choice between creating a stand-alone independent agency or an autonomous entity affiliated with USAID. If the goal is to ensure the success of the MCA in its own right, a new independent agency is the right way to go, even as this assumes heavy reliance on support from USAID. If the goal is to make U.S. foreign assistance and development policy more powerful, the creation of two federal agencies to administer development assistance defies policy and budgetary sense. The waste associated with bureaucratic redundancy, the potential for duplication and overlap, including in the field, and the likelihood of an implicit cross-subsidization from USAID to the MCC will be hard to avoid.

Recommendation: Affiliate MCA with USAID but Build in Safeguards

On balance, we find the case for designing the MCA to strengthen U.S. development policy compelling and therefore urge consideration of affiliating the MCC with USAID.

Although the administration is right to worry about the dangers of subjecting the MCC to the same type of restrictions and bureaucratic habits afflicting many programs at USAID, there are ways to minimize these risks. Building on the precedent established by the enterprise funds, the MCC could be established as an autonomous entity affiliated with USAID, with its own chief executive officer at a deputy administrator rank, an independent board, and a separate authorization from Congress.

Recognizing that the creation of a new agency is the more likely course, our recommendations are designed to apply to either type of entity equally.

Recommendation: Expand the Board to include Outside Representatives and USAID

An independent board should govern the MCC. Drawing on the experience of OPIC and Ex-Im, eight board seats should be divided equally between administration representatives and outside members recommended by Congress, on a bicameral and bipartisan basis, to serve six-year terms. We concur with the administration's proposal in recommending that the secretaries of state and treasury be on the board, but we disagree that the Office of Management and Budget would be an appropriate board presence, given its role as budget referee. Moreover the omission of USAID from the board is anomalous, especially given the extensive support envisaged from USAID and the importance of avoiding wasteful duplication and turf battles. A variety of possible agencies could be appropriate for the final board seat.

The experience of comparable independent agencies suggests that a board composed heavily of representatives of other federal agencies is a mixed blessing: Although it brings useful breadth of perspective, it may also subject the agency to political pressure to help further outside agendas. For this reason, budget transfer authority should remain with Congress (rather than being delegated to the MCC, as proposed by the administration) to diminish pressures to disburse MCA monies through other federal agencies.

We recommend that accountability and authority should be aligned by giving the CEO a seat on, and preferably leadership of, the board. The experience of OPIC and Ex-Im suggests that cabinet secretaries rarely, if ever, attend board meetings and instead delegate representation to lower-level officials.

Recommendation: Independent, Professional Staff

The MCC should be a lean organization, relying on outsourcing where it is cost effective and requiring fewer program staff than traditional U.S. assistance programs, because of the emphasis on country ownership and program support. Interagency detailing should be used to promote coherence and draw on expertise, as should limited term appointments from the private and nongovernmental sectors.

The administration's proposed staff size of 100 to administer $5 billion in grants annually nonetheless is unrealistic. A comparison with other bilateral aid agencies and private foundations suggests that program funding of $5 million per staff member per year is ambitious—a sobering contrast to the administration's implied $50 million per staff member per year. Given its similar operational approach, the Global Fund might be a rough guide. A more realistic staff size could be two to four times greater.

Both headquarters and overseas staff of the MCC should be detailed only on a reimbursable basis, to ensure that there are no hidden subsidies and that program evaluation is on the basis of all-in costs. Private sector entities should be prohibited from detailing paid staff to avoid conflicts of interest.

Recommendation: Build Recipient Capacity

The MCC should enhance the ability of MCA countries to implement grant programs by including training and capacity-building components in all technical assistance, financial management, and other relevant assistance programs. It should allow competition for procurement and other service contracts by MCA country institutions and expedite the registration process for these entities.

Driver 7: Greater Coherence in U.S. Foreign Assistance and Development Policy

Although the MCA presents an enticing opportunity, the risk is at least as great that it will simply add to the confusion of overlapping policies, agencies, aid programs, and eligibility criteria targeted at developing nations. Even a lot of money and a great idea will not be enough to make a difference to U.S. foreign assistance unless the MCA reflects the lessons from past aid failures. And even if it succeeds on its own terms, the MCA will fail in making the U.S. a more effective development partner unless it has a clear vision of how it can complement the operations and country coverage of existing U.S. programs for developing nations, particularly USAID.

Although the president's decision to establish an independent agency was a clear vote of no-confidence in the 10,000-strong USAID, the administration has not put forward any proposals to fix the agency, which will retain responsibility for providing foreign assistance to the vast majority of the world's poorest.

Since the inception of the Marshall Plan in 1948, six separate agencies have been created to address international development—only one of which exists today. Unlike past efforts, the MCC would create a new development agency without either replacing or triggering the reorganization of already existing foreign assistance programs.

It is ironic that, with clearly defined and separate missions, a greater preponderance of USAID programs would be directly related to foreign policy than ever before, while the MCC's mission would be relatively free of foreign policy considerations. Yet the administration proposes that the board of the development-oriented MCC be chaired by the secretary of state and not include the head of USAID.

Recommendation: Clear Division between USAID and the MCC

A clear division of labor must be articulated between USAID and the MCC (whether as a new agency or as part of an affiliated entity). The MCA should not rely on implicit cross-subsidization and support from USAID through details that are not reimbursed or support from USAID mission staff on the ground, as is currently envisaged in the administration's proposal. To do so would create wasteful duplication and needless turf fights, would muddy program evaluation, and would further diffuse USAID's mission and undermine morale. In a strict sense, this implies that, once a country qualifies for the MCA, with some transition period, USAID operations should shut down in that country.

The one sensible area of overlap between the MCC and USAID would be in those countries that fail to qualify for the MCA by virtue of one or two indicators or that are just below the median on several indicators. It is precisely in such near-miss countries that the promise of vastly increased foreign assistance could be catalytic in encouraging policy reforms, in contrast to poorly performing states, where the government is unlikely to possess the capacity to close the gap. Moreover this category is likely to include some developmentally important countries, such as Uganda, which has pioneered an effective development strategy but is plagued by severe deficiencies on governance. We recommend that limited MCA funding be made available as challenge grants to address those areas that are weak, but under USAID's supervision, to provide greater oversight.

Recommendation: Sharpen USAID's Mission

Greater clarity must be given to USAID's core mission. USAID would retain responsibility for five goals:

—providing humanitarian assistance;
—supporting development in geopolitically important countries;
—countering the threat posed by weak and failing states;
—helping postconflict countries through transitions; and
—addressing basic health, education, agriculture, policy, and governance challenges in moderate-to-poorly-performing poor countries.

Driver 8: Bringing Coherence to U.S. Development Policy

The creation of another independent agency to support international development with its own idiosyncratic conditions threatens to add to an already confusing proliferation of U.S. programs and agencies. U.S. development assistance will not achieve maximal efficiency and impact unless the aid is part of a coherent approach that includes debt relief, trade and investment programs, and the credit rating process. Especially for the most reform-oriented countries singled out by the MCA, the prospects for graduating rest centrally on improved trade and investment prospects. It makes little sense to grade a country on its trade openness, provide foreign aid to improve its trade regime, and then provide less favorable trade access than is available to other countries (who might be politically more important but less committed to market reform). This argues for an integrated approach to determining the appropriate terms on trade access, debt treatment, development assistance, and export and investment programs for each country.

Recommendation: Improve Development Policy Coordination

The administration should mandate a policy coordination process, led from the White House, using existing National Security Council and National Economic Council mechanisms, to ensure deployment of all the tools in the U.S. arsenal in a mutually reinforcing way to assist poor countries to make the transition to sustained growth. This should include foreign aid, technical assistance, debt relief, trade preferences or free-trade agreements, export credits, and investment support and agreements.

Driver 9: Financing Foreign Assistance

The administration's promised funding for the MCA represents a near doubling of existing U.S. bilateral development assistance, but existing levels are low, both relative to other donors as a share of income and relative to U.S. politically allocated economic assistance. It would increase the share of U.S. income devoted to overseas development assistance from the current 0.10 percent to nearly 0.15 percent, a significant increase but nonetheless well below the Organization for Economic Cooperation and Development average of 0.33 percent and the international target of 0.70 percent. The MCA could make an important but manageable contribution to the resources available to poor countries, and as such it represents a sizable but incomplete U.S. contribution to international efforts to address global poverty and achieve growth.

Recommendation: Prevent Budget Squeeze on Less Popular Programs

In the years ahead it will be important to examine the foreign aid budget in fine-grain detail to ward against the danger that programs with lower public salience will get squeezed. Traditional development assistance (DA) is particularly vulnerable, due to a combination of budget pressures and deterioration in the beneficiary pool, as the best performers migrate to the MCA, but DA is critically important in reaching some of the world's neediest populations. Already the administration has proposed cuts for funding for child survival and maternal health programs unrelated to HIV/AIDS to make room for the new priorities.

Recommendation: Prevent Geopolitical Creep

Continued scrutiny is also important to guard against the danger that the MCA may become the central source of economic assistance to geopolitically important countries that are part of the expanded lower-middle-income eligibility pool. Not only could this direct a disproportionate share of MCA resources away from the poorest nations, but it could also undermine the strict standards of the MCA, as political considerations creep in.

Recommendation: Deliver on the Promise

Finally, if a new agency is established to implement the MCA, it is unlikely that it will be able to disburse the promised amounts while maintaining high standards in its first year of operation and possibly longer. It is nonetheless critical for U.S. credibility internationally to deliver on the promised funding levels. Congress should use a combination of advance appropriations and no-year money to ensure that the promised funds will be available when there is the ability to use them well, without tying up resources that are badly needed elsewhere.

Already there are concerns that the MCA will not be fully funded. The administration's fiscal 2004 request for the MCA is 20 percent below the level initially proposed for the first year and falls well short of $5 billion in 2006. Moreover, Congress looks set to cut these levels further in the face of an overall budget squeeze and expectation of large additional assistance needs associated with war and reconstruction in Iraq.

Driver 10: Forging a Partnership with Congress

The administration's proposal to create a new agency, the Millennium Challenge Corporation, to implement the MCA should be understood as a reaction in part to the perceived failure of Congress and the president to work together effectively in the past on many foreign aid programs. Congress and the president have an enormous opportunity to initiate a new partnership in designing the agency and its mandate.

Recommendation: Appoint MCA Representative Now

To help Congress and the president define the terms of the new partnership that is needed for the MCA, the president should quickly designate a personal adviser who could represent the administration before Congress in crafting the MCA legislation. The president could consider announcing that this individual would be his likely nominee to be the CEO of the MCC, should Congress approve the creation of the agency. The experience with the authorization process for the Department of Homeland Security lends strong support to this recommendation.

Recommendation: Ensure Accountability to Congress

The MCC will need much of the flexibility that President Bush has requested but much more congressional policy input than the White House has acknowledged. To ensure the accountability of the MCC, Congress should prescribe and maintain input into the governing of the agency as well as the transparency of and public participation in the agency's decision-making. This should include mandating the following:

—a strong agency head, fully accountable for policy, with a seat on and preferably leadership of the board of directors, as at Ex-Im;

—a board of directors, selected with input from Congress, balanced between administration representatives and outside members, similar to OPIC;

—an adequate professional staff, some fraction of which should have civil service status, in the interest of institutional continuity and political independence, following Ex-Im and OPIC;

—independent agency status;

—the best monitoring and evaluation procedures;

—obligations to report regularly on priorities, expenditures, and performance, timed to coincide with reauthorization;

—a duty to notify Congress in advance in extraordinary circumstances, such as grants of an unusually large size (this could be the same 5 percent trigger as that necessitating exceptional board review); and

—obligations to solicit public participation through web postings and comment solicitation.

Recommendation: Establish a Limited Term and Regular Reauthorization

As with Ex-Im and OPIC, Congress should authorize the MCC for a limited term and require a regular reauthorization process. Balancing the need for congressional review to make adjustments to the MCC (especially in its early years) against the need to provide stable incentives for countries that are working to achieve eligibility suggests a six-year reauthorization cycle initially. The authorization process should do the following:

—Spell out, in general terms, political factors (such as respect for human rights) that must be met for a government to receive funding. The administration has proposed incorporating the basic conditions on assistance in the Foreign Assistance Act.

—Set out the principles for country selection criteria, and require the president to adopt regulations for implementing and subsequently modifying them, in order to create stable incentives and minimize the scope for political manipulation.

—Set out the principles of program areas and entities eligible to compete for funds, and require the president to adopt regulations laying out standard procedures for the review of grant proposals.

—Reflect findings from an external evaluation of the administering agency timed to coincide with the reauthorization process and undertaken by an independent entity, such as the General Accounting Office.

Recommendation: Define a Narrow Mandate

Congress should give the MCC a narrow and clear mandate that would protect it from taking immediate foreign policy considerations into account, just as Ex-Im is required to make funding decisions based solely on commercial criteria. The MCC should support growth, poverty reduction, and sustainable development by underwriting meritorious programs designed and implemented by poor nations with a demonstrated record of sound policy, social investment, and good governance.

Recommendation: Provide Operational Flexibility

Certain of Congress's historic practices on foreign aid—including earmarking and tying aid, extraneous political tests rooted in domestic debates, and procurement and contracting rules better suited to domestic agencies—would be fundamentally incompatible with the demand-driven, competitive grant-making logic of the MCA. Congress should grant the president significant operational flexibility to ensure that the MCC is responsive, efficient, and effective by doing the following:

—appropriating funds free of earmarks or ties, to the extent practicable;
—appropriating no-year funds;
—exempting the MCC from contracting and procurement rules (or enacting new waiver procedures); and
—avoiding advance notification requirements for routine grant decisions.

Achieving the MCA's Full Promise

These recommendations are offered in the spirit of making the MCA succeed, both in its own right and in strengthening the U.S. partnership with developing countries more broadly. It is vital that the new resources be used to pioneer a dramatically new and more effective approach, by underwriting the most promising development strategies proposed and implemented by poor nations committed to good governance and development. But success is by no means guaranteed. A failed MCA would quickly become yet another example—and the most expensive one—of wasted aid, and it could undermine political support for foreign assistance for decades to come. The United States must get it right the first time.

APPENDIX

Environment Assessments: The OPIC Model

Since 1985 the Overseas Private Investment Corporation has been required by statute to assess the environmental impacts of projects under consideration for political risk insurance and financing. OPIC's authorizing statute was also amended at that time to direct the corporation to decline assistance to projects posing a "major or unreasonable hazard to the environment, health, or safety" or resulting in the "significant degradation of a National Park or similar protected area." OPIC was also directed to operate its programs consistently with the intent of sections 117, 118, and 119 of the Foreign Assistance Act relating to environmental impact assessment, tropical forests, biological diversity, and endangered species.

Over the years OPIC has worked with counterpart organizations providing similar services to investors in the United States, overseas, and on a multilateral basis, as environmental procedures were developed. In OPIC's experience the progressive harmonization of standards and procedures similar to those used by these and other similar organizations worldwide has facilitated cofinancing and coinsurance arrangements and has made it simpler for clients to address environmental requirements.

The OPIC environmental review process entails the following steps:

1. OPIC screens the application to determine whether its support of the project would violate any categorical prohibitions required by OPIC's statute or policy to the extent possible at this early stage. OPIC will not support projects that would have a "major or unreasonable" adverse impact on the environment, health, or safety. Examples of such projects include large dams that disrupt natural ecosystems, infrastructure or raw material extraction in primary tropical forests, national parks, natural world heritage sites, and other internationally protected areas. If the project is ineligible, OPIC informs the applicant immediately so as to avoid any unnecessary effort or expense on the part of the applicant. (A more complete list of categorical prohibitions is included in appendix F of the OPIC *Environmental Handbook.*)

2. If the project is not categorically ineligible, OPIC continues to screen the application to determine the level of environmental sensitivity associated with the industry sector or site involved and requests the appropriate information from the applicant. During the screening process, OPIC's environmental staff categorizes projects. Category A and B projects receive the highest level of scrutiny.

Category A includes projects likely to have significant adverse environmental impacts that are sensitive (such as irreversible, effect-sensitive ecosystems or those that involve involuntary resettlement), diverse, or unprecedented. Such projects can be readily identified on the basis of industry sector or site sensitivity. A list of industries and sites in this category is provided in appendix E of OPIC's *Environmental Handbook.*

Category B includes projects likely to have adverse environmental impacts that are less significant than those of category A projects, meaning that few if any of the impacts are likely to be irreversible, that they are site-specific, and that mitigatory measures can be designed more readily than for category A projects.

3. If the project is identified as a category A project, an environmental impact assessment (EIA), an initial environmental audit (IEAU), or both, is required. Category B projects are subject to internal OPIC assessment based on information supplied by the applicant that need not take the form of an EIA. Category C projects do not have material impacts on the environment and are not subject to environmental assessment.

4. OPIC requires that applicants for category A projects submit the EIA or IEAU in a form that can be made public without compromising confidential information. With the consent of the applicant, the country and industry sector involved in a category A project (but not the name of the

applicant) are listed on OPIC's web site. The EIA or IEAU is made publicly available on request for a designated comment period of sixty days before any final OPIC commitment to a project. No application for a category A project can be processed without this public disclosure and review process. By statute, since 1985, environmentally sensitive projects have also been subject to host government notification prior to final commitment.

5. Concurrent with this public notification process, OPIC conducts an internal assessment of the project based on the EIA and other available information, including any comments it receives from the public. Category B projects are also subject to an internal environmental assessment. Through this review process, OPIC environmental staff assess the impacts of the project and the standards and mitigative conditions applicable to OPIC support.

6. These conditions are discussed with the applicant and included as representations, warranties, and covenants in the loan agreement or political risk insurance contract.

7. OPIC monitors project compliance with contractual conditions throughout the term of the OPIC loan agreement or insurance contract.

8. Category A projects are required to conduct at least one independent environmental audit during the first three years of OPIC support.

Source: OPIC *Environmental Handbook*, published on www.opic.gov.

APPENDIX

B

Congressional Budgetary Basics

Congress exerts important influence over U.S. foreign assistance policy through its constitutional controls over federal spending. In foreign aid, as in other areas of the federal budget, Congress has chosen to exercise its spending power through three separate types of congressional actions—budget resolutions, authorizations, and appropriations.

Each year Congress requires the president to submit an annual budget on or before the first Monday in February. In the proposed budget the president recommends spending levels for federal programs and agencies, including those relating to foreign assistance. In technical terms the president's proposed budget is a request for budget authority, the statutory authority to spend monies. Since the early 1970s, when its current budgeting procedures were established, Congress has required that it react to the president's budget by passing a concurrent resolution (scheduled for completion by April 15 of each year, although the deadline has rarely been met). Responsibility for completing the budget resolution lies in each house with its respective budget committee. Congress uses its budget resolution to establish its own spending priorities for each government agency and program, including foreign aid. While the budget resolution is not legally binding, the congressional leadership relies on the budget resolution to structure and constrain the formal appropriations process described below.

The Constitution requires that Congress alone appropriate federal monies.[1] Congressional appropriation acts grant the president the legal authority for the government to assume financial obligations and disburse funds during a particular fiscal year. How Congress organizes itself to consider appropriations is largely for it to decide. Each year Congress directs its appropriation committees and subcommittees to approve over a dozen appropriation bills covering the activities and programs of the entire federal government. These appropriations usually cover predetermined groups of departments and agencies, but supplemental bills are sometimes introduced to address unexpected and urgent budgetary needs, such as disaster relief or military action. Appropriation bills passed by the House and Senate are reconciled, approved by both houses, and then sent to the president for signature or veto. Once enacted, the appropriations represent the budget of the United States for the new fiscal year.

Under the procedures established by Congress, however, appropriation acts do not bestow upon the president the full authority necessary to expend any monies. Congress must also have authorized the relevant agencies to carry out the functions for which monies were appropriated. In short, Congress has chosen to make independent authorization acts necessary to establish, continue, or modify agencies and programs. Congress has delegated responsibility for drafting authorization bills to its various substantive congressional committees and subcommittees. In the Senate, for example, the Defense Department authorization bill is considered by the Armed Services Committee; the State Department and AID authorization bills are handled by the Foreign Relations Committee, and so on. Congress has the power to authorize agency action in perpetuity if it desires, but it has generally not done so in areas for which appropriations are required. Authorization acts usually cap what executive agencies can spend during a fiscal year, impose various substantive restrictions on the use of any subsequently appropriated funds, and stipulate that the authorizations enacted in the act expire at the end of the fiscal year.

Each year, before any money can be spent by any federal agency on itself or for any of its programs, the president must subject his policies to scrutiny by and receive multiple approvals from Congress. More specifically the president is dependent on Congress to grant the authority necessary to conduct the program in question and to provide independently an appropriation for the same expenditure. The cumbersome process created by Congress limits presidential discretion and creates a platform for Congress to advance its priorities. In addition the division of responsibility within Congress between the various budget, appropriations, and authorization committees helps to ensure widespread, although diffuse, participation among members of Congress in the budget process.

The foreign aid budget process, not surprisingly, follows the split authorization and appropriation procedures outlined above. Responsibility for considering foreign assistance authorization acts lies with the Senate Foreign Relations Committee and the House Committee on International Relations (the authorizers). Jurisdiction over the foreign assistance appropriations bills, in contrast, mainly rests with the Senate Appropriations Subcommittee on Foreign Operations, the House Appropriations Subcommittee on Foreign Operations, Export Financing and Related Programs (the appropriators). As in most other areas of federal spending, the appropriators generally approve funds one fiscal year at a time. The primary authorities for U.S. foreign aid agencies were consolidated and adopted in the Foreign Assistance Act of 1961. That act, as amended, grants these agencies many continuing (that is, permanent until changed) responsibilities and powers. In 1973 however Congress enacted legislation requiring that it pass an annual authorization act for foreign assistance. Also added at that time was the stipulation that without an annual authorization act there could be no expenditure of foreign assistance funds appropriated for that fiscal year without an explicit waiver of the requirement by Congress.[2] So after 1973 the basic foreign aid authorities in the Foreign Assistance Act too became contingent on the annual approval of Congress.

In reality the congressional foreign aid budgeting process has not always worked as envisioned. Though Congress begins each fiscal year with the stated intention of passing foreign aid appropriations and authorizations bills, it last enacted a comprehensive foreign assistance authorization act in 1985. Each year since then Congress has waived the requirement for an authorization act. Moreover appropriations acts have often contained provisions authorizing new activities and programs rather than merely approving annual spending levels. Ordinarily new aid activities should be approved in an authorization act.

Notes

Chapter One

1. George Bush, quoted in "The Millennium Challenge Account," fact sheet (www.globalhealth.gov [April 2003]).

2. George Bush, speech at Inter-American Development Bank, March 14, 2002.

3. There is considerable evidence suggesting that terrorism is not directly linked to poverty. For a discussion of the debate, see Lael Brainard, "A Turning Point for Globalisation? The Implications for the Global Economy of America's Campaign against Terrorism," *Cambridge Review of International Affairs*, vol.15, no.2 (July 2002), pp. 233–44.

4. "Report of the High-Level Panel on Financing for Development," United Nations, 2001 (www.un.org/reports/financing/full_report.pdf [March 2003]).

5. George Bush, speech at United Nations Conference on Financing for Development, Monterrey, Mexico, March 22, 2002.

6. "The Millennium Challenge Act of 2003," draft authorization legislation submitted by the administration to Congress on February 6, 2003.

7. Lael Brainard, "Compassionate Conservatism Confronts Global Poverty," *Washington Quarterly*, vol. 26, no. 2 (Spring 2003), pp. 149–69.

8. This is not the same as the list of the top five U.S. aid recipients.

9. Gene Sperling and Tom Hart, "A Better Way to Fight Global Poverty," *Foreign Affairs*, vol. 82 no.2 (March/April 2003), pp. 9–14.

Chapter Two

1. While the IMF does not have a mandate as a development institution per se, it is often viewed by the public as one. Thus when it does not succeed in preventing and fixing financial crises, which are at times extremely challenging, it is interpreted as a failure of development assistance, even though this is a misdiagnosis. The authors thank Lant Pritchett for making this important distinction.

2. William Easterly, "The Cartel of Good Intentions: Bureaucracy versus Markets in Foreign Aid," Working Paper 4, Center for Global Development, March 2003 (www.cgdev.org/wp/cgd_wp004_rev.pdf. [April 2003]).

3. James D. Wolfensohn, "Aid Donors Should Get Their Act Together," *International Herald Tribune,* February 24, 2003.

4. An extreme example of this is Eritrea, which turned down relationships with potential donors in order to limit entanglement and dependency. See Göte Hansson, "Building New States: Lessons from Eritrea," Discussion Paper No. 2001/66, United Nations University World Institute for Development Economics Research, August 2001 (www.wider.unu.edu/publications/dps/dp2001-66.pdf [April 2003]).

5. For an excellent discussion of the Dutch disease phenomenon as well as the case of Ghana, see Stephen D. Younger, "Aid and the Dutch Disease: Macroeconomic Management When Everybody Loves You," *World Development,* vol. 20, no. 11 (1992), pp. 1587–97.

6. There are also a host of other important venues for coordination among donors, including informal coordination among the G7/8, oversight of aid flows, and peer reviews by the OECD Development Assistance Committee; the authors thank Ann Richard for pointing this out.

7. Lael Brainard, "The Administration's Budget for Global Poverty and HIV/AIDS: How Do the Numbers Stack Up?" The Brookings Institution, February 24, 2003 (www.brookings.edu/views/papers/brainard/20030224.htm [April 2003]).

8. The lower figure is based on U.S. IMF and World Bank subscriptions, which make up approximately 17 percent of both IMF total member quotas and the World Bank's International Bank for Reconstruction and Development (IBRD) total subscriptions. "IMF Members' Quotas and Voting Power, and IMF Governors," January 24, 2002 (www.imf.org/external/np/sec/memdir/members.htm [April 2003]); "International Bank for Reconstruction and Development: Subscriptions and Voting Power of Member Countries," September 19, 2001 (www.worldbank.org/about/organizations/voting/kibrd/html [April 2003]). The upper figure is based on the U.S. share of OECD income based on Development Assistance Committee members' 2000 gross national income. Jean-Claude Faure, "Development Co-Operation, 2001 Report," *Organization for Economic Cooperation and Development DAC Journal,* vol. 3, no. 1 (2002), p. 284.

9. Colin I. Bradford Jr., "Toward 2015: From Consensus Formation to Implementation of the Millennium Development Goals—The Historical Background: The Consensus Formation Phase 1990–2002," Final Review Draft for the World Bank, Washington, December 2002.

10. For more on the eighth goal, see Nancy Birdsall and Michael Clemens, "From Promise to Pitfalls: How Rich Countries Can Help Poor Countries Help Themselves," Brief 2-1, Center for Global Development, April 2003 (www.cgdev.org [April 2003]).

11. www.un.org/millenniumgoal [April 2003].

12. The UN issues country-by-country progress reports. So far twelve country reports have been issued, and the objective is to have reports on all transition and developing countries by 2004. These are available on the UN website: www.un.org. UNDP, in conjunction with Jeff Sachs at Columbia University and a number of other academics, is also developing an extensive system of poverty mapping, in order to gauge more accurately where the most pressing poverty challenges are within countries. The World Economic Forum has launched a global governance initiative to assess the efforts being made by governments, civil society, international organizations, and the private sector to achieve the goals laid out in the Millennium Declaration. The initiative, directed by Brookings scholar Ann Florini, will grade the world on whether its efforts are commensurate with what would be needed to achieve those goals.

13. Bradford, "Toward 2015."

14. InterAction advocated a prominent place for the MDGs in the operations of the MCA in one of the earliest contributions on the MCA. "The Millennium Challenge Account: A New Vision for Development," InterAction Policy Paper, May 2002 (www.interaction.org/files.cgi/442_mcawhitepaper7.pdf [March 2003]).

15. For a description of the effects of the Jubilee 2000 campaign on the thinking about debt relief, see Nancy Birdsall, John Williamson, and Brian Deese, *Delivering on Debt Relief* (Washington: Center for Global Development and Institute for International Economics, 2002). For a view of the Jubilee 2000 campaign and of the PRSPs from the NGO community, see Alan Whaites, ed., *Masters of Their Own Development? PRSPs and the Prospects for the Poor* (Geneva: World Vision, 2002).

16. The IMF and the World Bank conducted a full-scale evaluation of the PRSP process in 2002. The report, "Poverty Reduction Strategy Papers and the Poverty Reduction and Growth Facility" (December 2002) can be found on the IMF's website: www.imf.org. See also "Poverty Reduction Strategy Papers: Progress in Implementation," report prepared by the World Bank and International Monetary Fund for the 2002 Development Committee meeting, September 2002 (www.imf.org/external/np/prsp/2001/042001.htm [March 2003]).

17. Background interview, fall 2002. Background interviews on a number of topics were held in January 2003 with Geoffrey Lamb, director of resource mobilization at the World Bank; Andrew Natsios, administrator of USAID; John Simon, deputy assistant director, Bureau for Policy and Program Coordination, USAID; and in the fall of 2002 with a number of officials involved in the PRSP process at the International Monetary Fund.

18. On the former, see William Easterly, *The Elusive Quest for Growth* (Cambridge University Press, 2001). On the latter see Gustav Ranis and Frances Stewart, "The Debt-Relief Initiative for Poor Countries: Good News for the Poor?" paper prepared for WIDER Conference on Debt, Helsinki, August 2001.

19. See, for example, Craig Burnside and David Dollar, "Aid, Policies, and Growth" (Washington: World Bank, 1996); Carol Graham and Michael O'Hanlon, "Making Foreign Aid Work," *Foreign Affairs,* vol. 76, no.4 (July/August 1997), pp. 49–52; and Carol Lancaster, *Transforming Foreign Aid: U.S. Assistance in the 21st Century* (Washington: Institute for International Economics, 2000).

20. In the United States, for example, a plethora of institutions provide independent oversight, such as the Congressional Budget Office (a government organization) and the Center on Budget and Policy Priorities (a nongovernmental organization). Such institutions also exist in some developing countries but are rare.

21. The G8 countries are Canada, France, Germany, Italy, Japan, Russia, the United Kingdom, and the United States.

22. The proposed amount was $8 billion a year through 2007. See provisional agenda item 13.1, *Report of the WHO Commission on Macroeconomics and Health,* Fifty-Fifth World Health Assembly, April 23, 2002.

23. The proposed amount was $5–10 billion. See "Abuja Declaration on HIV/AIDS, Tuberculosis, and Other Related Infectious Diseases," African Summit on HIV/AIDS, Tuberculosis, and Other Related Infectious Diseases, Abuja, Nigeria, April 24–27, 2001.

24. Through Round 2, the Global Fund has approved 160 programs in eighty-one countries, or about two per country.

25. Michael M. Phillips, "Disease-Fighting Fund Has Yet to Donate—Demand by U.S. and Others for New Delivery Systems Delays Aid," *Wall Street Journal,* August 5, 2002, p. A4.

26. See Lael Brainard, "Compassionate Conservatism Confronts Global Poverty?" *Washington Quarterly,* vol. 26, no. 2 (spring 2003), pp. 149–169.

27. Background interview, January 2003.

28. William Byrd, "Aid Management during Post-Conflict Reconstruction: Lessons from International Experience," speech at Preparing for Afghanistan's Reconstruction, a conference of the United Nations Development Program, World Bank, and Asian Development Bank, November 27–29, 2001 (http://lnweb18.worldbank.org/sar/sa.nsf/Countries/Afghanistan/0C4F54EACB53352985256 B110022BD5D?OpenDocument [April 2003]).

29. Jean DuRette and Glenn Slocum, "The Role of Transition Assistance: The Case of East Timor," Working Paper 322 (Washington: Center for Development Information and Evaluation, USAID, November 2001) (www.dec.org/pdf_docs/pnacn764.pdf [April 2003]).

30. Operations Evaluation Department, World Bank, "Aid Coordination and Post-Conflict Reconstruction: The West Bank and Gaza Experience," *Précis,* no. 185 (Spring 1999) (www.seerecon.org/Kosovo/KosovoReconstruction/185precis.pdf [April 2003]).

31. Debarati Guha-Sapir, "Lessons We Must Learn from El Salvador Quake," Relief Resources, Reuters Foundation, February 16, 2001 (www.alertnet.org/thefacts/reliefresources/231665 [April 2003]).

32. ReliefWeb, UN Office for the Coordination of Humanitarian Affairs. (www.reliefweb.int/help/whatwedo.html [April 2003]).

33. www.un.org/Depts/dha/res46182.htm [April 2003].

34. www.WHO.int/disasters/repo/7396.html [April 2003].

35. See Colin Bradford, "Anticipating the Future: A Political Agenda for Global Economic Governance," Department of Economics, American University, January 2003.

36. William Cline, "Financial Crises and Poverty in Emerging Market Economies," Working Paper 8 (Washington: Center for Global Development, June 2002).

Chapter Three

1. The president's speech is available at www.whitehouse.gov/news/releases/2002/03/20020314-7.html.

2. For an alternative methodology for choosing the MCA countries, written before the administration made its proposal, see Nancy Birdsall, "Selecting for Success and Reaching the Poor: MCA Eligibility Criteria Can Do Both," Center for Global Development, October 28, 2002 (www.cgdev.org/nv/eligibility.pdf).

3. Craig Burnside and David Dollar, "Aid, Policies, and Growth," *American Economic Review,* vol. 90, no. 4 (September 2000), pp. 847–68; Paul Collier and David Dollar, "Aid Allocation and Poverty Reduction," *European Economic Review* vol. 45, no. 1 (2002), pp. 1–26; World Bank, *Assessing Aid: What Works, What Doesn't, and Why* (Washington: 1998).

4. See, for example, Peter T. Bauer, *Dissent on Development: Studies and Debates in Development Economics* (London: Weidenfeld and Nicolson, 1971); Paul Mosley, John Hudson, and Sara Horrell, "Aid, the Public Sector and the Market in Less Developed Countries," *Economic Journal,* vol. 97 (September 1987), pp. 616–41; Hollis B. Chenery and Alan M. Strout, "Foreign Assistance and Economic Development," *American Economic Review,* vol. 56, no. 4 (September 1966), pp. 679–733; Peter Boone, "Politics and the Effectiveness of Foreign Aid," *European Economic Review,* vol. 40, no. 2 (February 1996), pp. 289–329. For a review, see Howard White, "Foreign Aid, Taxes, and Public Investment: A Further Comment," *Journal of Development Economics,* vol. 45 (1994), pp. 155–63.

5. William Easterly, Ross Levine, and David Roodman, "New Data, New Doubts: Revisiting 'Aid, Policies, and Growth,' " Working Paper 26, Center for Global Development, February 2003 (www.cgdev.org/wp/cgd_wp026.pdf).

6. The seven excluded IDA countries are Dominica, Grenada, St. Lucia, St. Vincent and the Grenadines, Samoa, Tonga, and the Maldives. These countries are part of a group of ten "small island exceptions" that are deemed eligible for IDA credits even though their incomes exceed the current operational cutoff of $875. For more on IDA eligibility requirements, see www.worldbank.org/ida.

7. "The Millennium Challenge Act of 2003," draft authorization legislation submitted by the administration to Congress, February 6, 2003.

8. The probability of passing the corruption indicator is 0.5. If country scores are completely random, the probability of passing two or more of the remaining five "ruling justly" indicators is 0.8125. The probability of passing two or more of the four "investing in people" indicators is 11/16, or 0.6875. The probability of passing three or

more of the six "economic freedom" indicators is 0.6562. The joint probability of achieving all four is (0.5*0.8125*0.6875*0.6562) = 0.1833, or 18 percent.

9. All these classifications use per capita incomes converted to U.S. dollars with average 2001 exchange rates. An alternative would be to compare incomes based on purchasing power parity (PPP). While this latter technique is widely acknowledged by economists as the superior methodology, in practice there are controversies about the accuracy of the underlying data and conversions in specific countries. These data are also not available for many low-income countries. As these data improve in the coming years, they will offer a more sound basis for comparisons of income across countries.

10. Steven Radelet, "Beyond the Indicators: Delivering Effective Foreign Assistance through the Millennium Challenge Account," Center for Global Development, September 2002 (www.cgdev.org/nv/features_MCA.html).

11. Specifically I regress average per capita income growth from 1990 to 2000 (g) on the initial level of income in 1990 (Y) and the average value of each indicator from 1990 to 2000 (i) as follows:

$$g = \alpha 0 + \alpha 1 * Y + \alpha 2 * i + \epsilon,$$

where $\alpha 0$ is a constant, $\alpha 1$ and $\alpha 2$ are the estimated coefficients on the initial income level and the indicator, respectively, and ϵ is an error term. I then repeat the process, substituting infant mortality and literacy for income growth as the left-side variable. Our focus of attention is on $\alpha 2$, the estimated coefficient for each indicator. The results in table 3-3 show both the sign and the statistical significance of the estimate for $\alpha 2$. Data for the regressions are drawn from all countries in the world where data are available. Note that this process is not meant to demonstrate causality from the indicator to the outcome, only the correlation after controlling for the level of income.

12. The KK indicators, along with four key papers by Daniel Kaufmann, Aart Kraay, and Pablo Zoido-Lobatón that describe the data and methodology: "Aggregating Governance Indicators," "Governance Matters," "Governance Matters II," and "Governance Matters III" can be found at www.worldbank.org/wbi/governance/. Kaufmann and Kraay have added a brief note dedicated to data issues in the MCA entitled "Governance Indicators, Aid Allocation, and the Millennium Challenge Account," which can be found at www.worldbank.org/wbi/governance/mca.htm.

13. Freedom House, *Freedom in the World* (www.freedomhouse.org/research/index.htm).

14. For more on the millennium development goals, see www.developmentgoals.org/.

15. "Achieving Education for All by 2015: Simulation Results for 47 Low-Income Countries," Human Development Network, Africa Region and Education Department, World Bank (www.worldbank.org/education/pdf/EFA percent20Complete percent20Draft.pdf).

16. Barbara Bruns, Alain Mingat, and Ramahatra Rakotomalala, *Achieving Universal Primary Education by 2015: A Chance for Every Child* (Washington: World Bank, 2003).

17. Ibid.

18. www.worldbank.org/data/onlinedatabases/onlinedatabases.htm [April 2003].

19. Lant Pritchett and Deon Filmer, "The Impact of Public Spending on Health: Does Money Matter?" *Social Science and Medicine*, vol. 40, no.10 (1999), pp. 1021–34.

20. The data are available (for purchase) at www.institutionalinvestor.com/premium/rr/index.htm.

21. Since data are missing for many countries, in some cases I have augmented the data with information from the World Bank's Country-at-a-Glance tables, available at www.worldbank.org.

22. The data are available at www.heritage.org/research/features/index/.

23. Simeon Djankov, Rafael La Porta, Florencio Lopez de Silanes, and Andrei Shleifer, "The Regulation of Entry," *Quarterly Journal of Economics,* vol. 117, no. 1 (February 2002), pp. 1–37. A slightly older version of the data can be downloaded from http://econ.worldbank.org/files/2379_wps2661.pdf. I received the most recent data directly from Mr. Djankov.

24. Michael Clemens and Steven Radelet, "The Millennium Challenge Account: How Much Is Too Much, and How Long Is Long Enough?" Working Paper 23, Center for Global Development, February 2002 (www.cgdev.org/wp/cgd_wp023.pdf).

25. Kaufmann and Kraay, "Governance Indicators."

26. Ibid.

27. Steven Radelet, *Challenging Foreign Aid: A Policymaker's Guide to the Millennium Challenge Account* (Washington: Center for Global Development, 2003). Note that the country lists differ slightly from the list originally presented in Steven Radelet, "Qualifying for the Millennium Challenge Account," Center for Global Development, December 2002 (www.cgdev.org/nv/features_MCA_cgddocs.html) because new data have become available for several indicators in the interim period.

28. The administration's fact sheet says that "a country would have to score above the median" to qualify on a hurdle (www.globalhealth.gov [April 2003]).

29. Paolo Pasicolan and Sara Fitzgerald, "The Millennium Challenge Account: Linking Aid with Economic Freedom," Backgrounder 1602, Heritage Foundation, October 2002 (www.heritage.org/research/Tradeandforeignaid/bg1602.cfm.)

30. Robert J. Barro, *Determinants of Economic Growth: A Cross-Country Empirical Study* (MIT Press, 1998); David Bloom and David Canning, "Cumulative Causality, Economic Growth and the Demographic Transition," in Nancy Birdsall, Allen C. Kelley, and Steven Sinding, eds., *Population Matters: Demographic Change, Economic Growth, and Poverty in the Developing World* (Oxford University Press, 2001); Kaufmann, Kraay, and Zoido-Lobatón, "Governance Matters II."

31. Palley, "Millennium Challenge Accounts."

32. United Nations Development Program, *Human Development Report 2002: Deepening Democracy in a Fragmented World* (Oxford University Press, 2002).

Chapter Four

1. For an excellent review of the evidence, see World Health Organization, "Macroeconomics and Health: Investing in Health for Economic Development: Report of the Commission on Macroeconomics and Health," December 2001.

2. Ibid.

3. Lael Brainard, "What Is the Role for Health in the Fight against International Poverty?" in Kurt Campbell and Philip Zellikow, eds., *Biological Security and Global Public Health* (Norton, forthcoming).

4. William Easterly, *The Elusive Quest for Growth: Economists' Adventures and Misadventures in the Tropics* (MIT Press, 2002); Robert J. Barro, *Determinants of Economic Growth: A Cross-Country Empirical Study* (MIT Press, 1998); Lant Pritchett, "Where Has All the Education Gone?" *World Bank Economic Review,* vol. 15, no. 3 (December 2001), pp. 367–91; N. Gregory Mankiw, David Romer, and David N. Weil, "A Contribution to the Empirics of Economic Growth," *Quarterly Journal of Economics,* vol. 107, no. 2 (May 1992), pp. 407–37.

5. "UN Millennium Development Declaration," UNGA A/RES/55/2, IV, September 18, 2000.

6. "Johannesburg Declaration on Sustainable Development," World Summit on Sustainable Development, September 2002 (www.johannesburgsummit.org/html/documents/summit_docs/13102_wssd_report_reissued.pdf [April 2003]).

7. Brett D. Schaefer and Aaron Schavey, "America's International Development Agenda," Heritage Foundation, Background Paper 1546, May 2002; Anna I. Eiras and Brett D. Schaefer, "Trade: The Best Way to Protect the Environment," Heritage Foundation, September 2001; Barun S. Mitra and Rakhi Gupta, "Sustainable Development versus Sustained Development," in Ronald Bailey, ed., *Global Warming and Other Eco-Myths* (Prima Publishing, 2002), p. 121.

8. Bjorn Lomborg, "The Skeptical Environmentalist 2001," in Bailey, *Global Warming.*

9. The great native prairies of the Midwest, with their tall grasses and abundant buffalo, elk, and other species, were altered forever in the 1800s, before the first U.S. conservation laws were passed in the early 1900s. Europe by and large lacks the enormous open spaces and large national parks we prize so much in the United States, because Europe's population exploded several centuries before the rise of strong national governments that could manage the resulting environmental changes and human migrations.

10. Charles Victor Barber and others, "The State of the Forest: Indonesia," World Resources Institute, Washington, 2002.

11. "Japan's Third National Communication under the United Nations Framework Convention on Climate Change," Government of Japan, May 2002; "Earth Trends," World Resources Institute, May 2002 (http://earthtrends.wri.org/ [April 2003]).

12. World Health Organization, "Children in the New Millennium, Environmental Impact on Health: Report of the Task Force on Children's Environmental Health," 2002.

13. See, for example, "Monterrey Consensus," Report of the International Conference on Financing for Development, March 2002 (www.un.org/esa/ffd/ [April 2003]).

14. "Monterrey Consensus," and "Plan of Implementation," World Summit on Sustainable Development, September 2002 (www.un.org/esa/ffd/ [April 2003]).

15. "International Energy Outlook 2002," table 25, Energy Information Administration, Department of Energy.

16. White House Executive Order 13141, November 1999.

17. John P. Birkelund, "Doing Good While Doing Well: The Unheralded Success of American Enterprise Funds," *Foreign Affairs,* vol. 80, no. 5 (September/October 2001).

18. See the Overseas Private Investment Corporation (OPIC) website (www.opic.gov [April 2003]).

19. See the Export-Import Bank of the United States website (www.exim.gov [April 2003]).

20. The one exception is Ex-Im's program to provide five-year financing for the purchase of HIV/AIDS medicines by countries of sub-Saharan Africa. Some have criticized the HIV/AIDS program, however, as adding to the midterm debt obligations of nations already overburdened with debt and debt-related expenses. The Ex-Im model of risk assumption does not allow it, even in programs aimed at the most disadvantaged, to escape limitations inherent in a model inextricably tied to legitimate but tangential American business interests.

21. Thomas Carothers, *Aiding Democracy Abroad: The Learning Curve* (Washington: Carnegie Endowment for International Peace, 1999).

Chapter Five

1. Carol Lancaster, *Transforming Foreign Aid: United States Assistance in the 21st Century* (Washington: Institute for International Economics, 2000). Despite its name, USAID country programs mostly fund specific projects rather than programs (for instance, sectorwide health or education programs). USAID sees these projects as together adding up to its "program" for the country.

2. Nancy Birdsall, Ruth Levine, Sarah Lucas, and Sonal Shah, "On Eligibility Criteria for the Millennium Challenge Account," Center for Global Development, September 12, 2002, www.cgdev.org/nv/MCA_criteria.pdf; Steven Radelet, "Beyond the Indicators: Delivering Effective Foreign Assistance through the Millennium Challenge Account," Center for Global Development, September 12, 2002 (www.cgdev.org/nv/MCA_indicators.pdf [April 2003]).

3. The full draft legislation and corresponding background documents can be found at www.cgdev.org.

4. The nomenclature for these actors can be confusing. *Civil society* is the generic term for nongovernmental, non-profit-seeking groups, which may be formal or informal. Nongovernmental organizations (NGOs) are formally organized, legally recognized entities that usually attempt, or at least claim, to serve a public interest. Governments will be expected to consult with civil society, including NGOs, as part of the contract preparation stage, but only the more formally constituted NGOs could be eligible for funding.

5. Andrew Natsios, administrator of USAID, remarks to the Council on Foreign Relations, February 4, 2003. The full transcript can be found at www.cfr.org/publication.php?id=5531 [April 2003].

6. The administration's draft legislation, sectional analysis, and background document can be found at www.cgdev.org/nv/features_MCA.html#usg [April 2003].

7. See Nancy Birdsall and others, "On Eligibility Criteria for the Millennium Challenge Account," Center for Global Development, September 12, 2002, and Steven Radelet, "Beyond the Indicators: Delivering Effective Foreign Assistance through the Millennium

Challenge Account," Center for Global Development, September 10, 2002, and testimony of Susan Berresford, president of the Ford Foundation, before the Senate Foreign Relations Committee, March 6, 2003.

8. A classic example is Kenya, which received nineteen World Bank adjustment loans between 1979 and 1996, with many of the same conditions repeated and never implemented, yet the funds continued to flow. See William Easterly, *The Elusive Quest for Growth: Economists' Adventures and Misadventures in the Tropics* (MIT Press, 2002).

9. Steven Radelet, "Beyond the Indicators."

10. Ibid.

11. For more on absorptive capacity in the MCA, see Michael Clemens and Steve Radelet, "The Millennium Challenge Account: How Much Is Too Much: How Long Is Long Enough?" Center for Global Development, Working Paper 23, 2003 (www.cgdev.org/pubs/workingpapers.html [April 2003]); Steven Radelet, *Challenging Foreign Aid: A Policymaker's Guide to the Millennium Challenge Account* (Washington: Center for Global Development, 2003); and Gayle Smith, "Absorptive Capacity: What It Is and What to Do about It," unpublished paper, 2002.

12. Michael Kremer, "Randomized Evaluations of Educational Programs in Developing Countries: Some Lessons," *American Economic Review: Papers and Proceedings*, forthcoming.

13. Paul T. Schultz, "School Subsidies for the Poor: Evaluating the Mexican Progresa Poverty Program," *Journal of Development Economics*, forthcoming.

14. Clemens and Radelet, "The Millennium Challenge Account: How Much Is Too Much."

Chapter Six

1. For instance, there are certain to be scale economies in sharing headquarters functions that cannot easily be outsourced, such as congressional relations, public relations, general counsel, and so forth.

2. Carol Lancaster reaches a different conclusion in "Where to Put the Millennium Challenge Account?" Center for Global Development, Oct 15, 2002 (http://cgdev.org/nv/where_MCA.pdf [April 2003]).

3. Larry Nowels, "The Millennium Challenge Account: Congressional Consideration of a New Foreign Aid Initiative," Congressional Research Service, January 3, 2002.

4. Ibid.

5. For a comprehensive list of government corporations, see "Government Corporations: A Guide to Internet Resources" (www.libsci.sc.edu/bob/class/clis734/webguides/corp.html [April 2003]). The authors thank Anne C. Richard for pointing this out.

6. Staff figures for all entities described here are approximate.

7. Personal communication from Norma Inge, human resources department, Export-Import Bank.

8. Personal communication from Jackie Barnes, Trade and Development Agency.

9. Personal communication from Monique Randolph, assistant secretary, Department of Agriculture.

10. Personal communication from Alex Wildy, vice president for communications, Ford Foundation.

11. Bylaws of the Global Fund to Fight AIDS, Tuberculosis, and Malaria.

12. Lancaster, "Where to Put the Millennium Challenge Account"; and Carol Lancaster, "The Devil Is in the Details: From the Millennium Challenge Account to the Millennium Challenge Corporation," Center for Global Development, December 11, 2002 (http://cgdev.org/nv/Devil_in_the_Details.pdf [April 2003]).

13. Susan Berresford, president of the Ford Foundation, also suggests that the proposed staff-to-disbursement ratio may be unrealistically high. The Ford Foundation's grant makers average approximately $3 million in disbursements per year. Berresford called the administration's proposed staff size "surprisingly small." Susan V. Berresford, testimony before Senate Foreign Relations Committee, March 4, 2003.

14. Andrew Natsios, USAID administrator, briefing, Council on Foreign Relations, February 4, 2003.

15. See "What's New in the ADS for January 2003," USAID (www.usaid.gov/pubs/ads [April 2003]).

16. Personal communication from Janet C. Ballantyne and Phyllis Forbes, former senior USAID officials.

Chapter Seven

1. Lael Brainard, "Compassionate Conservatism Confronts Global Poverty," *Washington Quarterly*, vol. 26, no. 2 (Spring 2003), pp. 149–69.

2. "A Portrait of the U.S. Development Assistance Program," draft paper, Washington, Center for Global Development, n.d.

3. Organization for Economic Cooperation and Development, *Development Co-Operation Review: United States* (Paris, 2002).

4. "U.S. National Security Strategy," White House, 2002.

5. See William Easterly, *The Elusive Quest for Growth: Economists' Adventures and Misadventures in the Tropics* (Oxford, 2002), and Carol Lancaster, *Transforming Foreign Aid: U.S. Assistance in the 21st Century* (Washington: Institute for International Economics, 2000).

6. "Foreign Aid in the National Interest," USAID, January 2003.

7. Lael Brainard, "What Is the Role for Health in the Fight against International Poverty?" in Kurt Campbell and Phillip Zelikow, eds., *Biological Security and Public Health* (Aspen, Colo.: Aspen Institute, forthcoming).

8. *Macroeconomics and Health: Investing in Health for Economic Development*, Report of the Commission on Macroeconomics and Health (Geneva: World Health Organization, December 2001), p. 44.

9. "Towards More Liberal Agricultural Trade," OECD Policy Brief, November 2001 (www.oecd.org/pdf/M00022000/M00022532.pdf [February 2003]).

10. "Facts about the Common Agriculture Policy," Catholic Fund for Overseas Development (www.cafod.org.uk/tradejustice/capfaq.shtml#3 [April 2003]).

11. *World Development Report, 2000/2001: Attacking Poverty* (Oxford University Press, 2001).

12. Brainard, "Compassionate Conservatism."

13. Experts have estimated the cost of rebuilding Iraq at between $25 billion and $100 billion. The administration has requested $3.6 billion in supplemental funds so far, claiming that the costs of reconstruction will largely be financed by oil revenues and international donors. The administration's supplemental request contains an additional $5.2 billion for bilateral aid to "supportive countries, or countries which may suffer consequences as a result of the war." See "Background Briefing," senior administration official on the supplemental, Washington, March 24, 2003; Mike Allen and Peter Behr, "Planning Postwar Iraq Aid; White House Says Oil Will Fund Rebuilding," *Washington Post,* March 29, 2003, p. A24; Diana B. Henriques, "Who Will Put Iraq Back Together?" *New York Times,* March 23, 2003, p. 31.

14. "U.S. Support for Plan Colombia," fact sheet, Department of State (usinfo.state.gov/regional/ar/colombia/ wwwhpcus.htm [March 2003]).

15. Paul Blustein, "Unrest a Chief Product of Arab Economies," *Washington Post,* January 26, 2002, p. A1; Fareed Ezz-Edine, "Egypt: An Emerging 'Market' of Double Repression," Middle East Report, Washington, Middle East Research and Information Project, November 18, 1999.

16. Personal communication from Nisha Desai, InterAction, February 4, 2002.

17. Similar pressures have affected U.S. contributions to the United Nations Population Fund. The authors thank Anne C. Richard for pointing this out.

18. Senator John McCain, statement on the Foreign Appropriations Bill for fiscal year 2002, October 24, 2001.

19. Carol Lancaster, *Aid to Africa: So Much to Do, So Little Done* (University of Chicago Press, 1999).

20. *Millennium Challenge Act of 2003,* 108 Cong. 1 sess., S571.

21. Larry Nowels, "The Millennium Challenge Account: Congressional Consideration of a New Foreign Aid Initiative," Congressional Research Service, January 3, 2003; and "Background Paper: Implementing the Millennium Challenge Account," USAID, February 5, 2003.

22. For a thorough analysis of the HIPC program, see Nancy Birdsall and John Williamson, assisted by Brian Deese, *Delivering on Debt Relief: From IMF Gold to a New Aid Architecture* (Washington: Institute for International Economics, 2002).

23. The administration's fiscal year 2004 request shows a $380 million decrease in funding for DA and CSH.

24. Andrew Natsios, USAID administrator, briefing, Council on Foreign Relations, February 4, 2003.

25. *Fiscal Year 2003 Budget of the U.S. Government,* Office of Management and Budget, 2002.

26. "U.S. National Security Strategy," White House, 2002.

27. Ibid.

28. Ibid.

29. Susan Rice, "U.S. Foreign Assistance and Failed States," working paper, Brookings, November 25, 2002.

30. "Human Development Report 2002: Summary," United Nations Development Program.

31. "Strategic" African countries cited in the NSS are Nigeria, Ethiopia, Kenya, and South Africa. Nigeria, Ethiopia, and Kenya do not qualify according to the policy-based criteria; South Africa is not poor enough to qualify in the first two years but would qualify in year three, assuming the income eligibility level is increased.

32. "2004 Budget," Mary E. McClymont, CEO, InterAction, Washington, February 4, 2003.

33. USAID's R4 process, where planning is done out in the field or at the country level, is an exception. The authors thank Anne C. Richard for this observation.

34. Gene Sperling and Tom Hart, "A Better Way to Fight Global Poverty," *Foreign Affairs,* vol. 82, no.2 (March/April 2003), pp. 9–14.

35. Rice, "U.S. Foreign Assistance and Failed States."

Chapter Eight

1. Edward S. Corwin, *The President: Office and Powers, 1787–1957* (New York University Press, 1957), p. 171.

2. Louis Henkin, "Foreign Affairs in the Constitution," *Foreign Affairs,* vol. 66 (Winter 1987–88), p. 287.

3. U.S. Constitution, art. 2, sec. 2 and 3.

4. U.S. Constitution, art. 2, sec. 3.

5. U.S. Constitution, art. 1, sec. 8.

6. Ibid.

7. Thomas E. Mann, *Making Foreign Policy: President and Congress* (Brookings, 1990) pp. 4–9.

8. Bruce W. Jentleson, "American Diplomacy," in Thomas E. Mann, ed., *A Question of Balance: The President, the Congress and Foreign Policy* (Brookings, 1990).

9. For a fact sheet on the Millennium Challenge Account, see www.whitehouse.gov/infocus/developingnations/millennium.html [April 2003].

10. Amy B. Zegart, *Flawed by Design* (Stanford University Press, 1999). pp. 7, 55, 107.

11. Ibid., p. 229.

12. Louis Brandeis, *Other People's Money* (New York: Frederick A. Stokes, 1933), p. 67.

13. 22 U.S.C. 635.

14. Ibid.

15. Larry Nowels, "The Millennium Challenge Account: Congressional Consideration of a New Foreign Aid Initiative," Congressional Research Service, January 3, 2003.

16. There are important exceptions. The authorizing legislation for the Freedom Support Act provides a broad mandate and minimal earmarks, restrictions, conditions, and directives. The authors thank George Ingram for this point.

17. This recommendation is supported by many but not all the authors.

Chapter Nine

1. This refers to the nondefense budget.

2. Average for 1999–2000, in 2001 dollars. Jean-Claude Faure, "Development Co-Operation, 2001 Report," *Organization for Economic Cooperation and Development DAC Journal,* vol. 3, no. 1 (2002), p. 207.

3. Andrew Natsios, USAID administrator, briefing, Council on Foreign Relations, February 4, 2003. The Center for Global Development recently has constructed an index ranking industrialized countries on six dimensions of their policies affecting low-income countries: aid, trade, investment, environment, migration, and security. The United States ranked twentieth out of twenty-one countries. For more on the Commitment to Development Index, see *Foreign Policy,* May/June 2003 (www.foreignpolicy.com) and the Center for Global Development website (www.cgdev.org).

4. "Americans on Foreign Aid and World Hunger: A Study of U.S. Public Attitudes," Program on International Policy Attitudes, February 2, 2001.

5. Lael Brainard, "Compassionate Conservatism Confronts Global Poverty," *Washington Quarterly,* vol. 26, no. 2 (Spring 2003), pp. 149–69.

6. "AIDS Epidemic Update," UNAIDS (www.unAIDS.org/worldaidsday/2002/press/Epiupdate.html [December 2002]).

7. "Report on the Global HIV/AIDS Epidemic," UNAIDS, Geneva, 2002.

8. "The AIDS Crisis," DATA (www.datadata.org/abouthiv.htm?1044892188078 [February 2003]).

9. "Sub-Saharan Africa Fact Sheet" UNAIDS (www.unaids.org/worldaidsday/2002/press/factsheets/FSAfrica_en.doc [February 2003]).

10. This discussion does not refer to politically motivated foreign aid, where support already was strong, such as aid to Israel or for counternarcotics cooperation.

11. Lael Brainard, "With Help from the Famous, Foreign Aid Resurges," *Los Angeles Times,* June 26, 2002.

12. This includes funds from the 150 function but excludes other important categories of U.S. aid funded through the Departments of Agriculture, Health and Human Services, and Defense.

13. Even aid skeptics such as Ann Krueger give due credit to foreign aid: "Without a doubt, U.S. aid significantly contributed to rapid and sustained growth in Korea and Taiwan." Testimony of David Gordon, director of the U.S. Policy Program, Overseas

Development Council, before the House Committee on International Relations, February 26, 1997.

14. *Recommendations of the High-Level Panel on Financing for Development* (New York: United Nations, 2001).

15. The lower figure is based on U.S. IMF and World Bank subscriptions, which make up approximately 17 percent of both IMF total member quotas, and the World Bank's International Bank for Reconstruction and Development (IBRD) total subscriptions. "IMF Members' Quotas and Voting Power, and IMF Governors," January 24, 2002 (www.imf.org/external/np/sec/memdir/members.htm [April 2002]); "International Bank for Reconstruction and Development Subscriptions and Voting Power of Member Countries," September 19, 2001 (www.worldbank.org/about/organizations/voting/kibrd.html [April 2002]). The higher figure is based on the U.S. share of OECD income based on Development Assistance Committee members' 2000 gross national income. Faure, "Development Co-Operation." Of the $50 billion, the panel estimates a gap of $10 billion per year to achieve the health targets. The WHO Commission on Macroeconomics and Health puts the price tag on health at more than double that amount, estimating that it will cost the international community roughly $22 billion by 2007 (or an additional 1 percent of GDP) to reach two-thirds of the population affected by HIV/AIDS and target the major communicable diseases and maternal and perinatal conditions in low-income countries. *Macroeconomics and Health: Investing in Health for Economic Development: Report of the Commission on Macroeconomics and Health* (Geneva: World Health Organization, December 2001). Some development experts do not find these numbers particularly compelling.

16. George Bush, speech at United Nations Financing for Development Conference, Monterrey, Mexico, March 22, 2002.

17. George Bush, speech at Inter-American Development Bank, March 14, 2002.

18. "On Budget Results for Fiscal Year 2002," joint statement of Paul H. O'Neill, secretary of the treasury, and Mitchell E. Daniels Jr., director of the Office of Management and Budget, press release, Department of the Treasury, October 25, 2002.

19. Pending supplemental legislation for fiscal year 2003 includes $5.02 billion to "support key coalition partners in the conflict with Iraq and in the global war on terrorism." In addition the supplemental legislation includes approximately $3.6 billion for reconstruction activities in Iraq. The Council on Foreign Relations has estimated that the actual cost could reach $20 billion a year for several years. See "Background Briefing," senior administration official on the supplemental, Washington, March 24, 2003; "G7 Daily Briefing," G7 Group, Washington, April 1, 2003.

20. Lael Brainard, "The Administration's Budget for Global Poverty and HIV/AIDS: How Do the Numbers Stack Up?" analysis paper, Brookings, February 20, 2003 (www.brookings.edu/views/papers/brainard/20030224.htm [March 2003]).

21. Carol Lancaster, *Transforming Foreign Aid: United States Assistance in the 21st Century* (Washington: Institute for International Economics, 2000).

22. Brainard, "Compassionate Conservatism."

23. Ibid.

24. White House Fact Sheet, "Millennium Challenge Account Update," June 3, 2002 (www.fas.usda.gov/icd/summit/WH%20MCA%20Fact%20Sheet%206-3-02.pdf [March 2003]).

25. *Fiscal Year 2004 Analytical Perspectives,* tables 25-1 and 25-2, pp. 482–83 and 502–03, Office of Management and Budget, 2003.

Appendix B

1. U.S. Constitution, art. 1, sec. 9.

2. State Department Basic Authorities Act of 1956, as amended (Public Law 84-885), sec. 701. Similar provisions exist for other foreign affairs agencies in their corresponding acts.

Contributors

Lael Brainard is the director of the Brookings Center for Global Development Project on the Millennium Challenge Account. She holds the New Century Chair in Economic Studies and Foreign Policy Studies at the Brookings Institution.

Carol Graham is vice president and director of the Governance Studies Program at the Brookings Institution, where she also directs the Global Poverty Reduction Initiative.

Nigel Purvis is the Brookings Scholar on Environment, Development, and Global Issues. He holds a joint appointment in economics, foreign policy, and governance studies.

Steven Radelet is a senior fellow at the Center for Global Development.

Gayle E. Smith was National Security Council senior director for African affairs during the Clinton administration and is now an independent consultant and a Brookings guest scholar.

Index

THE BROOKINGS INSTITUTION

The Brookings Institution is an independent organization devoted to nonpartisan research, education, and publication in economics, government, foreign policy, and the social sciences generally. Its principal purposes are to aid in the development of sound public policies and to promote public understanding of issues of national importance. The Institution was founded on December 8, 1927, to merge the activities of the Institute for Government Research, founded in 1916, the Institute of Economics, founded in 1922, and the Robert Brookings Graduate School of Economics and Government, founded in 1924. The Institution maintains a position of neutrality on issues of public policy to safeguard the intellectual freedom of the staff. Interpretations or conclusions in Brookings publications should be understood to be solely those of the authors.

The Center for Global Development is a nonprofit, nonpartisan institution dedicated to reducing global poverty and inequality through policy-oriented research and active engagement on development issues with the policy community and the public. The principal focus of the Center's work is policies of the United States and other industrialized countries, and of international institutions such as the World Bank and the World Trade Organization, that affect development prospects in poor countries. The Center seeks to identify policy alternatives that will promote equitable growth and participatory development in low-income and transitional economies and, in collaboration with civil society and private sector groups, seeks to translate policy ideas into policy reforms. The Center is supported by an initial significant financial contribution from Edward W. Scott Jr. and by funding from philanthropic and other organizations.